IRON ROADS
OF THE MONADNOCK REGION

Cheshire Railroad's second 16/*R. M. Pulsifer*, an American Standard (4-4-0) coal burner built by the Rhode Island Locomotive Works in 1883, is crossing Main Street with an eastbound train, Keene, NH, 1885–1890. Royal M. Pulsifer, owner/publisher of the *Boston Herald*, was a director of the road. The large house—still standing today—is the Dunbar House, the birthplace of Henry D. Thoreau's mother. Photo by J. A. French (assigned); Hist. Soc. of Cheshire County.

IRON ROADS
OF THE MONADNOCK REGION

—— VOLUME ONE ——

Railroads of Southwestern New Hampshire
and North-Central Massachusetts

by

Bradford G. Blodget and Richard R. Richards Jr.

BAUHAN PUBLISHING
PETERBOROUGH, NEW HAMPSHIRE
2020

This book is a selective history of the railroads in the Monadnock Region, focused on their operating years and their relationships to the communities they served. It is not intended to be a field guide to abandoned roadbeds and surviving railroad infrastructure and artifacts. Field exploration for such and the accompanying pleasures of discovery are reserved for the reader.

©2020 Historical Society of Cheshire County
ISBN 978-0-87233-305-5

Library of Congress Cataloging-in-Publication Data
Library of Congress Control Number: 2019954037
LC record available at https://lccn.loc.gov/2019954037

All photographs used by permission with credits in each caption.

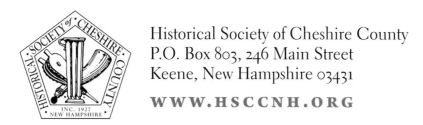

Historical Society of Cheshire County
P.O. Box 803, 246 Main Street
Keene, New Hampshire 03431
WWW.HSCCNH.ORG

PO BOX 117 PETERBOROUGH NEW HAMPSHIRE 03458

WWW.BAUHANPUBLISHING.COM

Book design by Henry James and Sarah Bauhan
Cover design by Henry James
Printed by Versa Press

FRONT COVER PHOTOGRAPH: In its twilight years, the B&M's Cheshire Branch, having no restrictions on over-dimension cars, was used mostly as a detour route for loads that the road didn't want to try squeezing through the Bellows Falls Tunnel. Here, B&M 4265, 1508, and 1514 are approaching the Rte. 12 Bridge in Walpole, NH, with a train of forty-four vats for a new Anheuser-Busch Brewery under construction in Merrimack, NH, Jan. 4, 1969. Frederick G. Bailey photo.

BACK COVER PHOTOGRAPH: Original Cheshire Railroad wax seal, auction photo, courtesy of Scott Czaja.

Printed in the United States of America

To

BRENT S. MICHIELS

railroad photographer, historian, archivist, and friend,

for his good counsel, encouragement, and indefatigable assistance in the preparation of this book,

and in recognition of his long-time sharing and service to the railfan community.

In the early 1980s, the B&M, employing MBTA commuter equipment, operated a number of popular railfan excursions for the Mass Bay Chapter of The Railroad Enthusiasts, Inc. One of these trips was the *Crotched Mountain Limited* which traveled out the Hillsboro Branch to the end of operable track in Bennington, NH The train, bracketed by F40s 1006 and 1002, marked the only time F-units were ever operated on the branch. Here, against the stunning backdrop of 2,055-foot Crotched Mountain itself, the special passes Powder Mill Pond in Bennington, April 23, 1983. Brent S. Michiels photo.

B&M RS2 1500, "the Queen of the Cheshire Branch," rests in Fitchburg Yard, N. Walpole, NH, May 1967. The little Alco was well-suited for service in the Monadnock Region and was well-liked by her crews. Photogr. unknown; R. R. Richards Jr. coll.

CONTENTS

A steam train crosses the Joslin Arch on a cold winter's day, Keene, NH, Feb., 1935. Beland Peirce photo; Hist. Soc. Cheshire Cty.

FOREWORD

On May 16, 1848, Keene changed forever. Cannons roared, bells rang, and people cheered as the first passenger train rolled across the town's Main Street and into the new brick train station. More than 5,000 people came into town to greet this new technological marvel. The railroad had arrived in central Cheshire County.

Few people realized on that day the impact the railroad would have on their community. Less than three decades later, trains were moving in and out of Keene in four directions, carrying tens of thousands of passengers and millions of tons of freight on the iron rails. The railroad truly made Keene what it is today—the economic and manufacturing center for all of southwest New Hampshire. The railroads connected Keene to the greater New England area, the nation, and the world.

Keene was only one of the dozens of towns touched by the railroads that traversed the Monadnock Region. This two-volume work tells the stories of those roads in a thirty-community area of southwest New Hampshire, as well as in seven towns in north-central Massachusetts, and two towns just across the Connecticut River in Vermont. The rail lines did not stop at county or state borders, but continued on to link up with other lines already in place or planned for the future.

Iron Roads of the Monadnock Region is the first publication to present comprehensive detailed histories of all of the region's railroads and street railways. For eight years, Brad Blodget and Dick Richards scoured the region for information and photographs to include in this history.

Blodget drove thousands of miles finding and following abandoned right-of-ways and visiting historical societies to review material. The authors also reviewed thousands of images in both public and private collections to illustrate how the roads operated, and interviewed numerous historians and former rail employees to uncover the rail story. Much of this information and many of these photos have never been published before.

In truth, the history included in this publication could not be duplicated even today. Some of the sources, people, and photos that made these volumes possible are no longer available a mere eight years after the project began. Brad Blodget, Dick Richards, and the Historical Society of Cheshire County unknowingly picked the most opportune moment to share this story—before it was lost.

The history of these railroads is a story of business, industry, and technology, but most of all it is a story of people. People who paid for or built the roads, traveled or worked on the roads, and transported goods or products in the freight cars of the eleven railroads whose rails touched the region. Almost all of these railroads have now been abandoned and have disappeared from the local landscape. Although much of the physical evidence of their existence is gone, their stories still survive. These two volumes, containing more than 500 pages and 750 photos, illustrate and recount a nostalgic story of a time when railroading in the Monadnock Region was described as a "glorious business."

Alan F. Rumrill
October 2019

In its last years of operation, the Cheshire Branch, having no clearance restrictions, was used as a detour route for over-dimension, "high-wide" cars. Here, B&M SW9 1230 is passing the former site of the State Line, NH station with what is probably Saturday-only train F-5 out of Fitchburg, MA making a "caboose-hop" to N. Walpole, NH, for cars. Behind the train, construction work is visible on the old Rte. 12, State Line NH, Dec. 1970. Photogr. unknown; R. R. Richards Jr. coll.

ACKNOWLEDGMENTS

As if all the challenges we faced in preparing this book weren't enough, nothing proved more daunting than trying to figure out how to extend our gratitude to the hundreds of people—wonderful people—who in so many ways enabled our work. The book you are about to read is truly a work of the many. We thank the numerous contributors who so generously shared with us their memoirs, important images, and special knowledge of railroad operations. Preparation of the book was an eight-year "being there" experience, a journey of learning and discovery through time. We would never have made it without you.

At the outset we must thank our sponsor, the Historical Society of Cheshire County in Keene, New Hampshire, which opened its archives for our use, provided office facilities and—most important of all—talented staff who assisted us in so many ways over for the last eight years. We thank you all so much for the faith you placed in us to complete this undertaking: Jenna Carroll, Andrea Cheeney, Chris Pratt, Alan Rumrill, Kathy Schillimat, and Rick Swanson.

When we set out to prepare this book, we assumed it would be a relatively straightforward project but doubted there would be enough good, unpublished photo material to support the work. We were wrong on both counts. First, elucidating important historical material—often well-embedded in history's fog—proved anything but straightforward. On the second count, the quantity of photo material that continually surfaced was so great it eventually forced us—in the interests of completing the book—to practically embargo any further incoming material! Our book is enriched by the work of over 89 photographers shared with us by 76 contributors, including many of the Monadnock Region's town historical societies. In lieu of listing them all here, their names appear in the photo captions. We took scrupu-

lous care to make correct attributions and apologize in advance if we have erred.

We thank the following people, many of them retired Boston & Maine Railroad employees as well as members of the Boston & Maine Railroad Historical Society, for their support and encouragement throughout the project and for sharing their knowledge of railroad history: Benjamin Campbell, Richard Conard, Alden H. Dreyer, the late Wayne Gagnon, J. R. Greene, Richard Hurst, Larry Kemp, Brent S. Michiels, Richard E. Miller, Russell F. Munroe, Frederick N. Nowell III, the late Ben Perry, Chris Pratt, John Alan Roderick, Dale O. Russell, Dwight Smith, Gareth Thomas, the late Craig Weed, Scott J. Whitney, Peter Wright, and Victor M. Zolinsky.

For our map production, after many stumbles, we discovered Dr. Christopher Brehme and his student Samantha Gaudette at Keene State College. Finding them was a miracle and we thank them for their wonderful work. We thank Robert Arnold, Bruce Davison, Cosette Dulmaine, and Brian Boisvert and his staff at L. B. Wheaton's in Worcester, Massachusetts, for helping us with negatives and digital images. Anna Tilton helped us greatly at the Cheshire County Registry of Deeds. Access to old newspapers was very important and we deeply appreciated the facilities and staff of the American Antiquarian Society in Worcester, the Keene Public Library, the Monadnock Center for History and Culture in Peterborough, and the Worcester Public Library. Harry L. York III was our go-to person for searching old newspapers in Keene and—believe us—he was indispensable. Thank you so much, Harry.

Lloyd Adams, Frederick G. Bailey, Catherine Behrens, Richard Butler, Robert W. Jones, Leo Landry, Brent S. Michiels, Richard E. Miller, Roberta Nylander, Alan Rumrill and Tom E. Thompson read sections of the manuscript and we are grateful for their comments and suggestions that improved the text materially.

At the end of our journey of discovery and writing we entrusted our work to the team at Bauhan Publishing in Peterborough, New Hampshire, to turn it all into a book. Sarah Bauhan, Henry James, and Mary Ann Faughnan all took a great interest in our project and were wonderful to work with. We thank them for their hard work and attention to so much detail.

We extend our thanks to Rick Swanson for his fundraising efforts and a very special thank you to the many people whose generous financial support helped make the book a reality.

And finally, we would like to say that while we have strived to document as much historical detail as possible about happenings on the railroads here in the Monadnock Region, the unfortunate reality is that errors and other goofs may await discovery. We regret such mistakes as may be found and accept responsibility for them. Errors in fact or judgement are ours and do not reflect upon our wonderful contributors. If you discover errors, please alert us by writing us c/o the Historical Society of Cheshire County, 246 Main Street, Keene, NH 03431. We will find a way to deal with them.

Bradford G. Blodget
Richard R. Richards Jr.

A westbound camp train of Pullman sleepers, drawn by F7 4268A/B, passes Gardner Tower, June 8, 1968. A train such as this one would normally be handed off to the New Haven at Worcester, MA, but this day was being detoured via Springfield on account of a derailment on the Worcester main line at Clinton. By this date, camp trains had become a rarity due to improved highways and rubber-tired alternatives, George C. Corey photo. See also photo on page 42.

EXPLANATION OF
CONVENTIONS AND ABBREVIATIONS

Throughout both volumes of this book, frequently used railroad names are abbreviated as follows:

B&A—Boston & Albany	MS&N—Monadnock, Steamtown & Northern
B&M—Boston & Maine	N&L—Nashua & Lowell
B&L—Boston & Lowell	NRR—Northern
BB&G—Boston, Barre & Gardner	NYC—New York Central
CRRR—Connecticut River	P&H—Peterboro & Hillsboro
CV—Central Vermont	V&M—Vermont & Massachusetts
FRR—Fitchburg	VC—Vermont Central
GMRC—Green Mountain	VTR—Vermont
M&K—Manchester & Keene	VV—Vermont Valley

We also abbreviate street railway names as follows:

A&O—Athol & Orange	TSRy—Templeton
GW&F—Gardner, Westminster & Fitchburg	KERy—Keene Electric
BF&SR—Bellows Falls & Saxtons River	NMSRy—Northern Massachusetts

In our discussion of various railroad lines, we use the timetable directions given in B&M Employee Time Tables (sometimes counterintuitive to compass directions). In B&M parlance, trains moving away from Boston, Worcester, or Springfield are referred to as *outward* trains; while trains moving in the opposite direction are *inward* trains. In our chapters we have tried to present stations in their correct order outward from Boston, Worcester, or Springfield.

Cheshire Branch trains traveling toward Bellows Falls are outward/westward, toward South Ashburnham inward/eastward; Ashuelot Branch trains traveling toward Keene are outward/northward, toward Dole Junction inward/southward; trains on the Worcester and Contoocook moving toward Hillsboro are outward/eastward, toward Worcester inward/westward; and Keene Branch trains traveling toward Keene are outward/northward, toward Nashua inward/southward.

Outward passenger trains carry odd numbers ("**Out**ward is **O**dd"), inward trains even numbers. Freight trains are designated by alphanumeric symbols ending in odd numbers for outward moves, even numbers for inward moves. For example, WX-1/XW-2 are the outward/inward symbols for freights between Worcester and Bellows Falls. For both specificity and brevity we use these symbols in the text, explaining them when they appear. Be advised that timetable directions and train numbers and symbols employed by B&M predecessor roads prior to 1900 may differ from those discussed above.

The decimalized numbers you will encounter in tables and timetables or sometimes in the text following (in parentheses) the names of stations, bridges, or signals, are B&M mileage points we have included for reference. We have drawn mileages primarily from *B&M RR ETT No. 1*, effective April 29, 1928. Mileages for the Fitchburg Route Main Line and Cheshire Branch are distances from North Station, Boston (B); for the Connecticut River Route Main Line from Springfield Union Station (S); for the Ashuelot Branch from either East Northfield (EN) or Springfield Union Station (S); for the Worcester and Contoocook from Worcester Union Station (W); and for the Keene Branch from Nashua Union Station (N).

On the Boston & Albany system's Ware River Branch, mileages are distances from Palmer drawn from the *B&A RR PTT*, effective February 2, 1925, and *B&A RR ETT*, effective April 29, 1956. Trains moving toward Winchendon were considered northward and were odd numbered, those moving toward Palmer southward and even numbered.

A number of other abbreviations appear frequently: CTC (Centralized Traffic Control), ETT and PTT (Employee and Public Time Tables), ICC (Interstate Commerce Commission), MP (mile post or mileage point), OD (over-dimension), and RRE (The Railroad Enthusiasts, Inc.). Following railroad custom, we may use the shortened versions for Hillsborough, Marlborough, and Peterborough (omitting "ugh") when the use of these names is directly connected to railroad operations.

Finally, we also use shortened names for newspapers and magazines frequently cited, viz., *B&M Bull.* for the *B&M Bulletin* published by the Boston & Maine Railroad Historical Society; *Sentinel* for all variations of the *New Hampshire* or *Keene Sentinel*; *Times* for the *Bellows Falls Times*; and *Transcript* for the *Peterborough Transcript*. Citations from the *Boston & Maine Railroad Employees Magazine* are codified as *EM* followed by the month, year, and page number, e.g., *EM* Jan49, 20.

Guilford Rail Systems GP40 377 on the Boston and Maine Railroad's Fitchburg Route Main Line (built between Fitchburg and Greenfield by the Vermont and Massachusetts Railroad in 1847–1850) at Gardner, MA, 1992. Guilford changed its name to Pan Am Railways in 2006 and partnered with Norfolk Southern Railway to form Pan Am Southern, LLC in 2008. Even as so much of the Monadnock Region's rail system is but a memory today, the original Vermont and Massachusetts route, passing through north central Massachusetts, remains an important rail corridor in the first decades of the twenty-first century. B. G. Blodget photo.

INTRODUCTION

THE MONADNOCK REGION

The Monadnock Region of southwestern New Hampshire and north-central Massachusetts is a glaciated area of rolling hills and moderately high elevation (500 to 1,600 feet). Mount Monadnock—the Grand Monadnock—in Jaffrey and Dublin, New Hampshire. is a focal point, dominating the landscape for miles around. South of the mountain is the relatively flat high elevation area known as the Monadnock Plateau and its extension, the Worcester Plateau that slopes southward into north-central Massachusetts. The Monadnock-Worcester Plateau is punctuated by occasional bedrock outcrops (monadnocks) that rise 800 to 1,800 feet above the surrounding landscape. The Grand Monadnock, at 3,165 feet, is the largest of these. East and north of the Grand Monadnock one finds a more continuous, rugged mountainous area dissected by rivers and mountain streams. Some have called the Monadnock Region "the tail end of the White Mountains."

The Monadnock Region is drained to the north, west, and southwest by the Ashuelot River, to the south by the

Otter and Millers Rivers, to the northeast by the Contoocook River, and to the southeast by the Nashua River. The Ashuelot, Otter, and Millers Rivers flow to the Connecticut Valley, the others to the Merrimack Valley. East of the Contoocook Valley is the Wapack Range, a steep ridge that begins with North Pack Monadnock in Greenfield, New Hampshire, and extends some forty-five miles south to Mount Wachusett in Princeton, Massachusetts.

These topographic features presented serious impediments to civil engineers tasked with building railroads into and through the Region. Surmounting the Wapack Range, drilling and blasting deep cuts through granite ledge, and building and filling trestlework over deep mountain stream valleys kept thousands of men employed for years—and presented the railroads with maintenance and operating difficulties for many years following. We will get into these matters in the appropriate chapters.

We believe it makes little sense—indeed it is impossible—to present the Monadnock Region's railroads as broken-off fragments of the vast system of which they formed a natural part. Thus, we will look at how and whence the Region's railroads sprouted, their junctions and relationships with surrounding lines, consolidations into larger systems, and subsequent declines.

For the purposes of this book, cautioning that we may stray at times, we define the Monadnock Region to include: 1) all of Cheshire County, New Hampshire; 2) the Contoocook Valley towns of Peterborough, Hancock, Bennington, Antrim, Deering, Hillsborough, and Greenfield in western Hillsboro County, New Hampshire; and 3) the towns of Westminster, Ashburnham, Gardner, Winchendon, Templeton, Royalston, and Athol in northern Worcester County, Massachusetts. We also reach out into the overlapping Wantastiquet Region, which straddles the Connecticut River, to pick up Brattleboro and Bellows Falls, Vermont—peripheral localities, yes, but nonetheless functionally important railroad gateways into the Monadnock Region. In the special cases of Brattleboro and Bellows Falls, we discuss only the railroads in those localities that crossed the river from New Hampshire.

Railroad Building in the Early Period

The first railroads in New England were the Boston and Lowell, Boston and Worcester, and Boston and Providence Railroads, all of which—radiating from Boston like spokes on a wheel—opened in 1835. The Nashua and Lowell extended the Boston and Lowell to South Nashua, New Hampshire, in 1838 and was the first railroad to enter the Granite State. The Concord Railroad extended this shoot of steel further northward to the capitol in 1842. In Massachusetts, the Fitchburg Railroad reached westward from Charlestown to its namesake city in 1845.

A total of eleven originally independent steam railroads would eventually lay rail in the Monadnock Region. Six of these roads were endemic to the Region. We examine all the original roads, organized by chapter in the order in which they were built, and discuss their operations and what happened to them. All the roads present strikingly different stories.

Railroad building in the Monadnock Region, reflecting a national pattern, fell into three periods that we will refer to as the Early (1835–1851), Middle (1868–1878),

and Late Periods (post-1890). In this volume we will discuss the original steam roads constructed in the Early Period—the Vermont and Massachusetts, Cheshire, Sullivan, and Ashuelot Railroads. Then in Volume II we will present the remaining seven original steam roads—six built in the Middle Period and one as an outlier in the Late Period and also cover the street railways and little-known quarry roads.

In the Early Period, the first reference to a railroad in the Region was a report that an application would be made to the Legislature to charter the "Keene Railroad Company" to build a line between Keene and Worcester or Lowell. Proponents cited "heavy teams constantly passing and five lines of stages well supported to Lowell and Boston and one to Worcester" as evidence of great and increasing travel that would benefit by completion of a railroad (*Sentinel* June 11, 1835). As actually chartered, the line was to be built from Brattleboro through Keene to Nashua (*Sentinel* Aug. 6, 1835). However, nothing happened because the costs were thought to be insurmountable, and the company was dissolved. Next, in June 1844, the Fitchburg, Keene and Connecticut River Railroad was chartered but subsequently rejected by the corporators. The Cheshire Railroad Co. was chartered later the same year and was organized the following year.

The extension of railroads into the Monadnock Region really began when the Vermont and Massachusetts Railroad (V&M), building west from Fitchburg, commenced grading work between Fitchburg and South Ashburnham in 1843. From South Ashburnham, the road would attack the steep eastern edge of the Wapack Range and reach the top of the grade at East Gardner in 1847. Meanwhile, the Cheshire Railroad, connecting with the then-abuilding V&M at South Ashburnham, built northwestward over the Monadnock Plateau. It would be the first railroad to enter Cheshire County, New Hampshire, reaching Troy in 1847 and Keene the following year.

By 1848, the major railroads were already entertaining various schemes to build or annex feeder lines. The Fitchburg Railroad, in particular, was intrigued by tap lines that would reach into the Merrimack Valley in southern and central New Hampshire—the state's capital district and industrial heartland. The Peterborough & Shirley Railroad built, from a connection with the

Road Name Orig. Charter Dates Total Mileage	Location Year(s) Built (Miles of Road in the Monadnock Region)	Owners/Operators
Vermont and Massachusetts 10/1843 (VT) 3-15-1844(MA) 4-16-1846(MA) 68.0	Fitchburg, MA to Brattleboro, VT 1843-1849 (*Westminster to Athol* 26.9)	The original main line was leased 1-1-1874 to the FRR, which disposed of the 21-mile "Brattleboro Branch" in 1880 by sale to the CV-controlled New London Northern RR. The remaining 57 miles became part of Hoosac Tunnel Route Main Line. Lease assumed by B&M in 1900.
Cheshire 12-17-1844 12-27-1844 53.6	S. Ashburnham, MA to North Walpole, N.H. 1845-1849 (53.6)	Construction between S. Ashburnham and Winchendon, MA was begun in 1845 by the V&M which sold this section to the Cheshire in 1846. Sold to FRR 10-1-1890; to B&M in 1900.
Sullivan 7-10-1846 26.0	Bellows Falls to Windsor, Vt. 1848-1851 (*Bellows Falls thru Walpole, N.H.* 1.5)	Controlled by NRR by 1858; leased to VC 1861-80; sold to VV 1880. Run by the CRRR under a 50-year operating agreement from 6-1-1881 until assumed by B&M 1-1-1893; consolidated with the B&M in 1949.
Ashuelot 12-27-1844 24.0	E. Northfield, MA to Keene, N.H. 1850-51 (24)	Operated by the CRRR 12-1-1851 to 12-31-1860; the Cheshire 1-1-1861 to 4-20-1877; and again by the CRRR 4-21-1877 to 2-6-1890; consolidated with CRRR on 2-7-1890; to B&M 1-1-1893.
Monadnock 12-13-1848; rechartered 1866 15.8	Winchendon, MA to Peterborough, N.H. 1870-71 (15.8)	Part of the Worcester & Contoocook Route. Leased by the BB&G 10-1-1874; leased by the Cheshire 1-3-1880; lease assumed by the FRR 10-1-1890; consolidated into FRR 10-1-1892; to B&M in 1900.
Ware River 5-24-1851 3/16/1867 3/15/1870 49.4	Palmer to Winchendon, MA 1868-73 (*Templeton to Winchendon* 10.3)	Leased by the Boston & Albany/New York Central System until 1961, when merged into NYC; briefly in PennCentral in 1968; road north of S. Barre abandoned except outer two miles sold to B&M in 1968
Ashburnham 5-5-1871 2.6	S. Ashburnham to Ashburnham, MA 1873 (2.6)	Purchased by FRR in 4-22-1885; to B&M in 1900.
Boston, Barre & Gardner 4-26-1847 5-12-1853 2-24-1872 36.4	Worcester to Winchendon, MA 1869-73 (*Gardner to Winchendon* 9.7)	Part of the Worcester & Contoocook Route. Consolidated with FRR 7-1-1885; to B&M in 1900.
Peterborough & Hillsborough 7-7-1869 18.1	Peterborough to Hillsborough, N.H. 1877-78 (18.1)	Part of the Worcester & Contoocook Route, controlled by the NRR; It was included in that road's lease to the B&L in 1884, then to the B&M in 1887; purchased by the B&M 12-1945.
Manchester and Keene 6-22-1864 29.6	Keene to Greenfield, N.H. 1876-78 (29.6)	Initially operated intermittently by the N&L 12-1878 to 12-31-1879; operations resumed 9-1-1880 to 8-31-1881 under lease to CRRR; purchased in bankruptcy by the Concord/B&L 50/50 consortium 10-26-1881 and operated by the B&L until leased to the B&M in 1887.
Connecticut River 4-7-1911 8.4	Dole Jct., N.H. to Brattleboro, VT 1912-13 (8.4)	Only section of road in the Monadnock Region actually constructed by the B&M (as CRRR lessee).

Quick Reference Table to the original steam railroads (excluding quarry roads) built in the Monadnock Region, arranged chronologically by year(s) built and showing their mileage and successive ownership and operators, 1843 to 1968. From 1913 to 1937, with all the roads in operation, there were about 200.5 track miles, 95 percent controlled by the B&M.

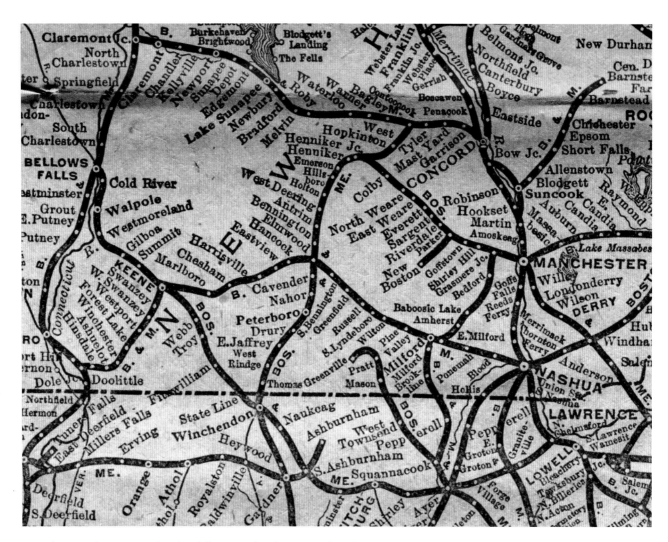

Map showing the steam railroads of the Monadnock Region after all except the Boston & Albany's Ware River Branch had been folded into the B&M system (*B&M PTT* Sept. 28, 1919).

Fitchburg at Ayer, Massachusetts, out as far as Greenville, New Hampshire, in 1850. Before it was even completed, the Fitchburg leased it to preclude any possibility that the Boston and Lowell might take control of the road and attempt to extend it. The Wilton Railroad built up the Souhegan Valley from Nashua, reaching Wilton in 1851. Both the Peterborough & Shirley and the Wilton were stopped by the Wapack Range and other physical impediments that effectively isolated Peterborough and other eastern Monadnock Region towns from connection with railroads for another twenty years. Meanwhile, stage lines flourished, connecting Peterborough and other isolated areas to railheads at Winchendon, Keene, Wilton, Hillsborough, and Greenville.

From the north, the Contoocook Valley Railroad built up its namesake valley from a connection with the Concord and Claremont Railroad at Contoocook to the doorstep of the Monadnock Region at Hillsboro Bridge in 1848–1849. Though it gave Hillsborough an all-rail route to Concord and Boston, it would remain a dead-end at Hillsboro for nearly thirty years until a link into the Monadnock Region was established. Plans surfaced in 1849 to extend the Contoocook Valley Railroad to Keene, where it would link up with the Ashuelot to provide Concord a direct route west. The New Hampshire Union Railroad received a charter July 2, 1851 to construct such a line, but the enterprise was abandoned.

By the end of 1851, the V&M, Cheshire, Sullivan, and Ashuelot Railroads were all completed—a decade before the Civil War.

During the Civil War, railroads in the Monadnock Region (in fact, New England railroads generally) did not experience the disruption and chaos suffered by those closer to the battlegrounds. None was taken over by the United States Military Railroads, created by an act of Congress in 1862 to operate lines under direct government control. By the end of hostilities, the US Military Railroads controlled about 2,000 miles of road, much of it in captured territory. Monadnock railroads actually flourished during the war. The Cheshire's gross revenues, for example, soared to record levels.

All the railroads in the Monadnock Region were built to standard gauge (4 feet, 8 1/2 inches between the rails), as were most of the roads in New England. Civil engineering and stonework construction were quite advanced in 1845, but mechanized construction methods were still in their infancy. The internal combustion engine was still a half century in the future. Teams of horses and oxen powered wagons and pulleys. Formidable granite ledges yielded only to armies of men whaling away with sledgehammers, pickaxes, and crowbars. Hand drilling and blasting were the order of the day to remove ledge. Hand drilling was done by two-man crews, one holding and rotating a star drill, the other swinging a twenty-pound sledgehammer. Then a "powder monkey" would stuff the holes two to three inches deep with black powder. On some days forward progress was measured in inches. Pneumatic hammers and steam drills did not come along until the 1860s, nitroglycerine not until 1866, and steam shovels for moving earth and rock debris not until the late 1870s.

Among the hundreds of construction workers in the labor pool—including notably large waves of Irish and Italian immigrants—there were some pretty hard characters, some of whom had difficulty staying within the law. Yet the construction work touched off economic boom times for hotels, boarding houses, and supply-chain purveyors of every name and nature.

In addition to the eleven original roads, another twelve roads at different times exerted differing degrees of influence in the formation of the Region's rail network or briefly operated in the Region via lease, stock control, trackage rights or other arrangements before most were absorbed by the Boston and Maine Railroad (B&M). In 1983 the B&M was itself acquired by

Guilford Transportation Industries and became a part of its Guilford Rail Systems (rebranded Pan Am Railways in 2006). Pan Am Railways' trackage in the Monadnock Region is now included in Pan Am Southern, LLC, a 50/50 partnership formed by Pan Am and Norfolk Southern Railway in 2008. We will discuss all these roads in the appropriate chapters.

Railroad Times

Before the railroad arrived, people had very little real mobility, and any long-distance travel was limited, sometimes arduous, and always slow. Most people lived tightly circumscribed lives. If you didn't own or borrow a horse to ride or hitch to a carriage, your travel options were limited. You would walk or take a stage. Earle (1900) provides insight into what travel was like in coaching days, before railroads—"the coming of the

Broadside for excursion to Bellows Falls "To see the High Water," April 22, 1869. Hist. Soc. Cheshire County.

cars"—revolutionized travel and expanded peoples' lives. Getting around by rail came to be seen as a necessity of life and "meeting the steam cars" soon became a preeminent social function of the populace. While local, horse-drawn coaches lingered long in remote areas— even to the turn of the century—stagecoach lines that ran longer distances between cities succumbed with astonishing rapidity as they were supplanted by railroads (Earle 1900, 337–339). Many stage coach drivers readily transitioned to railroad employment.

When the railroads opened for business in the Monadnock Region in the 1840s, passenger traffic was immediately important as an early source of revenue for the roads. The roads sought, particularly after the Civil War, to boost passenger revenues by marketing transportation to special events. Special fares—sometimes special trains—were promoted to all sorts of events, such as exhibitions, lectures, agricultural fairs, even political rallies. Some of these excursions were joint operations involving two or more roads. These weren't railfan excursions, but a normal part of everyday life.

We found many examples of such special excursions, operated by the Cheshire and Ashuelot Railroads, among broadsides in the Historical Society of Cheshire County Archives, including: November 17, 1868, to Keene to hear General J. S. Chamberlain's talk on "The Surrender of Lee;" August 1, 1869, to Bellows Falls to see General Grant at the Island House; September 2, 1869, to see the great Hoosac Tunnel (which, we note, did not even open until 1875!); February 27–29, 1872, to Keene to

The occasion is Keene's combined Sesquicentennial and Fourth of July Celebration, for which employees at B&M's Keene Shops created this parade float—"Engine 150, Train 1903"—to mark the event. The float, drawn by a team of four horses, was built of wood and engine parts scavenged at the locomotive shop. Also part of the day's events was an afternoon baseball game between the B&M's Mechanicville, NY, and Keene Shops (Keene lost). The railroad, Keene's largest employer at the time, obviously played a prominent role in civic life, July 4, 1903. Photogr. unknown; B. G. Blodget coll.

In a scene typical of any country depot, the local way-freight is in town waiting at the freight dock as a freight handler hustles outgoing freight across a span board to a waiting car. Way-freights ran like passenger trains except that they called at the freight house to drop and pick up freight instead of at the station for passengers. Running "wild" or "extra," they always had to make certain to be in the clear for scheduled trains. Henniker, NH, 1952. Dwight A. Smith photo; Brent S. Michiels coll.

see "The Grand Exhibition of the Battle of Gettysburg;" November 16, 1872, to Boston to see the ruins of the city's Great Fire; and April 11, 1876, to Swanzey for a Temperance Rally. On September 3, 1881, fourteen coaches with some 500 passengers departed Keene for Rocky Point on Narragansett Bay in Cranston, Rhode Island, to enjoy "shore dinners." Evidently even more cars were added en route, for "when the train got as far as Worcester as many cars as two locomotives could draw were filled with passengers" (*Sentinel* Sept. 8, 1881).

In 1901, fifteen B&M passenger trains departed Keene weekdays, including ten (five eastbound and five westbound) on the Cheshire Branch, two over the M&K Branch, and three over the Ashuelot Branch. It was three hours to Boston on the Cheshire via Fitchburg, three hours and forty minutes on the M&K via

Nashua. In Winchendon, sixteen trains departed weekdays: ten on the Cheshire Branch, four on the Worcester and Contoocook, and two on the Boston & Albany's Ware River Branch to Palmer, Massachusetts, via Barre and Ware. The Railroad Age was at hand and the roads built a robust passenger business.

However, while the public was enraptured by the glory and excitement of rail travel, railroads knew from their beginnings it was freight traffic that was going to sustain them in the long run—paying back their cost of capital and providing dividends to their shareholders. Yet as the railroad was a major technological invention, even its staunchest promotors could not foresee all the potential applications that lay ahead for the fledgling industry, let alone its coming role as an enabler of the Industrial Revolution. On the Cheshire Railroad in 1850, passenger and freight revenues accounted for 47 and 53 percent of combined revenues compared to 32 and 68 percent in 1889. Reflecting the growth of manufacturing, 54,969 tons of freight handled in 1850 grew to 661,375 tons in 1889 with corresponding revenues of $91,138 and $404,140 respectively.

The railroads ushered in an era of prosperity that would last over a hundred years and change the face of the area forever, introducing industrial manufacturing into a heretofore purely agricultural economy and connecting the Region to a westward expanding country. With transportation available, the Region suddenly found itself empowered by almost unlimited potential to produce and ship goods to market—everything from natural resources like lumber, blueberries, chickens, hogs, wool, ice, and granite to manufactured goods like shoes, textiles, pianos, toys, clothespins, furniture, woodenware, and industrial machinery. Throughout the text we present the names of consignees using rail at different stations in 1915—near the peak of railroad dominance—drawn from a B&M Traffic Department compilation (Atkins 1915) augmented by important customers we are aware of before and after that time.

Until highways in the Region improved after World War II, the railroads handled literally everything that moved in daily commerce. As commercial hubs, railroad stations were natural gathering places. They were where the telegraph office was located, where goods were received and shipped, and the portal through which people of every class arrived and departed town. They were the settings for scenes of happiness and sometimes great sorrow. News reporters were never far away, chronicling the comings and goings of people. Newspapers, mail, and express rode the rails. Four different Railway Post Offices (RPOs) staffed by US Government mail clerks operated on passenger trains running through the Monadnock Region. The much-anticipated daily arrival of the local way-freight brought petroleum products and coal, new appliances and automobiles, caskets, sacks of grain, livestock, household supplies, and goods of every description.

Today it is almost unimaginable how interwoven the railroad once was with the citizenry. Indeed, Francis A. Perry, retired master mechanic at the Keene Shops, even served as Mayor of Keene in 1901–1902. Railroads were the lifeblood of a community and cities and towns were either made or handicapped depending on whether or not they were connected to the nation by good rail service. Once the railroads became established, dependence upon rail service would extend well into the mid-twentieth century in many areas—including the Monadnock Region—where the highway system remained primitive. It continued to be faster and more efficient to travel and ship by rail. Not by coincidence, as highways were improved and built out, they often paralleled rail routes. It was along the railroads that communities, commerce, and industry had taken root and flourished.

The public's reliance upon railroads compelled a culture of self-sufficiency and dependability among the roads and their employees. The railroads were independent stockholder-owned companies. They were not government subsidized. There was zero tolerance for errors and members of the "railroad family" were expected to do their jobs flawlessly. Patalano (1997), even described most railroaders he worked with during his career (1941–1980) as "fanatically responsible." Shop forces home-built and repaired much of the roads' equipment. Sectionmen immaculately maintained the rights-of-way. Stations and freight houses were all built and maintained by special crews. In addition to maintaining their own signal systems and proprietary telephone and telegraph lines along their tracks, the roads moved company mail on their own trains, generated much of their own power at shop complexes and other large facilities, and made their own electricity in trackside battery tubs to power signals.

CHAPTER ONE

THE VERMONT & MASSACHUSETTS RAILROAD: THE "HOOSAC TUNNEL ROUTE"

Westminster (MP B54.99) to Athol, Massachusetts (MP B81.90)

The story of railroads in the Monadnock Region must begin with the seventy-seven-mile, Vermont & Massachusetts Railroad, a 26.9-mile section of which runs along the southern edge of the Monadnock Region, ascending and crossing the Worcester Plateau between Westminster and Athol, Massachusetts.

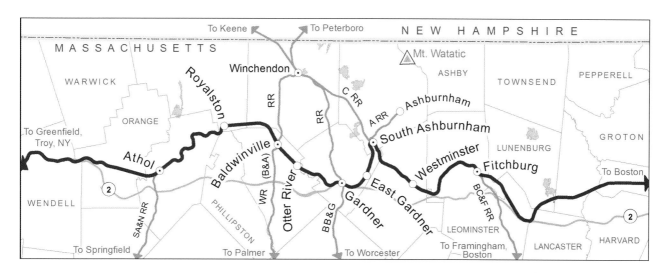

Boston, Mass. (North Station)	00.00	Royalston	75.58
Ayer	36.05	Pequoig Siding (Pequoig)*	77.96
Fitchburg (Jct. FRR, BC&F)	49.55	Athol (Jct. SA&N)	81.90
West Fitchburg	51.84	Tyter*	83.78
Wachusett	53.16	Millers Falls (Grouts Corner)[1]	97.34
Westminster	54.99	Greenfield (Jct. T&G, CRRR)	105.59
S. Ashburnham (Ashburnham) (Jct. Cheshire, Ashburnham RR)	59.90	Hoosac Tunnel	134.96
		North Adams, Mass.	142.39
East Gardner	62.14	Johnsonville, N.Y. (Jct. Troy Br.)	174.12
Gardner (Jct. BB&G)	64.66	Troy	190.40
Otter River (Dadmanville)	68.62	Mechanicville	187.06
Baldwinville (Jct. Ware R.)	70.53	Rotterdam Jct., N.Y.	209.34

Mileage table for the Vermont & Massachusetts Railroad (V&M), Fitchburg to Greenfield, showing stations, junctions with other railroads, and distances from North Station, Boston (Fitchburg Div., Main Line, *B&M ETT No. 1*, April 29, 1928). The shaded area denotes the section of the V&M included in our discussion. Trains on the V&M moving *away* from Boston are westward/outward trains; Trains moving *toward* Boston are eastward/inward trains.
[1]The "Brattleboro Branch," part of the original V&M, ran 21 miles from Millers Falls to Brattleboro. It was sold to the CV-controlled New London Northern Railroad in 1880.
*Not a passenger station stop; included for reference only.

The Independent Years, 1843–1873

Even before the earliest construction work on the Fitchburg Railroad had begun in 1842, its visionary president, paper mill magnate Alvah Crocker, was already seeking a way to link the road with the systems building in Vermont, Canada, and the Great Lakes. Crocker's influence had already led to the chartering of the Brattleboro and Fitchburg Railroad Company of Vermont on October 31, 1840 to build from Brattleboro to the Massachusetts state line (Vermont Legislature Act 56). Subsequently, with the backing of Crocker and the Fitchburg Railroad, the Vermont & Massachusetts Railroad Company (V&M) was chartered in Massachusetts on March 15, 1844 (M. G. L. Chapter 134 of the Acts of 1844) to build west from Fitchburg through the northern parts of Gardner and Templeton (Otter River and Baldwinville) and beyond to Athol and Grouts Corner (Millers Falls) in the town of Montague, Massachusetts. There it would take a right-angle turn and continue northward to the Vermont border. The two companies merged in November 1844 as the Vermont & Massachusetts Railroad Company. It was essentially a build-out of the Fitchburg Railroad.

Confident that it would in a timely manner receive its Massachusetts charter, the V&M boldly commenced grading work between Fitchburg and South Ashburnham in the summer and fall of 1843. Its charter was approved in due course, but in retrospect it appears the road's application for a charter had been premature. After receiving it, the road, confronted by the difficulty of surmounting the steep easterly face of the Wapack Range ("Ashburnham Hill"), decided to seek an amendment that would allow it to take a more advantageous northerly route up through Ashburnham to Winchendon where the road would follow the Otter and Millers River Valleys west to Baldwinville. Also, of course, the road was not blind to the financial benefit of interchanging with the then-abuilding Cheshire Railroad eight miles further west at Winchendon. The railroad appealed to the county commissioners to support such change in its charter even as—confident that approval would be forthcoming—it had already begun grading work westward via Winchendon in September 1845.

But uproar arose in Gardner and Templeton, which fought any change in the chartered route. When the commissioners offered no support, the railroad appealed directly to the Legislature in 1845 but was again rebuffed. The revised charter, signed into law April 16, 1846, required the road to turn southward at South Ashburnham and to pass through Gardner. And to quote Harlow (1946:240), "that turn was the making of Gardner." For the V&M, building toward Winchendon on the assumption a charter amendment would be granted had been a serious and costly miscalculation.

The V&M immediately sold (at a $10,000 loss) its largely graded but now useless alignment in Ashburnham and Winchendon to the Cheshire in 1846. With its first eight miles thus partially built for it by the V&M, the Cheshire continued construction northwestward over the Monadnock Plateau in 1847 and reached North Walpole, New Hampshire, in 1848. At South Ashburnham, the Cheshire built its own terminal facilities, including a turntable, engine house, woodshed, water tank, and yard tracks.

Meanwhile, forced to take a more southerly route, the V&M decided that its best alternative for attacking "Ashburnham Hill" was to construct a switchback at South Ashburnham. This was built in 1846–1847, allowing the road to reach the 1,112-foot divide at East Gardner. During its years as an independent road, the V&M would struggle with this switchback arrangement. The switchback reduced the grade, but it meant that V&M trains arriving at South Ashburnham had to have their engines cut off, turned, and hitched to the opposite end of their trains before they could continue. It was an annoyance to passengers, since when the direction of the cars changed it meant reversing the seats.

Engines were turned either by using the Cheshire's turntable or a wye formed by a short connecting track between the two legs of the switchback. Exactly when this connecting track was installed and the details of how it was used are unknown. Though it was short, steep, and made a tight radius curve, the standard American-type engines of the day probably used it without difficulty. Particularly for passenger trains, pre-turned engines may have been staged, ready to back onto trains. The American Railway Guide for 1851 shows running times between Fitchburg and Gardner as forty-five minutes westbound and forty minutes eastbound (Alden H. Dreyer, pers. comm.). When the Fitchburg took over twenty-three years later, running times were forty-nine minutes westbound, forty-five minutes eastbound (Fitchburg Railroad/V&M Div. ETT No. 1, March 9, 1874). Clearly, there was no diddling around at South Ashburnham.

Much of the switchback's upper leg runs along a high embankment, while its lower leg traverses a long cut. Today, most of the rights-of-way for the upper and lower legs of the switchback—as well as for the connecting track—survive well-preserved, if cloaked by forest, inside the horseshoe curve that replaced the switchback in 1877. Railroad-owned to this day (Town of Ashburnham Assessor's Office 2015), the rights-of-way skirt the edge of the High Ridge Wildlife Management Area in South Ashburnham and are easily walked.

West of Gardner, rails reached Baldwinville in September 1847. Construction work between Royalston and Athol proved very expensive, requiring five covered wooden bridges that crossed and recrossed the Millers

River at different points in Athol alone (Lord 1953). The first train to make it all the way out to Athol—a work train led by the locomotive *William Penn*—appeared on November 16, 1847. The road had planned on sending the *Athol* for this occasion, but on October 27, while drawing a work train consisting of two flatcars of iron rails, it was lost in the collapse of the Bearsden Bridge (about four miles east of Athol). The whole train landed in the Millers River. Five men were killed outright, the engine wrecked beyond repair (*Massachusetts Spy* Nov. 3, 1847).

On December 27 a special train arrived from Fitchburg carrying railroad officials and guests, and a celebratory banquet was served at the Pequoig Hotel to mark the completion of the road to Athol. Lord (1953) states that nearly the entire town turned out for the event. Regular service between Athol and Boston began January 1, 1848. An inspection train ran the full length of the road from Fitchburg to Brattleboro on October 16, 1848, and the first official train steamed into Brattleboro on February 20, 1849.

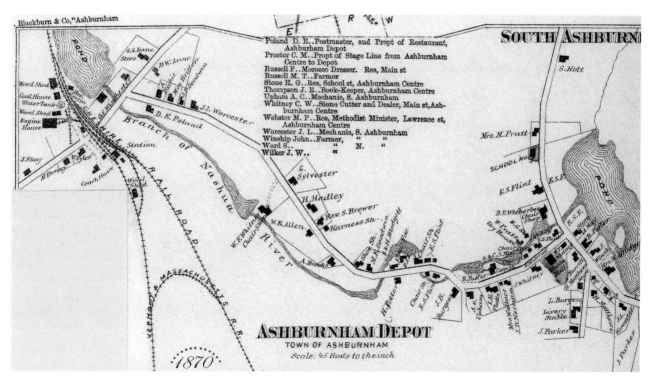

Track layout at S. Ashburnham in late V&M days. North is up. Note that while the V&M main line passed through S. Ashburnham, the yard infrastructure, including a turntable, engine house, and several wood-fueling stations, was Cheshire Railroad property. Note the two long switchback tracks (the right-hand, lower track leading eastward to Fitchburg, the left-hand, upper track westward to Gardner) and the tight radius connecting track, probably used for wyeing engines. The necessity of turning engines at S. Ashburnham ended in 1877 when the Fitchburg completed its horseshoe curve. F. W. Beers & Co. Atlas, 1870.

Even as the V&M's construction was underway, there was a buzz in the air about—of all things—a scheme to tunnel through the Hoosac Range in the Berkshires! No one knew for sure if this proposition would ever amount to anything, but just the talk of it was enough to alarm the Western Railroad. The Western, which merged with the Boston and Worcester to form the Boston & Albany (B&A) in 1867, quickly came to view the V&M as a potential competitor and bitterly opposed its plans at every turn. The V&M certainly did nothing to ease tensions when in 1850 it built an eight-mile branch from Grouts Corner to Greenfield. Construction of this branch had so stressed the road's finances that, in order to raise cash, a proposal to sell the road's east end between South Ashburnham and Fitchburg to the Fitchburg Railroad was briefly considered—and dismissed (Annual Report 1850). Obviously, the road felt an urgency to get the branch built, and indeed the branch would later become part of the Hoosac Tunnel Route main line.

As originally built, the V&M was a single-track main road, with passing tracks at all stations. More than 7,500

V&M lantern. Bob Arnold photo, courtesy of Fitchburg Hist. Soc.

tons of 56-pound iron rail from Liverpool had gone into construction of the road (Annual Report 1850). There were fifty-seven bridges twenty-five feet or more in length, aggregating to over 6,000 feet. Thirty-one of the bridges were Howe covered wooden truss bridges, the remainder masonry. A large engine house and turntable plus the road's shops were located in Fitchburg. There was a smaller engine house and turntable at Brattleboro and turntables at Gardner and Athol. The road paid rent to the Connecticut River Railroad (CRRR) for the use of its track and engine facilities at South Vernon, Vermont. Inexpensive wooden stations were constructed along the road. The road was fenced its entire length. The road owned hundreds of acres of woodlands that supplied the fuel for its locomotives. As early as 1860, the road began converting its locomotives from wood- to coal-burners (Annual Report 1861).

The V&M and the Fitchburg, both "Crocker roads" headquartered in Fitchburg, were natural end-to-end partners and, despite squabbles from time to time, maintained a tight relationship. Immediately after the V&M was chartered, Crocker was briefly president of both roads. Yet the two roads were separate companies and while it did not control it, the Fitchburg clearly took a familial interest in the V&M. In the late 1840s, the Fitchburg briefly leased the V&M, doubtless to help the financially strapped road get up and running.

Beginning in August 1851, the V&M and the Cheshire entered into a one-year trial arrangement that granted the Cheshire trackage rights over eleven miles of the V&M between South Ashburnham and Fitchburg for an annual rent of $32,000. In subsequent years, the Cheshire paid the V&M $39,000 (increased to $51,000 in 1869) annually for the trackage rights as well as for use of the V&M's engine house, station, water tank, and other terminal services and facilities in Fitchburg. In 1869 there was talk of granting the Cheshire permanent rights into Fitchburg in exchange for rights to Winchendon, but this never happened.

In its earliest years, V&M passenger service consisted of one through-trip over the road each way between Fitchburg and Greenfield, later further west to Shelburne Falls and Hoosac Tunnel Station. Thus, a one-day round trip was not possible or practical between most stations. Daily commuting was not practiced at the time.

However, on May 16, 1864, a second train each way "was placed on the road" (Annual Report 1865) and continued into the Fitchburg years.

The road's freight business reflected the wood-based economy of the day. An early mainstay was the woodenware industry, especially chair shops and other furniture makers.

In its early years, the V&M could have thrown Boston freight to the Fitchburg and Worcester Railroad (F&W) at Fitchburg or (after 1871) to the Boston, Barre and Gardner Railroad (BB&G) at Gardner. Both the Boston, Clinton and Fitchburg Railroad (which took over the F&W in 1869) and the BB&G brazenly included "Boston" in their names even though the city was never on their chartered routes. This was a marketing ploy to attract Boston traffic that either road could have handed to the B&A. However, this never happened as the V&M's loyalties rested securely with the Fitchburg.

By the late 1860s both the V&M and the Fitchburg were in full planning mode for the opening of the tunnel. The Commonwealth of Masachusetts had purchased the Troy and Greenfield Railroad (T&G) in 1862 to expedite its and the tunnel's construction, and on October 8, 1866, the V&M and the Fitchburg jointly leased the still unbuilt T&G between Greenfield and the east portal of the tunnel. The lease—calling for an exorbitant annual rent of $30,000—would be valid only until the tunnel was completed. The V&M furnished and began operations over the line as far west as Shelburne Falls on January 1, 1868, and to Hoosac Tunnel Station in July 1868 (Annual Report 1869). The road was in service only a little more than a year before a devastating flood damaged the track and bridges October 3–4, 1869. Service over the line was suspended and was not restored until July 1870 (Schexnayder 2015, 400, 416).

Even though the Hoosac Tunnel would not open for business until 1875 (Byron 1995), the Fitchburg, V&M, and Troy and Boston (T&B) roads began promoting through-passenger service over the "Great Hoosac Tunnel Route" between Boston and Troy, New York. Actually, ten miles of the trip—over Hoosac Mountain between Hoosac Tunnel Station and the T&B station in North Adams—was in a six-horse Concord Coach. The stage service, never profitable, began August 17, 1868, and continued until the tunnel opened.

The T&G was really a dead end for the next seven years. As Baker (1937, 183) observed, "The Troy & Greenfield served merely to keep the Fitchburg and V&M in the forefront of the Tunnel line project while the leased road was practically useless as a traffic producer." However, after the T&G opened, significant benefits "immediately accrued" to the small towns west of Greenfield, and the road played a crucial role in moving heavy equipment and supplies to the east bore (Schexnayder 2015, 208, 401).

In 1867 the V&M granted the Connecticut River Railroad trackage rights on the ten miles of track between South Vernon and Brattleboro. Ostensibly this was to allow the Connecticut River to run through-freights between Springfield and Brattleboro—an arrangement the V&M thought "satisfactory for the Connecticut River line." But at the same time, it appears the V&M also agreed to pay the Connecticut River to haul its traffic between South Vernon (possibly Greenfield) and Brattleboro—a sign it was not very profitable for the road (Annual Report 1868).

Even though the opening of the tunnel was still years away, the road grew confident its destiny lay westward and it began to lose interest in its line between Grouts Corner and Brattleboro (what it was by then calling its "Brattleboro Branch"). In 1870 it leased the branch to the Rutland Railroad for fifteen years. Before the year was out, the Rutland was in turn leased by the Vermont Central on December 30, 1870 (Baker 1937, 236).

Other changes were made by the road to prepare for the expected surge in freight and passenger traffic that would follow upon the tunnel's opening. In 1872–1873, on the eve of its lease to the Fitchburg, the V&M replaced its original wooden station in Athol with a new brick station. Athol was an important stop, located about midway on the line. Since the road had no dining cars, the new station was restaurant-equipped and became the road's primary station for meal stops. The company originally planned to move its general offices to the new building. However, before the new station was completed the road reached an agreement to lease itself to the Fitchburg Railroad and decided to keep its offices in Fitchburg (Lord 1953).

On Thanksgiving Day, November 27, 1873, in the presence of a large crowd of politicians and railroad officials, the Hoosac Tunnel headings met 10,134 feet from the west portal, completing a rough, 4.75-mile bore through the mountain. There was still much work to be done and the tunnel wouldn't open to traffic until 1875. (Schexnayder 2015, 458, 459).

During the V&M's years of independent operation, it suffered one notably serious accident. This accident occurred June 16, 1870, at Long Bridge—a covered bridge about halfway between Royalston and Athol—when the westbound passenger local came upon trackmen with a section car in the bridge. The section car was pushed along thirty feet, pounding the ties and cracking the bridge's floor timbers. Engine 11/*Thomas Whittemore* fell through the bridge and into the Millers River, taking with it the baggage and mail car and two other coaches (Lord 1953; Fletcher letters 1963 and 1965; Kyper 1987). Miraculously, no fire engulfed the wreck. There were three fatalities and twenty-two people injured (Mass. Railroad Comm. Report 1872). The bridge was repaired only to later burn on April 19, 1881 (*Athol Chronicle* April 21, 1881).

As an independent road, the V&M was never very profitable. Unlike the Western Railroad, the V&M never received a dime of state assistance. It was built with private capital and construction costs had drastically exceeded projections. Unfortunately, a railroad-building bubble in Britain had blown up in 1847, affecting interest rates and the availability of capital (Schexnayder 2015, 113–118). Struggling for capital, much of the road was mortgaged and the road was forced to issue bonds—which had the effect of increasing future operating costs.

In addition to the hangover from its construction costs (including damages), in its early years the V&M suffered from a general lack of freight! It was built through a sparsely populated area and though the road advertised some twenty-four miles of rivers along its route that could be harnessed for waterpower, trackside industrialization did not happen overnight. In its first decade, here is what the road candidly reported to its shareholders (Annual Report 1856, 11):

> Among the early mistakes in Railroad business, in which this Company was involved with all the rest of the Roads, was that of attempting to carry passengers and freight at rates far less than would pay an actual living

profit. All over the world railroads were new. Managers of roads then had no experience to guide them. They were launching out upon an unknown business. Had the prices of transportation been kept up, as they were before the railroads were built, the ruinous consequences we have been obliged to meet would not have come upon us. The public were [*sic*] most sadly deceived by the splendid fallacies that an iron road was going to last almost forever; that the cost for repairs would be very small; that the deterioration of iron wheels and iron machinery would be scarcely perceptible, and that the profits of railroads would be immense . . . it is scarcely necessary to say, that all this was a fatal mistake.

Financially, as Kirkland (1948, 1:415–416) summed it up, the road "was a weakling at birth and years had not strengthened it." Eventually, on the eve of the tunnel's opening, the V&M—in desperate need of capital—surrendered its independence, leasing itself to the Fitchburg Railroad for 999 years effective January 1, 1874.

In its last year of independent operation, the road carried 139,370 tons of freight, including 83,132 tons of lumber (its single biggest commodity) and 30,000 tons of finished goods.

The Fitchburg Years, 1874–1900

At the time of its hand-over to Fitchburg management, the V&M's rolling stock included thirteen Hinkley American (4-4-0) locomotives in working order, nineteen passenger and seven baggage/mail cars, 155 8-wheel boxcars, 120 8-wheel flatcars, two snowplows, two derricks, and a drovers' saloon.

With the lease of the V&M, the Fitchburg secured direct access to the state-owned Troy and Greenfield Railroad (T&G), thereby extending itself from Greenfield west to Williamstown. The V&M and the T&G became the Fitchburg's Vermont & Massachusetts Division. The opening of the Hoosac Tunnel had been expected to occur in 1874, but structural problems delayed the opening into the following year. On February 9, 1875, the first train—a work train drawn by the *N. C. Munson*—crept through the tunnel from daylight to daylight. The first

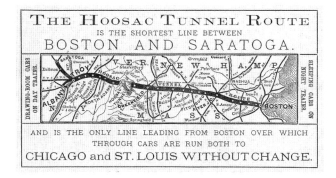

Map of the Hoosac Tunnel Route of the Fitchburg Railroad and the Troy & Boston Railroad. Public Time Table, 1878. Fitchburg Hist. Soc.

revenue freight, an eastbound drawn by the *Deerfield*, passed through the bore April 5, 1875 (Schexnayder 2015, 482–484).

"The completion of the five-mile Hoosac Tunnel was one of the great engineering achievements of nineteenth century America" (Schexnayder 2015, ix). Long anticipated as a gateway to the west, the tunnel's opening, after nearly thirty years of sometimes deadly struggles, was truly one of the great railroad events of the day. The Hoosac Tunnel Route now threatened to become what the B&A had long feared: a real competitor for western traffic.

Soon after leasing the V&M, Fitchburg management unleashed major capital investments to upgrade the road. One of its first priorities was to speed up operations on Ashburnham Hill by replacing the obsolete switchback and turning arrangements at South Ashburnham with a horseshoe curve. When the town of Westminster got wind of this, it immediately saw an opportunity to redress what it considered a long-standing grievance: the V&M had bypassed the center of town. It was a two-mile stage ride to reach the town's station. Thus, the town sponsored a meeting in the Town Hall on December 23, 1874 that attracted some fifty officials and business leaders from Fitchburg, Gardner, and other nearby towns. Citing the desirability of straightening as much as possible the Great Hoosac Tunnel Route between Wachusett and Gardner, they proposed a route that would shorten the distance by two miles and pass closer to Westminster Center (*Fitchburg Sentinel* Dec. 24, 1874). Even though

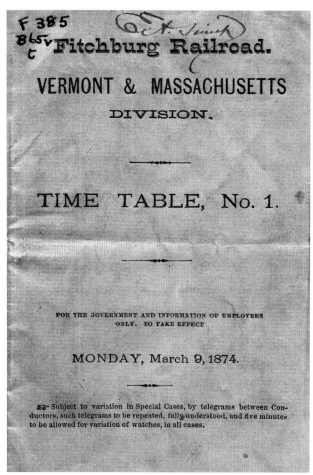

Fitchburg Railroad/V&M Div. ETT No. 1, March 9, 1874. This was the first ETT issued for the governance of the road after the Fitchburg leased the V&M. Through service between Fitchburg and Hoosac Tunnel Station (at the tunnel's east portal; the tunnel had not yet opened) was limited to No. 6 East departing Hoosac Tunnel at 7:30 a.m., arriving Fitchburg at 12:20 p.m., and No. 2 West departing Fitchburg at 1:20 p.m., arriving Hoosac Tunnel at 6:00 p.m. Train No. 11, a Monday-only cattle train, departed Greenfield at 11:50 a.m. and arrived Fitchburg at 6:26 p.m. Fitchburg Hist. Soc.

some preliminary survey work had found a feasible alignment, the route no doubt entailed much higher costs and nothing came of it.

The Fitchburg proceeded with its plans, authorizing construction of a horseshoe curve that would permit continuous operation through South Ashburnham. Completed in 1876–1877, the curve allowed 1.41 miles of steady, 1.05 percent grade between MP59.34 and MP60.75. West of MP60.75, where the grade to East

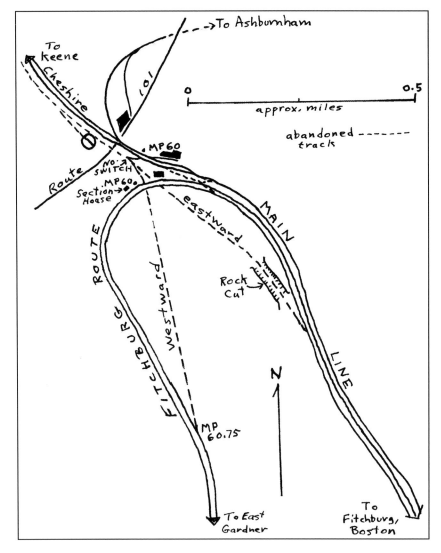

This sketch, adapted from Goodwin (1976), shows the horseshoe curve at S. Ashburnham ca. 1940. The dotted lines show the old V&M eastward (lower) and westward (upper) legs of the switchback arrangement that the curve replaced.

percent grade. While the eastward grade was not as severe as the westward grade, it was longer and complicated by the fact that eastbound trains on the system were generally heavier than westbounds. Illustrating this point, the eastbound pusher district was forty miles, compared to fifteen miles for the westbound pusher district.

In addition to the Ashburnham Hill project, the Fitchburg urgently rushed along other projects intended to increase speeds and capacity on the V&M Division. In 1876–1877 the road laid 3,000 feet of second iron between Athol and South Royalston. As a part of this project, the road was realigned along the Millers River, the river channel moved, and two bridges eliminated. To facilitate the construction work, Pequoig (French-Indian for "land along the Millers River") was established as a train register station and telegraph office about halfway betwixt Royalston and Athol. (Note: In Chapter 2 we will encounter a different Pequoig in Winchendon.) By 1886, fifty-four miles of the road's fifty-six-mile main line between Fitchburg and Greenfield were already double-tracked.

The Fitchburg replaced many of the old dilapidated stations (described by some as "mere hovels") it had inherited from the V&M. New stations were installed at South Ashburnham in 1874 and Fitchburg in 1877. From the late 1870s into the mid-1880s, the V&M's original wooden bridges were gradually "ironized."

In 1880 the road disposed of the V&M's old "Brattleboro Branch" by outright sale to the Central Vermont-controlled New London Northern Railroad. As Baker (1937, 183) observed, Fitchburg management presciently recognized that a struggle was emerging for Vermont to New York traffic in the Connecticut Valley and deemed

Gardner summit (MP62.14, 1,112 feet) steepens to 1.20 percent, the project made no changes. In its total climb from Fitchburg (MP49.55, 440 feet) to East Gardner, the road rises 672 feet in 12.59 miles, for an average grade of about 1.01 percent.

Trains ascending the Worcester Plateau from the west, even with the assist of the Millers River Valley, also struggled. Eastbound trains faced a long grade from Athol (MP81.90, 541 feet) to East Gardner, climbing 571 feet in 19.76 miles, an average grade of 0.55 percent. The ruling eastward grade was "Royalston Hill," seven miles from MP81 to MP74 that included a brief section of one it wise to sell while the selling was good. This sale, however, gave the Central Vermont control of the section of the Connecticut River main line between East Northfield and Brattleboro, an arrangement that, as we will discuss further in Chapter 14, would one day present difficulties for the B&M.

In 1887 the Fitchburg purchased the Troy & Boston and Boston, Hoosac Tunnel & Western Railroads, further extending its reach west to Troy and Rotterdam, New York. At the same time, it purchased (for $10 million in Fitchburg stock and bonds) the Hoosac Tunnel and the Troy and Greenfield Railroad from the Commonwealth of Massachusetts. After these acquisitions, the road reorganized into three divisions: the Fitchburg, Tunnel, and Western Divisions. The V&M became part of the Tunnel Division, which included the main line and all branches between Fitchburg and Williamstown, Massachusetts.

As mentioned earlier, the V&M had built a new brick station at Athol in 1872–1873, which was roughly at the road's midpoint. Unfortunately, a fire, which started in the station's restaurant kitchen, broke out on July 22, 1892, destroying the station's second floor and roof (Lord 1953). An old passenger coach was rushed out to serve as a temporary station, and a replacement station was built in 1892–1893. Since the line was now part of a longer route, the Hoosac Tunnel Route, the Fitchburg chose to shift the restaurant/dining stop westward about twenty-four miles to Greenfield.

In 1895–1896 the antiquated station at Gardner was replaced by a new brick station at the crossing of the Worcester Branch. It was built alongside and with a connecting canopy to the Boston, Barre & Gardner Railroad station there. Finally, Gardner had a "union station," even though by this time the Fitchburg controlled both lines. A grand opening celebration was held March 24, 1896.

The Boston & Maine Railroad leased the Fitchburg system on July 1, 1900 and it naturally became the B&M's Fitchburg Division. The underlying V&M lease, its term changed from 999 to ninety-nine years, came along with the deal. In 1901, under terms of the lease, the B&M purchased all the Fitchburg stock held by the Commonwealth of Massachusetts. Finally, the state was completely out of the railroad business (Bradlee 1921, 70).

The Boston & Maine Years, 1900–1983
"The Route of the Minute Man"

The crown jewel in the Fitchburg lease was the road's prized main line between Boston and Mechanicville, New York. In the twentieth century, the Fitchburg Division would become the B&M's chief revenue-producing division, with Mechanicville the road's principal western gateway, and the Fitchburg Route Main Line its busiest route in tonnage. Now at the very heart of a much larger system, the V&M had become a very valuable property. In this segment we touch on some of the historical highlights, particularly those that apply to our defined area along the southern edge of the Monadnock Region.

Upon leasing the Fitchburg, the B&M had acquired 221 locomotives, 263 passenger cars, 5,162 freight cars, and miscellaneous other rolling stock (Frye 1982). Among the locomotives, Moguls (85), Americans (78), and Consolidations (25) predominated (Edson 1982).

The Fitchburg Railroad of 1900 was a run-down property, still governed by remarkably primitive operating procedures. This was exemplified in a talk presented by B&M Historian William J. Fletcher (1890–1981) to a Railroad Enthusiasts group in Boston on November 16, 1961. Fletcher, who grew up along the railroad in Fitchburg, Massachusetts, described how in the early years of the nineteenth century, watching freight trains making a run for Ashburnham Hill was a spectator sport:

> People in Fitchburg used to make it a point to watch fast-freights 253–257 and 259 as they passed through the city around five in the evening. Moguls 646–653 and 620 used to haul them. They ran only a few minutes apart and just as fast as they could go. There were no block signals to guide them, but every crossing tender, switchman, sectionman, and many others would hold up 1-2-3-4-5 fingers to the engineers to warn them how close they were to the train ahead. Pushers used to be set in the Middle [Track] at Fitchburg and as soon as the buggy of one of the trains would go by, the switch would be opened and we would see the pusher chase after the train to assist it on the hill. It was all risky business. If one of the trains should stop suddenly, its buggy would be smashed and men hurt.

Type B double-arm, lower-quadrant automatic block signals were installed on the Fitchburg Route Main Line in 1908–1910 (Goodwin 1976). To speed up traffic on "Ashburnham Hill," five miles of third iron were laid between Westminster station and South Ashburnham in 1920. It served as both a long lead for the Cheshire Branch and a running track for westbound freight drags, allowing faster traffic to move on the main line.

With a fresh infusion of capital, the V&M began to see many long-overdue upgrades in the mid-1920s, after years of underinvestment and deferred maintenance. In 1925 a new steel bridge was installed in Athol and other bridges were strengthened to allow operation of heavy Santa-Fe (2-10-2) power east of East Deerfield. Deep rock-ballasting followed and, in compliance with ICC orders, an Automatic Train Stop system was installed in 1926 (*EM* Aug26, 3).

Infrastructure improvements led to a speed-up in passenger trains and the establishment of several named trains on the system, including the Fitchburg Division. In May 1926 the *Minute Man* with a through-sleeper to Chicago was inaugurated (*EM* June26, 3–6). It ran express to Fitchburg and also stopped at Gardner and Athol in the Monadnock Region. The *Berkshire Flyer*, a day express between Boston and Troy, New York, was added in September 1927.

In 1930–1931 the road installed twelve sections (totaling 159 miles) of Centralized Traffic Control (CTC), the first installation of its kind in New England and the largest in the world at that time (*EM* AprMay31, 8, 14). Included were the 26.9 miles in our defined region over the Worcester Plateau between Westminster and Athol. This installation and that later installed along the Connecticut River Route Main Line in 1964–1965 would be the only CTC installations ever made in the Monadnock

This rare image, shot from atop the Temple-Stuart Company's water tank, shows Train 58, the eastbound *Minute Man*, on the road in Baldwinville, ca. 1930. The train is drawn by either Pacific 3681 or 3688. These two engines, christened the *Wm. Dawes Jr.* and *Paul Revere*, respectively, received a special "buff and blue" paint scheme shortly after the train's debut in May 1926. The curved track at right is the spur into the Temple-Stuart plant. George A. Miller photo, courtesy of Richard E. Miller.

Region. The light density traffic on all the other lines did not justify the expense of such an installation.

The B&M's first diesel, brand-new Alco switcher 1102, passed over V&M rails in September 1934 on a break-in run from Mechanicville to Lowell (*EM* Jul–

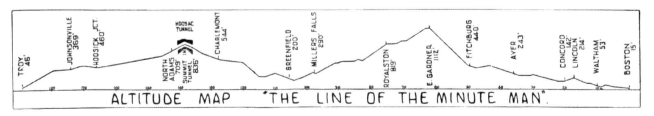

Profile chart of "The Route of the *Minute Man*" on the Fitchburg Route Main Line and the Troy (NY) Branch showing the rise in the road over the Worcester Plateau between Fitchburg and Athol. Westbound the grade was steepest, but the eastbound grade was much longer (B&M PTT April 24, 1938).

EMD FT 4219AB and a trailing F2 are on Boston to Rotterdam Jct., NY, symbol freight BR-1 at Gardner, Aug. 10, 1951. Photogr. unknown; R. R. Richards Jr. coll.

Sep34, 9–10). Not far behind it came B&M's new Budd streamline train 6000 on its maiden trip on B&M rails from Mechanicville to Boston on February 9, 1935. General Motors/Electro-Motive demonstrator, FT road diesel 103, made test runs on the line September 5–15, 1940 (Byron 1994).

The floods of March and April 1936 and the hurricane of 1938 inflicted serious damage to the line. In response to these devastating floods, the Army Corps of Engineers Birch Hill Dam Project came along in 1940–1941. Track was raised thirty-five feet over a 4.5-mile stretch in Winchendon, Templeton, Phillipston, and Royalston. Work included a big forty-foot deep rock cut and a new three-span, 210-foot bridge over the Otter River in Winchendon (EM Sum41, 9–13).

World War II brought a surge in both passenger and freight traffic on the B&M. Nowhere was the traffic heavier than on the Fitchburg Route, where the road's heaviest steam power, T1 Limas (2-8-4; 4000–4024) and R1 Baldwins (4-8-2; 4100–4117) purchased in 1928–1929 and 1935–1941 respectively, were called upon to move huge wartime manifests (Goodwin 1976). In need of even more power, the road leased six Mikados (2-8-2) from the Delaware, Lackawanna and Western Railroad (DL&W) in December 1942. Railroad photography was wartime restricted and images of these units working on the B&M are virtually non-existent. Even though they could move freight the fastest, all the "big steam" still required pushers, usually K8 Consolidations, on Ashburnham and Royalston Hills.

The B&M's first diesel road engines, EMD FTs 4200–4224 (A/B sets), began arriving during the war in 1943. They were immediately pressed into service moving wartime tonnage on the Fitchburg Route Main Line. Their performance exceeded expectations, allowing the Mikados to be returned to the DL&W in May 1943. On October 26, 1943, the new diesels set a record run: Boston-Mechanicville in six hours and twenty-five minutes with 125 cars, 3,839 tons. Keene resident Lloyd S. Seaver was fireman on that much-celebrated run. By the end of 1946 the Fitchburg Route Main Line was completely dieselized, as was the entire Fitchburg Division by the end of 1952.

Photographer George C. Corey says he climbed atop a boxcar to take this image—back in the days when such didn't seem to bother anyone! Pilot "Bluebird" 1744 and three Erie Lackawanna U25Bs on PB-W lean into the curve at S. Ashburnham at sunset, June 21, 1968. Note the Cheshire Branch leads at left.

In the mid-1950s, a period of contraction began. Close to 800 tons of steel rail was salvaged in the removal

B&M GP9 1704 leads two muscular-looking Erie Lackawanna SD45s on PB-99 a B&M-D&H-Erie Lackawanna pooled-power piggyback train at Gardner Yard. The SD45s on these trains marked one of the early appearances of six-axle freight power on the B&M, ca. 1969. Richard E. Miller photo.

of the third iron between Westminster and South Ashburnham in 1957 (*EM* MayJune57, 16). Then in 1961, seven miles of second iron from Parkers (MP66.51), through Otter River and Baldwinville, to Wrights (MP77.65) was lifted and, in the early 1980s, another ten miles of second iron—between Westminster and Gardner—was removed.

In late April 1952, streamline train 6000 was taken off the *Cheshire* and assigned to the Fitchburg Route Main Line where it would run most of its final years as the *Minute Man* between Boston and Troy, New York. The streamliner made its final run from Troy to Boston on May 7, 1957 and was retired without fanfare. Not long afterwards, the last passenger train to operate west of Fitchburg departed Boston April 23, 1960 at 9:30 p.m. and arrived Greenfield at 12:05 a.m. the following morning.

In the 1960s, joint B&M-D&H-Erie Lackawanna through service using pooled power between Boston and Chicago was tried. These trains—PB-W/PB-E (later resymboled PB-99/PB-100)—marked one of B&M's early, joint-marketing efforts with western roads to tap exploding demand for piggyback service between New England and the Midwest. Regular freight also could move on these trains. The pooled power arrangement made for interesting train watching. For power, Erie Lackawanna usually supplied SD45s, but GP35s, U25Bs, and even a few Alcos made appearances. The power sets were always led by a B&M engine—usually a GP9—since they had the cab signals required at the time. The pooled power trains were discontinued in late 1970 (letter, Richard Anderson to Brent Michiels, Jan. 8, 2016).

In 1970 the B&M entered bankruptcy and a thirteen-year revenue-based reorganization began. Passenger service was restored as far west as Gardner on January 18, 1980, when the MBTA and B&M instituted service to the Chair City. Unfortunately, this arrangement only lasted through December 1986. The B&M, having lost the MBTA commuter rail contract to Amtrak, terminated commuter rail operations over its track west of Fitchburg on January 1, 1987. The service marked the only time the MBTA ever reached into the Monadnock Region.

Westminster—B54.99

The Westminster station was located on Bathrick Road in the eastern part of town, about two miles from the center of town. The town operated a stage to connect passengers, mail, and express between the station and Westminster Center, as well as to Wachusett Park, a nearby resort and recreation area at the base of Mount Wachusett. The stage was taken off after the Gardner, Westminster & Fitchburg Street Railway began operations in 1899.

The original station, built in 1846, was a two-story building. The station agent and his family occupied an apartment on the second floor. The station burned to the ground March 16, 1908 (*Fitchburg Sentinel* March 16, 1908). The family lost everything in the fire except their lives (Cousins 1958). A replacement station was built in 1908.

Station Agent Daniel J. Burns poses in front of the second Westminster station, ca. 1910. Postcard; Westminster Hist. Soc.

Seventeen cars on X2659 East have piled up at the Westminster station after a wheel broke on a loaded coal hopper. Both mains were fouled, the station pushed off its foundation, and a hobo riding the cars critically injured. One hundred men worked twelve hours to reopen the line. During the outage, Cheshire Branch passenger trains were detoured both ways via Worcester, April 30, 1914. Postcard; Westminster Hist. Soc.

Being in a rural area less than two miles west of Wachusett station, passenger traffic was light and Westminster was dropped as a passenger stop by 1930. However, Westminster remained operationally important as a train-order station. The station was situated near the base of Ashburnham Hill, where trains began their attack on the eastern slope of the Worcester-Monadnock Plateau. An agent-operator was on duty here twenty-four hours a day, signaling or hooping-up train-orders to as many as sixteen scheduled freight and twelve passenger trains daily in each direction, plus extras (Bachelder 1984).

Five miles of third iron, starting here at Westminster station and extending to South Ashburnham, was installed in 1920 to get slow-moving westbound freights grinding their way up the hill out of the way and allow faster traffic to move on the main line. Installation of Centralized Traffic Control (CTC) between Westminster and Athol in 1930–1931 was a major modernization that further increased fluidity on the main line. With CTC, Westminster was less important, but still warranted an agent-operator until 1939 when the station was finally closed (Bachelder 1984).

Westminster, richly endowed with many natural ponds and lakes, was mostly high in elevation and lacked the falling water necessary to turn mill wheels. As a result, the town was predominantly an agricultural community. As in other towns further north in the Monadnock Region, blueberries were a signature crop here and the annual harvest provided important income to many residents. In season, berries brought to the station during the day, often more than 150 bushel-sized crates, would be shipped on the night express to Boston, consigned to the L. B. Blanchard Co. at Fanuiel Hall Market (Cousins 1958).

Consignees at Westminster included the Dawley and Shepard Co., which received flour and shipped the famous Westminster Crackers; E. H. Merriam, a grain and grocery dealer; and C. L. Smith, the local coal and lumber dealer. A shoddy mill near the station received carloads of rags. J. C. Goodridge, a manufacturer of box shooks, and chairmaker M. E. Pierce used the station team track. Another chair manufacturer located in nearby East Princeton, Temple-Stuart Co., drayed raw materials and finished products between its plant and the station.

South Ashburnham
—MP B59.90

In V&M days this station was known as Ashburnham. It became South Ashburnham a few years after the Fitchburg took control in 1874. The station was razed in 1951. A small detached baggage building was modified as a stand-in final station (see photo 3-10 in Chapter 3). On August 15, 1958, the agency at South Ashburnham was discontinued and it became a carload-only, prepaid station under the jurisdiction of the agent at Gardner.

A heavy westbound freight, with Consolidation 2711 pushing, has just cleared South Ashburnham station on the way to East Gardner summit. Note the SRLX (Swift Refrigerator Line) car ahead of the buggy, Feb. 1940. H. W. Pontin photo; Brent S. Michiels coll.

Even with her shiny nose, E7 3815 (below) certainly looks nice on the point of Train 57, an all-stops, all-coach train to Troy, NY, as she passes South Ashburnham. This train only stopped at "South Ash" on a flag signal, Summer 1950. Photogr. unknown; Dale O. Russell coll.

A westbound troop train, led by B&M Mountain (4-8-2) 4102, leans into the curve at South Ashburnham. The station is the large building with the small detached baggage room to its left. At the extreme left, a woman and little girl are next to the section house taking in the action. The smoke stack is for the W. F. Whitney & Co. power plant, ca. 1943. Raymond E. Tobey photo; B&MRRHS Archives.

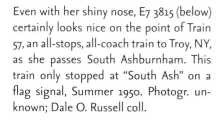

East Gardner—MP B62.14

East Gardner station looking inward. This was a small station that existed chiefly to serve nearby Gardner State Hospital, which at its peak had a population of about 1,800. The B&M delivered coal to the hospital's power plant, visible beyond the station, Spring 1951. Photogr. unknown; B&MRRHS Archives.

Gardner—MP B64.66

At Gardner, the V&M was crossed at grade by the Boston, Barre & Gardner Railroad. Both roads had their own stations until Gardner Union Station opened in 1896. In 1874 the V&M was leased by the Fitchburg and the BB&G consolidated with the Fitchburg in 1885. Fifteen years later the B&M would take over the Fitchburg system.

In steam days, eastbound (East Deerfield to Gardner) or westbound (Fitchburg to Gardner) pushers were regularly assigned to assist heavy trains to the East Gardner summit. The pushers would cut off in Gardner, be spun on the turntable, and then drift back down the hill for their next assignments. The turntable lead at Gardner was just off the westbound siding a short distance east of the station.

In 1900–1925 the B&M interchanged cars at Gardner with the Northern Massachusetts Street Railway (or predecessor roads), especially carloads of coal destined for the street railways' power plants in East Templeton and Westminster Center, neither of which locations were served by a steam road.

In 1868–1878 more than two million chairs were produced in Gardner annually and shipped all over the country (Herrick 1878, 174). In 1897, P. Derby & Co. alone ranked as the second largest chair manufacturer in the world. In addition to Derby & Co., the following chair manufactories were served by sidings off the V&M: Wyman & Upham Co., John A. Dunn Co., E. Wright & Co., and Knowlton Chair Co. (Richards 1898). Other major chairmakers in the city had sidings off the BB&G line (see Chapter 11). At one time, Gardner ranked as the second busiest shipping point on the B&M system (EM Winter41, 28). Due to the large volume of LCL shipments—chiefly chairs and other furniture—handled here, the road installed a freight-handling conveyor system to speed cross-dock transfer of freight from trucks to rail cars. Up to eighteen boxcars spotted at the freight house dock could be loaded simultaneously (EM Feb50, 1–4).

There were, of course, other shippers in Gardner besides chairmakers. Atkins (1915) listed the Children's Vehicle Co. (baby carriages), Gem Crib and Cradle Co., G. E. Hoglund Co. (foundry), L. G. McKnight & Son (machinery), and Royal Steam Heater Co. (heaters and boilers) among important consignees at Gardner.

Depot Square, Gardner, at the junction of the Fitchburg's main line and Worcester Branch as it appeared ca. 1885. At left center is the fine brick station built by the BB&G ca. 1880, at right center the Fitchburg's old wooden main line station that it inherited from the V&M. Photo from Moore (1967).

Roughly the same view showing the Fitchburg's new Gardner Union Station shortly after it was built in 1895. It was architecturally harmonious with the BB&G station and included a clock tower. Gardner Tower would later be built just east of the water tower. Photogr. unknown; Photo courtesy The Gardner Museum.

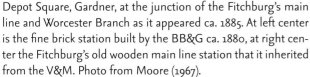

Union Square and Station, Gardner, Mass.

Gardner Union Station, Union Square, ca. 1920. Note the giant "Derby Chair," located on the lawn area east of the station, which fittingly welcomed visitors to "The Chair City of the World." It was donated by P. Derby & Co., one of the city's seventeen chair manufacturers that used rail service. Postcard; B. G. Blodget coll.

At left, E7 3811 has arrived Gardner Union Station with Boston–Troy, NY Train 57. At right, workers move carts of mail and express left by the train to waiting trucks, June 11, 1954. Nash-Ludlow photo; S. J. Whitney coll.

Westbound B&M GP9 "Bluebird" 1735 and three sisters are crossing the Peterboro Branch diamond at Gardner Union Station with a Boston-to-Mechanicville, NY, freight. The road's fifty GP9 road switchers (1700–1749), bought new in 1957, were the backbone of the road's main line power for the next quarter century. That is the connecting track to the Peterboro Branch at lower right. Note the early piggyback cars on the train's head end, 1959 (shortly before the station was razed). George C. Corey photo.

Gardner Union Station is now only a memory as GP18 1753, one of six GP18s purchased new by the B&M in 1961, leads a quartet of "Bluebirds" on a westbound freight at Gardner, June 5, 1961. Gardner Tower (left) contained a lever plant that controlled switches in the Gardner Yard and a Centralized Train Control machine that allowed dispatchers to control all train movements over twenty-eight miles of road between Westminster and Tyler. Donald S. Robinson photo; Brent S. Michiels coll.

With East Gardner Summit still 2.5 miles ahead, a quartet of GP9 "Bluebirds" led by the 1713 roars past Gardner Tower with Mechanicville-to-Boston freight MB-2. The 1713 is about to cross the Peterboro Branch diamond. By this time the branch had been cut back to Heywood. The two orderboard masts on the tower are for main line trains (left) and the branch, Oct. 15, 1961. Donald S. Robinson photo; Brent S. Michiels coll.

Otter River (Dadmanville) —MP B68.62

In early V&M years, this station was called Dadmanville—for C. E. Dadman, the stationmaster. B&M customers here in 1915 included livestock shipper Young & Son, the Otter River Brick Co., the Otter River Board Co., and Lord & Stone Foundry and Stove Works. Since it was only two miles from Baldwinville, the Otter River station was an early candidate for elimination, and it was closed in 1926. It burned and was sold in 1935. The midnight whistling of a passing train had given warning of the fire, but the station was lost (*Gardner News* Aug. 15, 1935). Both the passenger station and freight house are gone today, but freight trains still call at Otter River for outbound loads of paper from Seaman Paper Co., which operates a modern warehouse facility at the site.

Here at the vine-covered Otter River station and freight house, it would appear someone took pains to maintain a pleasant, garden-like environment—even with a swing to relax in—on the station grounds. Note the B&M stock car spotted at the east end of the freight house, probably for stock dealer Young & Son, ca. 1910. Photogr. unknown; Narragansett Hist. Soc., Templeton.

Baldwinville—MP B70.53

Baldwinville, named after Jonathan Baldwin, who settled in the area in 1767, was once a busy little industrial village. The Boston & Albany's Ware River Branch crossed the double-tracked V&M here on diamonds that were protected by a ball signal until, with the coming of CTC in 1931, it was replaced by color light signals. The two roads shared the station, but each maintained their own freight house. While each road had captive customers, they also interchanged traffic and competed for business in Baldwinville.

B&M customers here in 1915 included A. L. Adams Paper Co. (tissue paper) and five chairmakers, including Temple-Stuart Co. and Bishop & Dickinson, Inc. Today, except for a busy, single main line track, all the railroad infrastructure is gone. Passenger service ended here in 1960 and the station was razed in the late 1960s. Shortly before midnight on January 7, 1969, a derailment sent two flatcars with trailers right through the freight house, demolishing it (*Gardner News* Jan. 8, 1969). Thousands of boxes of Ritz Crackers were strewn about the tracks. (We'll have more to say about Baldwinville in Chapter 12.)

Baldwinville station and freight house (left) looking east on the B&M's Fitchburg route main line. The B&A diamonds, difficult to see in this image, are east of the station. Further east on the main line, note the signalman's shanty, section house, and one of the station's two 50,000-gallon water tanks. The high Otter River Bridge is southward (right, out of view) on the B&A (see Chapter 12). The boxcars at right are standing on one of two team tracks on the street side of the station, ca. 1910. Postcard; photog. unknown; Brent S. Michiels and Gordon Poirier colls.

B&M facilities east of the crossing diamonds as viewed from the east end of the freight house. The B&M pumped water from Depot Pond (on the opposite side of the tracks, not visible) to fill the big water tanks.

This overview is looking eastward from the Bridge St. overpass (note the "telltale" chains). The station, on the engineer's side east-bound, is at center-right across the tracks from the freight house. The track at right reached two team tracks on the south side of the station. The team tracks at left were accessed from the westbound main. July 16, 1949. Alan Thomas photo; B. G. Blodget coll.

Baldwinville station looking west, Nov. 6, 1954. L. S. Twombly photo; Brent S. Michiels coll.

[Opposite page] Looking from the US Rte. 202 bridge, west-bound F7 4268A/B approaches with a camp train, detouring due to a derailment on the Worcester main line. EF-2, the E. Deerfield-to-Fitchburg local freight, is in the clear on a rem-nant of the old eastbound main. Known by crews at the time as "the dead track," it was used as a runaround while switching. The tracks at left lead into the plant of furniture maker Temple-Stuart Co., once an important B&M customer. Baldwinville, June 28, 1968. Richard E. Miller photo.

Another eastward view at Baldwinville. Note the distant CTC color light signals, ca. 1940. Photogr. unknown; courtesy Narragansett Hist. Soc., Templeton.

Royalston station was located in the southern part of town—South Royalston village—along the Millers River. That's the Royalston House (hostelry) west of the station. Notice the open countryside above the station, ca. 1900. Postcard; B. G. Blodget coll.

Royalston—MP B75.58

Royalston station was situated in the extreme southeast corner of the town, four miles from the center, in the village of South Royalston. Here the railroad shared a narrow, steep-sided valley with the Millers River. By 1865, South Royalston had become a thriving village of small mills, turning out lumber, chairs, pine furniture, and textiles. Unfortunately, the village had a history of devastating floods and fires. A big fire in 1904 nearly took out the whole village.

The Whitney Woolen Co., which grew to become the dominant manufacturing enterprise in the village, was destroyed in the 1904 fire. The business was assumed and the mill rebuilt by the American Woolen Co. In 1915, manufacturing businesses included the woolen mill and at least three lumber mills. The American Woolen Co. plant was later purchased by the Mason-Parker Manufacturing Co., a maker of diverse products including toys, dollhouse furniture, beach chairs, and pool tables. Mason-Parker, the last of South Royalston's manufacturing mills, burned in 1939.

Business through Royalston station also included a strong agricultural component. In 1915, farm consignees—including three wood dealers, two shippers of hides, a livestock shipper, and eight dealers in poultry and eggs—used the station team track.

Royalston station showing much of the village across the Millers River, ca. 1908. Postcard; Gordon Poirier coll.

The "new" Royalston station that replaced the old station in 1941. The Rte. 68 bridge over the Millers River is visible at right, undated. Donald S. Robinson photo; Brent S. Michiels coll.

Athol—MP B81.90

The westernmost station on the V&M included in our discussion is Athol, aptly nicknamed "Tool Town" for two rail customers—the L. S. Starrett Co. (machine and precision measuring tools) and Union Twist Drill—that grew to become the town's largest employers. But before we continue, a bit more background on Athol's early, pre-B&M railroad history.

Here at Athol, the Boston & Albany's Athol Branch (originally the Springfield, Athol & Northeastern Railroad) met—but did not cross—the V&M. As was the case at Baldwinville, both roads interchanged and competed for traffic here. Originally, each road had its own yard, engine facility, and freight house. Passenger facilities were shared with the V&M under a union station agreement. Three hotels—the Pequoig Hotel, Athol House, and Leonard Hotel—were within walking distance of the station for the accomodation of travelers (Greene 2007, 197).

The B&A's Athol Branch ran eastward along the south side of the V&M for about a half mile to the station. Along this stretch were a lead to the B&A's three-stall, brick roundhouse, a 973-foot runaround track, and switches for several freight house sidings. In 1935, the B&A was forced to abandon the northernmost twenty-nine miles of the branch, from Bondsville to Athol, as the time drew near when the Swift River Valley would be flooded to create the Quabbin Reservoir. The last B&A train, the regular mixed, departed Athol Union Station on June 1, 1935. When the reservoir reached capacity in 1946, some eleven miles of the old branch were under water (Greene 2007).

The V&M's original facilities in Athol were all located on the north side of its main line. In its earliest years the V&M also had a turntable here, located at the western end of its yard. In the B&M years, a long, brick freight

The V&M replaced its early wooden station at Athol with this very ornate second station in 1872–1873. In addition to the clock tower, there was a similar tower on the building's south side and four smaller towers at each corner—all six towers festooned with, as Lord (1953) put it, "many doodads and much ornate iron grill work." Another unusual feature of this station was a large bell mounted atop the clock tower. Perhaps it was rung to herald the arrival and departure of trains. The station burned in 1892 and was immediately replaced. Photogr. unknown; photo from *Athol Illustrated* (ca. 1875), Linotype Printing Co., Gardner, MA.

An eastbound Fitchburg train is in Athol Union Station, as B&A Train 475, drawn by American 181, makes ready for its departure down the Athol Branch to Springfield, ca. 1885. B&MRRHS Archives.

Athol's third station, built by the Fitchburg in 1892–93, incorporated some of the second station's first-floor walls that had survived the fire. Note the smokestack for the L. S. Starrett Company's powerplant east of the station, ca. 1910. Postcard; B. G. Blodget coll.

Passenger service in Athol ended in 1960. Here is the same station and view as the preceding, ca. 1951. Nash-Ludlow photo; S. J. Whitney coll.

house was located just west of the station. When B&A service to Athol ended, the V&M/B&M purchased the road's terminal facilities and assumed the accounts of its shippers. Having no use for the roundhouse, the B&M leased it to others and eventually sold it. Remarkably, it survives today, a nearly forgotten relic of the old Springfield, Athol & Northeastern.

Upon its opening, the V&M looked to ship its share of the town's woodenware output—some 500 tons of table legs and leaves, chair seats, settee backs, barrels, kegs, boxes, shingles, etc. (Annual Report 1849). Exemplifying the diversity of Athol industries using rail service in the early B&M years, the road listed the Athol Comb and J. Wilcox Cos. (combs for textile machinery), Athol Gas & Electric Co., Athol Machine Co. (foundry), Athol Pump Co. (brass castings), Athol Table Co., National Printing Co. (printing presses), Bates Bros. (wallets), N. D. Cass Co. (toys), and Lee Bros. (shoes) as important customers (Atkins 1915). The B&M began serving the Diamond Match Co., one of several former B&A customers, in 1935 and, in 1946, began serving the Athol Wholesale Beverages Co., which built a large warehouse along the old Athol Branch connecting track (Greene 2007, 229).

Guilford Rail Systems/Pan Am Railways, 1983–2008

Pan Am Southern, LLC, 2008–

On June 30, 1983, the B&M was purchased out of bankruptcy by Guilford Transportation Industries and it became part of Guilford Rail Systems. In 2006, Guilford Rail Systems renamed itself Pan Am Railways. The V&M, the last of the original predecessor roads that made up the B&M system, was legally dissolved January 14, 1991. (Interestingly, the corporation was revived May 6, 2006, for a period of one year, not for the purposes for which it was originally organized, but for the purpose of conveying real property.)

More changes followed in 2008 when Pan Am Southern, LLC, a 50-50 joint venture of Pan Am Railways and Norfolk Southern Railway, was created to own and operate the 155-mile former B&M Fitchburg Route Main Line between Ayer, Massachusetts and Mechanicville, New York, including the original V&M between Fitchburg and Greenfield.

Though most of the Monadnock Region's original lines are gone, the B&M Fitchburg Route (ex-V&M) main line—now owned by Pan Am Southern, LLC—has survived. The Providence and Worcester (P&W), which purchased the old Boston, Barre & Gardner road between Worcester and Gardner from the B&M in 1974, interchanges traffic with Pan Am Southern at Gardner. Here Pan Am Southern train EDPO, the East Deerfield-to-Portland freight, meets P&W train WOGR, the Worcester-to-Gardner freight, March 18, 2016. Zachary Carlson photo.

A Pan Am Southern coal train with Norfolk Southern power is stopped on the main line at Gardner, awaiting a crew that will take it to Bow, NH, Aug. 16, 2016. Chuck Heidorn photo.

CHAPTER TWO

THE CHESHIRE RAILROAD:
THE "MAIN LINE OF CHESHIRE COUNTY"

South Ashburnham, Massachusetts (MP B59.90)
to Bellows Falls, Vermont (MP B113.83)

The Independent Years, 1845–1890

Chartering and Construction. The Cheshire Railroad Company, first projected by Keene businessmen in 1843, was chartered by the New Hampshire Legislature December 17, 1844, to build a line of rail from the Massachusetts border to Bellows Falls, Vermont. An organizational meeting of the corporation was held on January 10, 1845, at which time the charter was accepted and Salma Hale was elected the road's first president (*Sentinel* Jan. 15, 1845). On May 15, 1845, the company's first annual meeting was held, at which shareholders elected seven directors (*Sentinel* May 21, 1845). While Hale would continue as a director, Thomas M. Edwards of Keene, a tireless proponent of the railroad, was appointed president.

In one of the company's first orders of business, it sought and the Massachusetts Legislature granted

a charter on March 13, 1845, in the name of the "Winchendon R. R. Co.," to build from the state line to a connection with the Vermont and Massachusetts Railroad (V&M) at South Ashburnham, Massachusetts. Then in August of the same year, the Winchendon Railroad, never more than a paper railroad, was merged into the Cheshire Railroad.

As discussed in Chapter 1, the Cheshire purchased the first eight miles of its alignment from South Ashburnham to Winchendon, the grading already nearly completed, from the V&M in 1846. The road completed this section in the fall of 1847. Meanwhile, as early as August 1845 grading contracts had been awarded for work between Winchendon and Keene, and the railroad built northwestward over the Monadnock Plateau, reaching

Boston, Mass. (North Station)	*00.00*	Webb (Marlboro)	85.30
Fitchburg	*49.55*	E. Swanzey* (Golding-Keene Co.)	—
Wachusett	*53.16*	Joslin (Swanzey, South Keene)	89.22
Westminster	*54.99*	Keene (*Ashuelot, M&K*)	91.28
S. Ashburnham (*V&M, ARR*)	59.90	Summit*	97.08
Astor House Crossing/Bridge*	63.42	Tenth Section*	99.28
Naukeag (North Ashburnham)	64.03	Gilboa (East Westmoreland)	100.36
Winchendon, Mass. (*WR, W&C*)	67.92	Westmoreland	103.66
State Line, N.H.	70.93	Walpole	109.82
Fitzwilliam	76.28	Cold River	112.57
Putnam*	78.34	N. Walpole, N.H.* (*Sullivan*)	113.50
Rockwood Siding/Passing Track*	79.22	Connecticut River Bridge*[1]	113.60
Troy	81.55	Bellows Falls, Vt. (*Rutland*)	113.83

Mileage table for the Cheshire Railroad, South Ashburnham to Bellows Falls, showing stations and locations, junctions, and distances from North Station, Boston (Fitchburg Div., Cheshire Branch, *B&M ETT No. 1*, April 29, 1928). Trains moving *away* from Boston are outward/westward trains; Trains moving *toward* Boston are inward/eastward trains.

[1]End of B&M ownership on the Vermont shore; final 0.23 miles to Bellows Falls station via trackage rights on the Rutland Railroad.

*Not a passenger station stop; included for reference only.

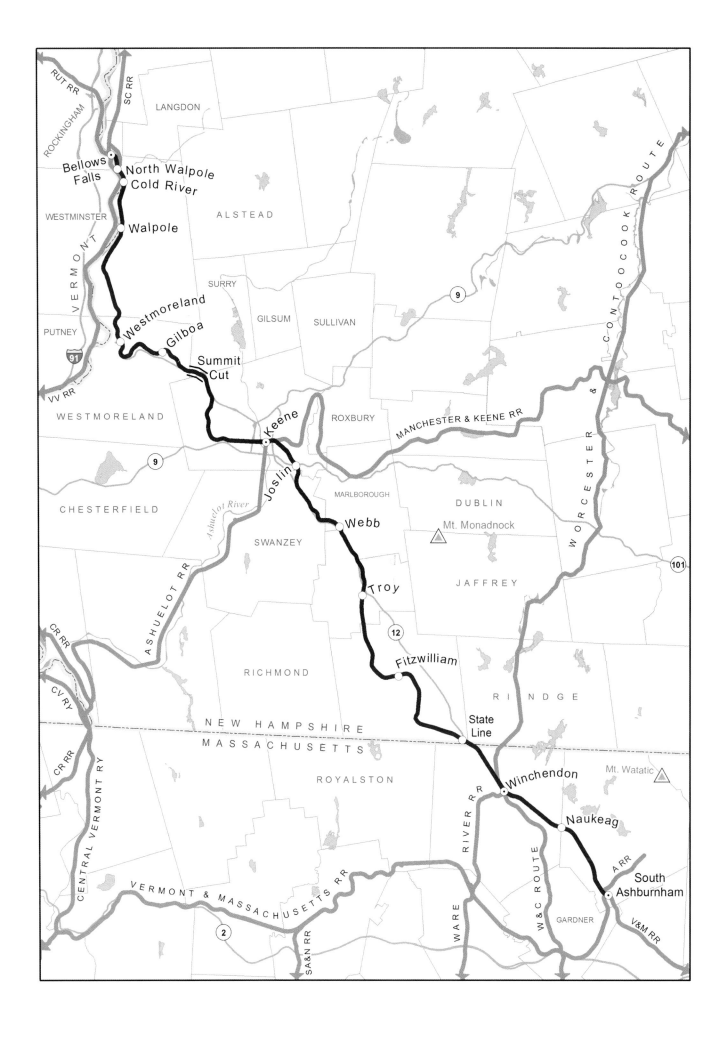

Troy, NH, in December 1847. Regularly scheduled service from the connection with the V&M at South Ashburnham out to Troy began in the same month, with a stagecoach connection beyond to Keene.

North of Troy, the topography becomes more mountainous and construction workers there had to deal with an enormous granite ledge and the deep gorge of the Ashuelot River's South Branch. The road followed the steep-sided river valley—at times along granite shelves cut into the hillsides—down into the Keene lowlands. Cutting and filling work to arrive at the final grade through Marlborough, and construction of a high, granite arch bridge over the East Branch of the Ashuelot River in South Keene (the "Joslin Arch"), delayed the road's opening to Keene. During a powerful storm that raked much of New England on October 13, 1846, "the great framework" built to support the erection of the arch collapsed in ruins. It was a major setback, but the keystone was finally set December 9, 1846, and the bridge completed in 1847.

Meanwhile, in anticipation of the cascading benefits to be delivered from the opening of the road, a building boom had gotten underway in Keene. An anonymous shareholder noted that twenty new buildings had been built in the city in 1847, and more new ones, exclusive of railroad buildings, were under construction in early 1848 (*Sentinel* May 25, 1848).

The road officially opened to Keene, and the first train, heralded by the sounds of cannon fire echoing among the hills south of the city, rolled in from Boston May 16, 1848, amid a huge celebration. More cannons boomed as the train rounded the curve from Water Street. Shops closed, church bells rang out, and a crowd of 5,000 met the train as it pulled into the station. Many had never seen a train. One old-timer is famously reported to have exclaimed, "Now, oh Lord, I'm ready to go!" It was arguably the greatest transformative event in the history of Keene. A new era was

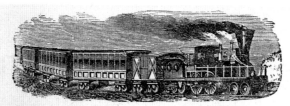

CHESHIRE RAILROAD.

Bellows Falls, Vt., to Fitchburg, Mass., 64 miles.

CONNECTIONS.

At Bellows Falls, with Central Vermont R. R. Line for all points North and West. At Keene with Ashuelot R. R. for Brattleboro, Springfield, Palmer, New York. At Winchendon, with Monadnock, Boston, Barre & Gardener, and Ware River Railroads. At South Ashburnham with Vt. & Mass. R. R. At Fitchburg, with F R. R. for Boston, Lowell, Nashua, &c. Also, with B. C. & F R. R., for Worcester, Providence, New Bedford.

R STEWART, *Gen. Manager*

F. H KINGSBURY, *Gen. Ticket Agent and Cashier*
General Office, Keene, N H

WM. A. RUSSELL, Prest. J. W DODGE, Gen. Freight Agent.

F. A. PERRY, Master Mechanic. H. H. STONE, Purchasing Agent.

R. HYLAND, Road Master and Wood Agent. D. C. HOWARD, Train Dispatcher.

Cheshire Railroad advertisement. Keene City Directory, 1879. Hist. Soc. Cheshire Cty.

dawning not only in the city, but in all the communities along the new road as well.

The train of fifteen cars, festooned its entire length with flags and boughs of evergreens, was drawn by two engines—Americans 5/*Cheshire* and 6/*Monadnock*—freshly delivered from Hinkley & Drury Locomotive Works in Boston. The conductor was Gardner Hall, born in Keene in 1809, a former stage driver between Fitchburg and Keene. On board were many prominent citizens, among them Mayor Quincy of Boston, Fitchburg Railroad President Alvah Crocker and other railroad officials, as well as many of the road's stockholders. The Boston Suffolk Brass Band led a procession of stockholders from the station to the Town Hall for a business meeting and then back to the station, where tables had been set up under a canopy and a feast for 1,600 people, recalled by locals as "the big lunch," was served. The train was turned, and returned to Boston at day's end.

The opening of the road to Keene had not come easily. Early opposition had come from farmers, fearing their markets would be ruined. Tavern owners and turnpike and stagecoach operators were rightfully concerned about what the railroad would do to their businesses. The road had to contend with political prejudices, opposition of the V&M, and difficult negotiations for the purchase of land—

The famed Barry Faulkner mural, *Advent of the Railroad*, 1848, depicting the arrival of the first train in Keene, May 16, 1848. The mural can be seen today at the Historical Society of Cheshire County.

initially without the power of eminent domain—from reluctant landowners. Then, as a shareholder remarked, "serious difficulties were presented: 1st to get into our valley, 2d to get out of it, and 3d to procure the means" (*Sentinel* May 25, 1848).

Now with a continuous line of rail between Boston and Keene open for business, the directors of the Cheshire gushed about the soon-to-be-completed rail system from northern Vermont to Boston in their Annual Report for 1848:

> . . . we shall be ready as soon as the other roads constructing above us shall be completed, to receive their business and to pass it along to its destination; with the Rutland, the Sullivan, the Central, the Passumpsic, the V&C [Vermont and Canada], and the Ogdensburg roads—all passing on to completion, and in the business of all of which our road must participate, in a greater or less degree—we can want no incentive to urge us on our work, and can entertain no distrust, that when the road shall be completed, the amount of business which shall be done on it will exceed any expectations which have been entertained by its most sanguine friends.

Construction of the road west of Keene, begun in 1846, dragged on through 1848, drilling and blasting through over 3,000 feet of granite ledge (up to a depth of fifty feet) in West Keene, Surry, and Westmoreland. This was the Summit Cut, where the road reached its highest elevation between Keene and the Connecticut River at 830 feet in Surry. Even with the benefit of the huge cut, the road west of Keene required a maximum grade of 1.42 percent to reach the divide near MP98 before descending with a maximum grade of 1.14 percent to a point in Walpole near MP110.

The contractors hired for the difficult job of cutting through the ledge brought in several hundred immigrants, mostly Irishmen, to supply the labor. This dangerous work took almost three years and the difficulties caused several contractors to fail financially.

As if the construction work itself was not difficult enough, the housing of hundreds of workers and their families was a real problem for the railroad, especially when the work advanced into sparsely populated areas. To address the need, the railroad built scores of rough lumber "shanties." Despite the term, they were sturdily built and strong enough to shelter workers through the cold, snowy Monadnock winters. They were generally twenty-five-feet long by fifteen-feet wide, and of course

J. A. French's "Around the Curve," Surry, 1868. Even though the Cheshire barely entered the town of Surry, a defining feature of the road was found here—the Summit Cut, within which the top of the grade was reached at 830 feet. In its totality, Summit Cut extends over 3,000 feet, reaching depths of 50–60 feet, beginning with Dickinson's Cut in West Keene and continuing through the London Cut in Westmoreland. For many years, trackwalkers' shanties at both ends of the cut were manned around the clock, especially in winter, to watch for and warn trains of dangerous ice conditions and fallen rock on the track. Of course, the shanties had stoves, but still, it must have been a cold, lonely job. We may be looking at one of the trackwalkers in this image. . . . Do you see him? Hist. Soc. Cheshire Cty.

had stoves for heating and cooking. Some were larger and functioned more like dormitories for unmarried men.

Shanties sprang up at various places along the railroad right-of-way and were physically moved along with the progress of construction. When the occupants moved, they took not only their belongings, but they took their homes with them! In some places the shanties were clustered in groups in the virgin forests along the right-of-way while in other places they took the form of fair-sized villages on the outskirts of towns. Near Summit, the Irishmen and their families lived in an encampment that came to be called "Irish Village." Because of the difficulty of the ledge work here, it remained long enough (about three years) to warrant a school in which sixty children were taught by volunteers from Keene. The laborers were an excitable lot, and from time to time there was fighting among them and labor unrest. A serious riot, fueled by liquor, broke out in the camp in the autumn of 1848 when the workers were not paid. In this case the Keene Light Infantry was called upon to bring the situation under control.

The shanties served their purposes well and then gradually faded from the scene as they were moved, razed, or appropriated for other uses. After the railroad construction work ended, many of the workers assimilated themselves into the towns along the new railroad, becoming farmers or finding work in the mills.

The road opened January 1, 1849 to the east bank of

The Cheshire Railroad's covered wooden bridge (left) and the Tucker Toll Bridge, looking upstream at the Great Falls of the Connecticut. The river is aboil with snowmelt from the mountains after a very snowy winter, Walpole, NH, May 1, 1888. The Tucker Toll Bridge was built in 1840, replacing the first bridge built over the Connecticut River here in 1785. J. A. French photo; Hist. Soc. Cheshire Cty.

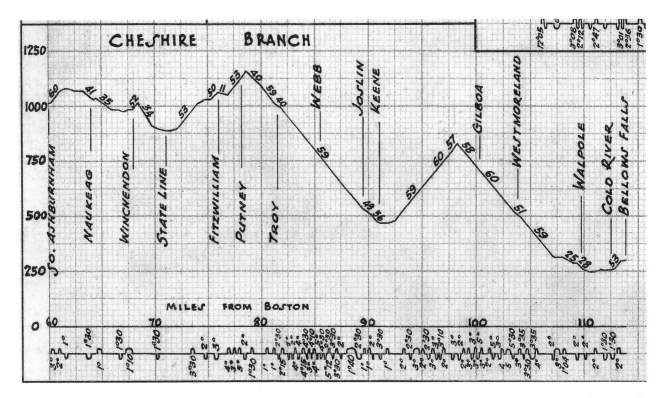

Profile chart for the Cheshire, showing mileages from Boston and elevations. Figures on the grade line are the rise in feet per mile. Note the location Putnam on the chart is misspelled Putney. Office of Chief Engineer, Boston, 1930. Ron Rand coll.

the Connecticut River where a temporary Bellows Falls station near the North Walpole, New Hampshire, end of the Tucker Toll Bridge had been built. On the opening day, a passenger train carrying dignitaries arrived at this station from Keene, amid great excitement and jollifications. On January 8, 1849, regular passenger and freight service began. The road had six locomotives: its original 11-ton workhorse (the 1/Rough and Ready) plus three 18-ton passenger and two (20- and 22-ton) freight locomotives.

For the next six months, the temporary station was used while the road's bridge over the Connecticut River was being completed. Passengers were conveyed across the toll bridge into Bellows Falls by stagecoach. The Cheshire chose to erect its bridge at the river's narrowest point—at the Great Falls—where the river surges through a fifty- to sixty-foot deep chasm worn into the bedrock over thousands of years. It was a covered wooden, arched truss bridge with stone portals at each end. The bridge's completion in June 1849 allowed for the extension of rail service the final 0.2 miles to the station in Bellows Falls proper. The Cheshire was the first railroad to enter

Bellows Falls. In 1851 a telegraph line, part of which ran along the Cheshire, had already been installed between Boston and Rutland.

The Cheshire was engineered to a gold standard and built to last a millennium. It was widely hailed as one of the great engineering feats in New England. A single-track road, its total length from South Ashburnham to Bellows Falls was 53.75 miles, plus eight miles of passing tracks and sidings. Most of the stations had passing tracks. There were no weight or clearance restrictions. The roadbed and bridgework were built to accommodate a second track should it ever be warranted. Section houses were located about every five miles, each with four to six sectionmen depending on track maintenance requirements. The section houses were often near stations to be near the telegraph. There were extensive yard facilities and turntables with roundhouses at South Ashburnham, Keene, and North Walpole. Rail was 60-pound laid on timber crossties, and the roadbed gravel and cinder ballasted. The maximum grade per mile was 59.66 feet (1.13 percent) and the total rise and fall in the road 2,377 feet. The road reached its highest elevation at 1,147 feet in Fitzwilliam, just west of Putnam. The highest point between Keene and the Connecticut River was 830 feet at Summit. There were 31.28 miles of straight track, 39 crossings at grade, and an aggregate 1,939 feet of wooden bridges. The road was fenced its entire length.

According to the Annual Report for 1849, the cost to build the railroad was $2,081,000. The Annual Report for 1851 adjusts the total, reflecting final construction work and costs of furnishing the road for operation, to $2,777,843.89. The directors, sparing nothing to get a quality road, assessed the road's 9,519 original stockholders an additional $10/share—ten times! Total excavations for the entire road were 4,294,000 cubic yards or eight million tons, of which 63,530 cubic yards were for high-quality masonry.

The Granite Arch Bridges. The Cheshire is deservedly well-known for the impressive granite structures it built along its right-of-way. The road's cut granite bridges and culverts are considered models of civil engineering.

Arguably the most impressive structure on the Cheshire is the Joslin Arch (B89.41), a granite, single-arch keystone bridge spanning the East Branch of the Ashuelot River in South Keene. It was designed and erected in 1847 under the supervision of Lucius Tilton, the Cheshire's chief engineer, using granite drawn from the Thompson Farm a half mile away in Roxbury, New Hampshire (Keene Hist. Comm. 1968). It is the largest of some twenty stone arches constructed along the railroad, the largest stone arch ever built in New Hampshire, and ranks among the most impressive masonry arches built in the United States before 1850.

The Joslin Arch has an inside diameter of sixty-eight feet, a height of forty-five and a half feet above the riverbed at the keystone, and is twenty-seven-feet wide face-to-face. Its beautiful wingwalls curve outward ninety degrees, retaining massive volumes of earth behind them to resist any spreading tendency of the vault. The total length of the structure, including the wingwalls and their extensions, is about 186 feet. A small arch filled

R. R. Bridge. South. Keene. N. H.

An eastbound B&M passenger train steps smartly across the Joslin Arch. That's the D. R. Cole grist mill visible through the arch, South Keene, ca. 1905. Postcard; B. G. Blodget coll.

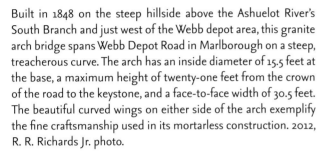

Built in 1848 on the steep hillside above the Ashuelot River's South Branch and just west of the Webb depot area, this granite arch bridge spans Webb Depot Road in Marlborough on a steep, treacherous curve. The arch has an inside diameter of 15.5 feet at the base, a maximum height of twenty-one feet from the crown of the road to the keystone, and a face-to-face width of 30.5 feet. The beautiful curved wings on either side of the arch exemplify the fine craftsmanship used in its mortarless construction. 2012, R. R. Richards Jr. photo.

with cut stone of the same type as the wall is built into the bridge's northwest wingwall extension. It is mostly buried in the earthen embankment, but the top of the arch is visible (inspected by the authors, May 20, 2015) and it is estimated to have a width of eighteen to twenty feet. This is believed to be a "relieving arch" installed at the time of construction to strengthen the wingwall extension. The other three wingwall extensions are so deeply buried with earth that their relieving arches—if they exist—are not exposed (CHA, Inc. 2009).

The Union Pacific Big Boy (4-8-8-4) X4012, one of the largest locomotives in the world, was towed, with spacers for weight distribution, across the Joslin Arch on September 23, 1964, en route to Steamtown at N. Walpole (see Chapter 7).

Other remarkable, surviving granite arches include: a double arch over Damon's Brook in Fitzwilliam, New Hampshire (B71.08), a triple arch at Scott Brook in Fitzwilliam (B73.32), the arch over the Ashuelot River in Troy (B83.24), the arch over Webb Depot Road just west of Webb Depot in Marlborough, New Hampshire (B85.34), and the arch over Chesterfield Road in West Keene (B94.57). A granite arch at Swanzey Factory Road in Keene (B89.34) has been dismantled. Some of its remnants rest in the nearby woods.

The Cheshire's granite arch bridge at Chesterfield Road, West Keene. Hist. Soc. Cheshire Cty.

Keene Shops and Roundhouse. In the Cheshire's early years, the company had wooden shop facilities in Keene that employed about sixty men and handled only light repairs. Heavier repairs on locomotives were made in the shops of their builders. Later the home shops became well-enough equipped to rebuild engines, but still lacked boiler casting capability. In 1859, the shops turned out their first rebuilt engine, the 4/*New Hampshire*, followed in 1860 by the 3/*Winchendon*. The 6/*Monadnock*, which had blown up at Fitzwilliam on September 4, 1857, killing the engineer, emerged from the shops with a new boiler from the Boston Locomotive Works in 1863 as second 6/*Thomas Thatcher*. (Thatcher was the road's second president.) In 1866, the 11/*President* was released as second 11/*David Upton*.

Most of the early wooden facilities were replaced by brick shops, designed and built in 1866 for $50,000 under the supervision of master mechanic Frank A. Perry. Perry had come to work for the Cheshire from the Hinkley Locomotive Works. The following year the locomotive roundhouse was built for $66,000. To celebrate the opening of the new shops, a dedicatory supper and dance lasting into the wee hours of the night was held on April 3, 1867. Special trains were run for the 800-plus attendees. The new shops consisted of a machine shop (193 by 65 feet), blacksmiths' shop (110 by 52 feet), and a carpenters' shop (112 by 56 feet) built in a continuous line but each distinct and complete in itself. Later—and into the B&M years—other shops were added to the complex, including car shops, a spring shop, a tank shop, and a frog shop.

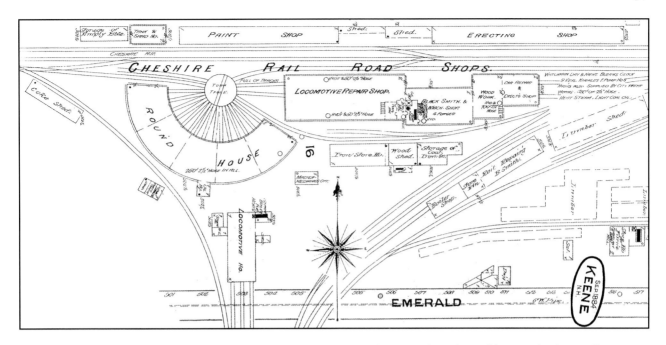

Layout of the Cheshire Railroad's Keene Shops and Roundhouse between the east and west legs of the wye. The three stall "Locomotive House" shown south of the roundhouse belonged to the Ashuelot Railroad. Sanborn Insurance Map, Sept. 1884.

Cheshire Railroad American (4-4-0) second 11/*David Upton*. Upton, a former master mechanic, was so pleased to have the locomotive named after him that he presented the fine headlight to the Cheshire Railroad. Eventually the practice of naming locomotives ended and numbers were used instead.

Keene Shops in Cheshire Railroad days, looking west, ca. 1885. A. A. Clough photo; Hist. Soc. Cheshire Cty.

Another westward view of the Keene Shops complex. The brick shops (center) were primarily for locomotive repair work, while the wooden building (right) housed the car shops, Keene, 1886. W. P. Allen photo; Hist. Soc. Cheshire Cty.

These were high-quality, state-of-the-art shops that—now with boiler casting capability—could build entire locomotives. Eight American-type (4-4-0) engines were built here in 1868–1880. The first to be completely built in the new shops was the 22/*Murdock*, built in 1868 and named to honor Ephraim Murdock Jr., Esq. of Winchendon, the road's third president. Two locomotives were built in 1870: the 25/*F. A. Perry*, named in honor of master mechanic Perry, and the 26/*Samuel Gould*. There followed the 28/*Fitchburg* in 1871, second 5/*Cheshire* in

1872, the 29/*Ashburnham* in 1873, and the 31/*Monadnock* in 1875. The last engine turned out was second 9/*Keene* in 1880. In November 1882, a new, stronger turntable for handling the heaviest locomotives was installed at the roundhouse.

By 1877–1878 the road already had converted ten engines from wood to coal burners. The Annual Report for 1878 notes that for the year, the road's fuel needs—including such for heating purposes—required a staggering 17,602 cords of wood (almost fifty cords per day) and 2,582 tons of coal. The wood came from both company-owned and private woodlands along the line. In June 1885 the shops completed the task of converting all the road's engines to coal burners. The sight of wood trains, expansive wood sheds, and great piles of wood at fueling points disappeared, and the men who had cut and furnished the wood were done. The Annual Report for the year ended September 30, 1888 reported the road's fuel needs were almost totally met by coal—19,582 tons of it.

Before the new shops were built in 1866, the road's power was largely supplied by the Hinkley companies or the Boston Locomotive Works. The road also sampled products from other builders including Taunton, Schenectady, and Manchester. Then, in 1868–1880, even as the road built eight engines in its own shops, it also took delivery of five Americans from Hinkley & Williams.

Cheshire Railroad employees take a break from their labors at the roundhouse, built in 1867, Keene, ca. 1880. J. A. French photo; Dale O. Russell coll.

Cheshire American 22/*Murdock* at Keene, undated. Hist. Soc. Cheshire Cty.

In the road's final decade of independence, it looked exclusively to the Rhode Island Locomotive Works in Providence for its needs, purchasing twelve engines in 1880–1890: one American (4-4-0), two Moguls (2-6-0), and nine Ten-Wheelers (4-6-0). Clearly, the road had begun to upgrade its fleet with more powerful engines.

Purchased in 1883, second 16/*R. M. Pulsifer* was the most powerful American the road ever owned. The last engine purchased before the practice of naming engines went out of style was Ten-Wheeler second 2/*W. H. Hill Jr.* purchased in 1887. The last acquisitions were Moguls 34 and 35 in 1889 and Ten-Wheelers 36 and 37 in 1890. At the time of consolidation with the Fitchburg Railroad in 1890, thirty-three of the Cheshire's locomotives, many relatively new or rebuilt, were incorporated into the Fitchburg numbering system (Edson 1982). Nine of these, all Rhode Islands (the two Moguls and seven of the Ten-Wheelers), survived in Boston and Maine Railroad (B&M) service until the 1911 renumbering, at which time or shortly thereafter they were scrapped.

Cheshire American 24/*Peterborough*, her brass appointments all polished, poses on the turntable at Keene. Photogr. unknown.

Cheshire Ten-Wheeler second 8/*F. H. Kingsbury*, brand new as delivered from the Rhode Island Locomotive Works, poses on the table at the Keene roundhouse, 1883. She was named in honor of Keene native Frederick H. Kingsbury, first treasurer of the road. Photogr. unknown; Hist. Soc. Cheshire Cty.

The last two former Cheshire engines in service in the B&M era were the 1939 (ex-1052; ex-Fitchburg 202; ex-Cheshire 2/*W. H. Hill Jr.*) and 1915 (ex-1048; ex-Fitchburg 233; ex-Cheshire 33/*E. C. Thayer*), scrapped in 1913 and 1916, respectively.

Operations. The Cheshire management's early exuberance about all the western traffic it expected to start moving over its line soon dissipated like hot air from a balloon. In the Annual Report for 1852, the road's directors soberly explained that in July 1852 the Vermont Central, to prevent any possible diversion of its traffic at White River Junction for Boston via the Sullivan-Cheshire-Fitchburg Route, had begun restricting interchange of through east-west traffic with the Sullivan Railroad and, effective September 1, 1852, cut off all such traffic.

In 1854 the Vermont Central formalized a traffic agreement with the Northern Railroad of New York and the Northern Railroad of New Hampshire to protect what would become known as the "Great Northern Route," a main line between Concord, New Hampshire, and Ogdensburg, New York. In the 1870s this agreement expanded to include the Concord, the Nashua and Lowell, and the Boston and Lowell Railroads. This consortium of six roads, referred to in the Cheshire's Annual Reports

as "the Trunk Lines," effectively set a pattern whereby the Cheshire and its successors were forced to live off online business and such interchange as the Rutland Railroad could deliver at Bellows Falls. The Vermont Central also reduced interchange of through traffic with the Rutland at its Rouses Point, Vermont, gateway. The Cheshire, lamenting the loss of through traffic and the ruinous low rates forced by the Trunk Lines, reflected an increasing tone of desperation in its Annual Report for 1881: "The great strife and changes going on in connection with through business makes the future of our road, as with all short roads that are mere links in a through line, somewhat uncertain." These difficulties went on for years, but despite their seriousness the Cheshire's management met with some success in growing online business and reported net profits for all years except 1875.

Starting in August 1851, for annual rent of $32,000, the Cheshire began running all its trains the extra eleven miles between South Ashburnham and Fitchburg under agreement with the V&M for use of its tracks as well as for use of its engine house, station, water tank, and other terminal services and facilities in Fitchburg. In the early 1870s the rights conveyed in the agreement were deemed more valuable as the opening of the Hoosac Tunnel Route neared, and the rent increased to $51,000.

The Cheshire and the V&M together installed a new turntable at South Ashburnham in 1867 (Annual Report 1868). Another new turntable—a brand new Boston Bridge Works 60-foot, 112-ton-capacity, wrought iron turntable—was installed by the Cheshire on the eve of the Fitchburg takeover. The Fitchburg would later move it to Keene in 1895 as a part of its expansion of the repair shops there (*Sentinel* Oct. 15, 1895).

By about 1876, the road had begun pulling up iron rails and replacing them with steel rails. Thirty-eight miles of road were converted by early 1878 and this work was completed in the early 1880s. The Cheshire operated

Going South and East.

LEAVE	No. 1, P. M.	No. 3, A. M.	No. 19, A. M.	No. 5, A. M.
St. Albans,........	7.00			6.20
White River Jc.	1.30	4.20		12.20
Rutland,..........	12.50			12.01
B. Falls,..........	3.50	6.35		2.30
Cold River,.......	—	6.38		—
Walpole,..........	4.00	6.45		2.40
Westmoreland,..	4.14	6.58		2.53
E.Westmor'land	4.23	7.07		3.00
KEENE,..........	4.55	7.33	9.00	3.26
So. Keene,........	—	7.37	9.08	—
Marlborough,....	5.08	7.46	9.28	3.40
Troy, ...	5.17	7.54	9.45	3.49
Fitzwilliam, ...	5.29	8.06	10.17	4.02
State Line,........	—	8.18	10.40	—
WINCHENDON,....	5.48	8.25	10.55	4.21
N. Ashburnham,	5.56	8.34	11.12	4.30
So. Ashburnh'm,	6.06	8.43	11.35	4.40
Westminster,...⸴	6.16	8.55	11.49	—
W. Fitchburg,..⸴	6.22	9.03	11.57	—
FITCHBURG,........	6.30	9.10	12.05	5.05
BOSTON,.....Arrive	8.35	11.05	2.23	7.10
	A. M.	A. M.	P. M,	P. M.

—— Does not stop.
⸴ Stops only to leave passengers.

Going North and West.

LEAVE	No. 2, A. M.	No. 4, A. M.	No. 24, P. M.	No. 6, P. M.
BOSTON, ...	7.30	11.10	2.35	5.30
FITCHBURG,........	9.20	1.25	5.10	7.35
W. Fitchburg,..†	—	1.36	5.20	7.42
Westminster,...†	—	1.47	5.30	7.51
So. Ashburnh'm,	9.43	2.10	5.55	8.04
N. Ashburnham,	—	2.20	6.05	8.14
WINCHENDON,....	9.59	2.32	6.15	8.25
State Line,........	—	2.40	6.23	—
Fitzwilliam, ...	10.16	2.53	6.38	8.45
Troy, ...	10.27	3.06	6.50	8.58
Marlborough,....	10.35	3.15	6.58	9.07
So. Keene,........	—	3.30	7.10	—
KEENE,..........	10.50	3.40	7.15	9.30
E.Westmor'land	—	4.03		9.53
Westmoreland,..	11.19	4.12		10.02
Walpole,..........	11.32	4.27		10.15
Cold River,.......	—	4.34		—
B. Falls,...Arrive	11.40	4.37		10.25
Rutland,..........	2.05			1.45
White River Jc.	1.20	8.10		12.56
St. Albans,........	6.30			5.50
	P. M.	P. M,	P. M.	A. M.

—— Does not stop.
† Stops only to take passengers.

Cheshire Public Time Table, May 3, 1875. Basil B. MacLeod coll.

its express passenger, accommodation, and freight trains at speeds of 25, 22, and 12 miles per hour, respectively, about average for New England railroads of the day.

The road's fleet of cars as of April 1, 1878, gives a good indication of the character of the road's business at the time. In addition to 22 passenger, 8 baggage, and 2 postal cars, the road owned 419 merchandise cars, including 194 box, 27 hay, 34 stock, 138 platform (flat), 10 gravel, and 11 wood cars, plus 5 short saloons (cabooses or buggies). The road also owned 2 derrick cars, a drover's saloon, a wood sawyers saloon, and 2 snowplows (Annual Report 1878). Many of the cars were built in the home shops. A decade later the road reported owning 25 passenger cars, 2 combines, and 11 baggage, express, and mail cars. The freight car fleet had grown to 506, consisting of 232 box, 25 stock, 4 coal, 179 flat, and 66 "other" freight cars (Annual Report 1889).

During its forty-five years of independent operation, the Cheshire never pursued a policy of aggressive expansion. However, on two occasions the Cheshire leased connecting roads, probably for defensive purposes. It took over the Connecticut River Railroad's lease of the Ashuelot Railroad in 1860, and operated that road for seventeen years until the Ashuelot's shareholders, alleging mismanagement, canceled the lease and returned it to Connecticut River. Then in 1880, after the financially strapped Boston, Barre and Gardner Railroad (BB&G) had suspended its lease payments to the Monadnock Railroad in February 1879, the Cheshire stepped in and assumed the Monadnock lease. When the Fitchburg Railroad swallowed the Cheshire in 1890, the Monadnock lease went along with it into the Fitchburg system.

Stock Trains. One area of online business scarcely recalled today was livestock. Livestock—cattle, sheep, horses, and hogs—was an important early commodity handled by the railroads in agrarian days. Before the advent of "western beef" in the late 1870s and the introduction of refrigerated cars, meat for local consumption was derived exclusively from stock raised at small farms all over the New England countryside. Many stations had stockyards where cattle, hogs, and other stock were held and could be watered and fed. From the 1850s and until the appearance of trucks, it was not uncommon to see herds of livestock being driven right through the towns to the stockyards. There, railroad livestock agents handled the paperwork. This was a wonderful service to area farmers, providing them steady, reliable access to the market.

Monday was generally stock train day on the Cheshire. The stock train departed Bellows Falls just after the arrival of Train 515 at noon and made all station stops to load stock. Many stations had stockyards, with those at Cold River and Walpole notably important (Frizzell 1963). The drovers rode in the buggy. By 9:00 p.m. the train would be in Winchendon, where the cars would be set off to be picked up later at night by a through stock train. This train carried a sleeping car made from an old Cheshire Railroad coach for the accommodation of the drovers. Bill Fletcher remembered that in his early years (1910–1911) on the B&M, a retired conductor was caretaker of the car and kept it in immaculate condition. He also recalled ASPCA Officer Jennie B. Powers, who inspected stock trains in Keene. If she discovered an animal that had been trampled and was suffering, she would make them take it off and she would draw her revolver and shoot it. (Fletcher letter, Dec. 28, 1973).

A note in the December 16, 1880 *Sentinel* gives some idea of the importance of stock to the railroads: "Stock trains over the road were unusually heavy this week. One hundred cars were handled from Bellows Falls to Fitchburg on Monday the 13th, an unusual amount in a single day. . . . On Saturday the 18th the Central Vermont and Cheshire roads will operate a special train to carry Christmas poultry to Boston." This was in the period before June 1, 1881, when the Sullivan County Railroad was leased by the Central Vermont.

"Western beef" presented a totally new paradigm and would prove to be a game-changer for the railroads, which had always enjoyed a very profitable business moving livestock. Noting that they would be left with a fleet of useless cars and forced to invest in new refrigerated cars, the roads fought a losing battle against "western beef." Rail movement of stock continued through the 1930s and there was a last surge in business during World War II. A freight schedule dated April 28, 1946 shows Train 5500 handling stock on Sundays (Nimke 1991). But in the postwar years, improved roads and explosive growth in trucking proved a *coup de grâce* and railside stockyards disappeared.

The Fitchburg Years, 1890–1900

The Cheshire was consolidated into the Fitchburg Railroad October 1, 1890, by an exchange of shares, and it became the Fitchburg's Cheshire Branch. At the time of the merger, the Fitchburg reorganized itself into three divisions, the Fitchburg, Tunnel, and Western Divisions. The Cheshire Branch was in the Tunnel Division that included the main line and all branches between Fitchburg and Williamstown, Massachusetts.

Layoffs, then Expansion, at the Keene Shops. Though the building of new locomotives had ended

Fitchburg passenger tariff schedule for its Cheshire Division and Monadnock Branch, Oct. 1, 1890. Rindge Hist. Soc.

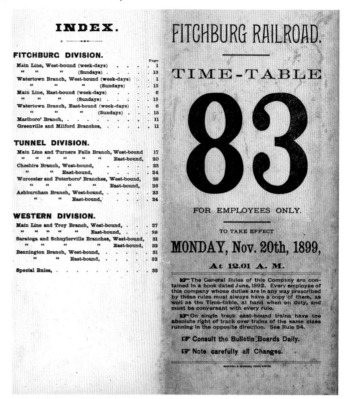

(left) Time Table for Boston to Montreal service via the Fitchburg and connecting roads. Fitchburg PTT, 1898. Fitchburg Hist. Soc.
(below and following page) Cheshire Branch trains shown in Fitchburg ETT No. 83, Nov. 20, 1899. Hist. Soc. Cheshire Cty.

BOSTON TO MONTREAL
— VIA RUTLAND. —

Boston to Bellows Falls, Fitchburg Railroad.
Bellows Falls to Burlington, Rutland Railroad.
Burlington to St. Johns, Central Vermont Railroad.
St. Johns to Montreal, Grand Trunk Ry.

See Map on page 34.

STATIONS.	MAIL. No. 15	DAY EXPRESS No. 17	PASS'R No. 13	NIGHT EXPRESS No. 5
Leave BOSTON	8.00	11.00	3.05	7.00
" Waltham	8.19	......	......	......
" Lincoln	8.31	......	3.34	......
" Concord	8.37	......	3.40	......
" Concord Junction	8.42	......	......	......
" South Acton	8.50	......	3.50	7.44
" Ayer	9.08	11.57	4.11	8.03
" North Leominster	9.26	......	4.26	......
" Fitchburg	9.40	12.29	4.38	8.39
" South Ashburnham	10.04	......	5.04	9.06
" Winchendon	10.20	1.07	5.21	9.27
" Fitzwilliam	10.39	1.21	5.35	9.43
" Troy, N.H.	10.51	1.29	5.45	9.54
" Marlboro	11.00	1.38	5.53	10.02
" Keene	11.14	1.50	6.06	10.17
" Westmoreland	11.42	f 2.22	6.28	f10.42
" Walpole	11.55	2.35	6.40	10.55
Arrive Bellows Falls	12.05	2.45	6.50	11.04
" Chester	12.37	3.22	7.41	11.55
" Ludlow	1.05	3.49	8.13	12.36
" Cuttingsville	1.37	......	8.48	1.26
" Rutland	2.00	4.40	9.10	2.00
" Proctor	2.17	......		
" Brandon	2.37	5.12	......	2.53
" Middlebury	3.10	5.42	......	3.21
" New Haven Junction	3.26	......	......	......
" Vergennes	3.35	6.04	......	3.45
" Shelburne	4.05	6.27	......	4.10
" Burlington	4.20	6.40	......	4.21
" Essex Junction	4.43	7.00	......	4.41
" Milton	5.12	......	......	5.04
" Georgia	5.19	......	......	5.10
" St. Albans	5.40	7.55	......	5.25
" Highgate Spa.	6.19	......	......	5.58
" St. Armand	6.30	......	......	6.07
" St. Johns, P.Q.	7.15	9.17	......	6.50
" St. Lambert	8.00	9.55	......	7.22
" MONTREAL	8.20	10.15	......	7.40

Through Car Service, on page 42.
Meal Stations, Fitchburg, Bellows Falls, Rutland and St. Albans.
Trains run daily except Sunday.

INDEX.

FITCHBURG DIVISION.

	Page
Main Line, West-bound (week-days)	1
" " " (Sundays)	13
Watertown Branch, West-bound (week-days)	1
" " " (Sundays)	13
Main Line, East-bound (week-days)	6
" " " (Sundays)	15
Watertown Branch, East-bound (week-days)	6
" " " (Sundays)	15
Marlboro' Branch,	11
Greenville and Milford Branches,	11

TUNNEL DIVISION.

Main Line and Turners Falls Branch, West-bound	17
" " " " East-bound,	20
Cheshire Branch, West-bound,	23
" " East-bound,	24
Worcester and Peterboro' Branches, West-bound,	25
" " " " East-bound,	26
Ashburnham Branch, West-bound,	23
" " East-bound,	24

WESTERN DIVISION.

Main Line and Troy Branch, West-bound,	27
" " " " East-bound,	29
Saratoga and Schuylerville Branches, West-bound,	31
" " " " East-bound,	32
Bennington Branch, West-bound,	31
" " East-bound,	32
Special Rules,	33

FITCHBURG RAILROAD.

TIME-TABLE

83

FOR EMPLOYEES ONLY.

TO TAKE EFFECT

MONDAY, Nov. 20th, 1899,

At 12.01 A. M.

☞ The General Rules of this Company are contained in a book dated June, 1892. Every employee of this company whose duties are in any way prescribed by these rules must always have a copy of them, as well as the Time-table, at hand when on duty, and must be conversant with every rule.

☞ On single track east-bound trains have the absolute right of track over trains of the same class running in the opposite direction. See Rule 84.

☞ Consult the Bulletin Boards Daily.

☞ Note carefully all Changes.

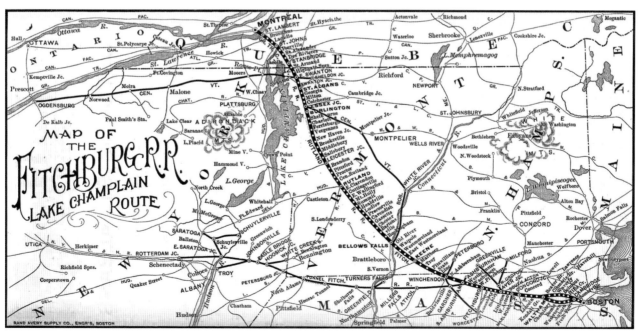

Map of the Fitchburg's *Lake Champlain Route*, incorporating the Cheshire Branch, from Boston to Montreal, Quebec. This route and the road's trademark *Hoosac Tunnel Route* between Boston and Rotterdam Junction, NY, split at South Ashburnham. Fitchburg PTT, 1898. Fitchburg Hist. Soc.

23

TUNNEL DIVISION.—Cheshire Branch.

			First-Class.				WEST-BOUND TRAINS.		Second-Class.		Third-Class
No. of Train....			21	15	1	13	5	151	173	203	227
A ‡ in this line is a reminder to look for marginal note of same number as the train.			Daily Ex. Sun	Daily Ex. Sun	Daily Ex. Sun	Daily Ex. Sun	Daily Ex. Sun	Sundays Only.	Sundays Only.	Daily Ex. Sun	Daily Ex. Sun
Miles from Boston.	Miles between Stations.	**STATIONS.**	Bellows Falls Passenger	Mail Passenger	Montreal Express Passenger	Rutland & W.R.Jc. Passenger	Montreal Night Exp. Pass.	Press and Passenger	Bellows Falls Passenger	Fast Freight.	Local Freight.
			A.M.	A.M.	P.M.	P.M.	P.M.	A.M.	P.M.	A.M.	A.M.
59.99		So. Ashburnham lv.	s 7 37	s 10 04	12 50	s 5 04	s 9 09	s 4 16	s 10 10	12 35	8 00
63.89	3.90	N. Ashburnham .	f 7 47	f 10 11	12 56	f 5 13	f 9 17	f 4 28	f 10 18	12 47	8 16
67.76	3.87	Winchendon	s 7 57	s 10 20	s 1 08	s 5 25	s 9 29	s 4 36	s 10 26	1 02	9 15
70.80	3.04	State Line	f 8 02	f 10 27	1 13	f 5 30	f 9 34	f 4 41	f 10 31	1 11	9 31
76.11	5.31	Fitzwilliam	s 8 12	s 10 39	f 1 21	s 5 39	s 9 44	f 4 50	s 10 41	1 27	10 00 14 / 10 39 15
81.38	5.27	Troy.............	s 8 23	s 10 51	s 1 29	s 5 48	s 9 55	f 5 00	s 10 51	1 44	11 13
85.11	3.73	Marlborough	s 8 32	s 11 00	f 1 38	s 5 55	s 10 03	f 5 06	s 10 59	1 55	12 00
89.09	3.98	South Keene	f 8 39	f 11 07	1 44	f 6 02	f 10 10	f 5 12	f 11 06	2 07	12 28
91.09	2.00	Keene	s 8 45	s 11 14	s 1 50	s 6 08	s 10 18	s 5 19	s 11 13	2 20	1 20
97.02	5.93	Summit...........	8 58	11 29	2 04	6 19	10 31	5 29	11 24	2 45	2 04 17 / 2 17 18
99.02	2.00	Tenth Section	9 04	11 32	2 12	6 22	10 34	5 32	11 28	3 04	2 25
100.16	1.14	E. Westmoreland..	s 9 07	f 11 35	2 15	s 6 24	f 10 36	f 5 34	f 11 31	3 09	2 34
103.48	3.32	Westmoreland	s 9 13	s 11 42	2 22	s 6 29	f 10 41	f 5 39	s 11 37	3 20	2 52
109.61	6.13	Walpole...........	s 9 25	s 11 55	2 35	s 6 40	s 10 51	f 5 51	s 11 48	3 40	3 22
		Riverside									
112.36	2.75	Cold River	f 9 31	12 01	2 41	f 6 46	f 10 56	f 5 56	f 11 54	3 50	3 33
113.61	1.25	Bellows Falls ..Ar.	s 9 35	s 12 05	s 2 45	s 6 50	s 11 00	s 6 00	s 11 59	3 55	3 45
			A.M.	P.M.	P.M.	P.M.	P.M.	A.M.	P.M.	A.M.	P.M.
			Ex. Sun	Ex. Sun	Ex. Sun	Ex. Sun	Ex. Sun	Sundays	Sundays	Ex. Mon	Ex. Sun
No. of Train....			21	15	1	13	5	151	173	203	227

13.   No. 20 takes siding at Winchendon for No. 13.   This applies only at Winchendon.

Time-Table No. 83.

TUNNEL DIVISION.—Cheshire Branch.

24

			First-Class.				EAST-BOUND TRAINS.		Second-Class.		Third-Class.
No. of Train....			12	22	14	2	20	156	150	240	228	234
A ‡ in this line is a reminder to look for marginal note of same number as the Train.			Daily Ex. Mon	Daily Ex. Sun	Daily Ex. Sun	Daily Ex. Sun	Daily Ex. Sun	Sundays Only	Sundays Only	Daily Ex. Sun	Daily Ex. Sun	Daily Ex. Sun
Miles from Bellows Falls.	Miles between Stations.	**STATIONS.**	Montreal Night Passenger	Bellows Falls Passenger	Cen. Vermont Passenger	Mail Passenger	Montreal Express Passenger	Milk and Passenger	Bellows Falls Passenger	Freight.	Local Freight.	Freight.
			A.M.	A.M.	A.M.	P.M.	P.M.	A.M.	P.M.	A.M.	A.M.	P.M.
		Bellows Falls ..Lve	s 2 30	s 5 30	s 8 30	s 1 40	s 3 55	s 6 25	s 3 00	6 00	7 10	6 50
1.25	1.25	Cold River	2 33	s 5 35	s 8 33	f 1 43	3 58	s 6 28	s 3 03	6 05	7 25	6 55
		Riverside										
4.00	2.75	Walpole...........	2 40	s 5 43	s 8 40	s 1 50	s 4 03	s 6 34	s 3 09	6 13	7 50	7 05
10.13	6.13	Westmoreland	2 53	s 6 01	s 8 53	s 2 03	4 13	s 6 50	s 3 21	6 34	8 30	7 30
13.45	3.32	E. Westmoreland..	3 01	s 6 10	s 9 01	f 2 10	4 19	s 6 58	s 3 29	6 47	9 01 11 / 8 37 21	7 45
14.59	1.14	Tenth Section	3 04	6 13	9 04	2 12	4 21	7 00	3 31	6 51	9 13	7 50
16.59	2.00	Summit............	3 09	6 17	9 09	2 17	4 24	7 04	3 35	7 01	9 23	7 58
22.52	5.93	Keene	s 3 23	s 6 29	s 9 23	s 2 31	s 4 38	s 7 16	s 3 48	7 35	10 25	8 30
24.52	2.00	South Keene......	3 27	s 6 33	s 9 28	f 2 35	4 42	f 7 20	s 3 52	7 42	11 07	8 36
28.50	3.98	Marlborough	f 3 36	s 6 44	s 9 38	s 2 46	f 4 51	s 7 30	s 4 02	7 58	12 00	8 56
32.23	3.73	Troy..............	f 3 46	s 6 54	s 9 48	s 2 56	s 5 00	s 7 38	s 4 10	8 23	12 45	9 16
37.50	5.27	Fitzwilliam	3 58	s 7 04	s 10 00	s 3 08	f 5 10	s 7 48	s 4 20	8 43	1 21	9 44
42.81	5.31	State Line	4 09	f 7 13	f 10 11	f 3 18	5 19	s 7 58	f 4 30	8 59	1 52	10 00
45.85	3.04	Winchendon	s 4 20	s 7 23	s 10 20	s 3 27	s 5 25 / 5 29	s 8 06	s 4 38	9 15	2 30	10 21
49.72	3.87	N. Ashburnham ...	4 28	f 7 30	f 10 27	f 3 36	5 38	f 8 13	s 4 46	9 30	2 45	10 35
53.62	3.90	So. Ashburnham Ar	s 4 37	s 7 37	s 10 35	s 3 45	f 5 47	s 8 20	s 4 55	9 45	3 00	10 50
			A.M.	A.M.	A.M.	P.M.	P.M.	A.M.	P.M.	A.M.	P.M.	P.M.
			Ex. Mon	Ex. Sun	Ex. Sun	Ex. Sun	Ex. Sun	Sundays	Sundays	Ex. Sun	Ex. Sun	Ex. Sun
No. of Train....			12	22	14	2	20	156	150	240	228	234

12 Engineman of this train must stop at the flag stations if passengers are seen who are evidently waiting for the train, even if the signal is not set.
20 No. 20 takes siding at Winchendon for No. 13. This applies only at Winchendon.
22 Stop at Hall Crossing between Walpole and Westmoreland to receive milk.
156 Stop at Hall Crossing between Walpole and Westmoreland to receive milk.

---

a decade earlier, the Keene Shops, now populated by Fitchburg power, continued in operation. At the time of the consolidation, the shops complex employed about 250 men (Wilber 1937). After taking possession of the road in October 1890, the Fitchburg instituted various efficiency improvements, including consolidation of all car-building at its West Fitchburg Car Shops. This marked the end of car-building in Keene, and twenty carpenters were discharged. Also, now with freight trains mostly originating at

Fitchburg or Bellows Falls, some twenty engineers, firemen and brakemen were no longer based at the Keene engine house.

Citing a sharp downturn in traffic, another seven positions—the house foreman, one night wiper, and one day hostler at the engine house plus two machinists' helpers, a blacksmith, and a carpenter at the locomotive shops—were terminated May 13, 1891 (*Sentinel* May 14, 1891). However, while the Fitchburg had its own locomotive repair shops in Charlestown, Massachusetts, the road had nothing that could compare with the Keene Shops' engine repair facilities and the skilled labor force there. Thus, it is not surprising that in 1895 the Fitchburg announced a major expansion of the Keene Shops,

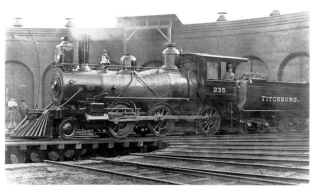

Examples of Fitchburg power at the Keene roundhouse during the Fitchburg era, 1890–1900, include (clockwise, above) American (4-4-0) 183, Mogul (2-6-0) 235 (ex-Cheshire 35), Ten-Wheeler (4-6-0) 232 (ex-Cheshire 32/*Wm. A. Russell*), and Consolidation (2-8-0) 93. Below, enginemen pose with Fitchburg Ten-Wheeler 212, ex-Cheshire 12/*J. W. Dodge*, at the Keene Shops. Photogr. unknown.

People and freight await the arrival of a train at the old Keene station in Fitchburg Railroad days. This is the less frequently seen west end of the train shed, showing the extended platform and canopy added in 1895. Hist. Soc. Cheshire Cty.

doubling the capacity of the main locomotive repair shop (*Sentinel* April 17, 1895). This was accomplished by expanding the east end of the roundhouse and connecting it to the repair shop. The Keene Shops became the largest locomotive repair works on the Fitchburg system.

The shops were reequipped with modern, state-of-the-art machinery, hydraulic lifts, and electric hoists. Sections of the roundhouse were partitioned and repurposed for the erecting and boiler shops. Only thirteen years after the Cheshire had installed a heavier turntable at the Keene roundhouse, the Fitchburg, needing an even bigger turntable capable of handling their heaviest locomotives, moved the South Ashburnham turntable to Keene (*Sentinel* Oct. 15, 1895).

The old Ashuelot engine house that was located between the east and west legs of the wye was blocked and moved further east, converted into a new blacksmith shop, and connected to the main repair shop. It was equipped with two new steam hammers. A larger power plant, including a new chimney, was built. The Stores Department moved into expanded quarters. In August and September 1895, blacksmiths, machinists, and boiler makers were transferred to Keene from the Fitchburg's Charlestown Shops. Then a year later the Fitchburg moved tools, machinery, and stock from its Mechanicville, New York, Shops to Keene. Machinists and other tradesmen, as well as several foremen, were relocated from Mechanicville to Keene (*Sentinel* Aug. 14 and Sept. 11, 1896).

The Fitchburg sent locomotive 357 (originally 176, renumbered in 1895) out to Keene to handle the increased switching duties at the shops (*Sentinel* Nov. 6, 1895). The 357 was a diminutive 2-4-2 Forney switcher built by the Grant Locomotive Works. It was small enough to ride the turntable with another locomotive and thus was very useful for shuffling engines about the complex. Originally built for the Manhattan Railway in 1878, it was acquired by the Boston, Hoosac Tunnel, and Western Railroad for its Saratoga, New York, business in 1881 and ended up on the Fitchburg when it purchased the road June 1, 1887. After the B&M took over the Fitchburg on July 1, 1900, it briefly wore B&M number 1094 before being scrapped in November 1900 (Edson 1982).

To appreciate the magnitude of the expansion of the Keene Shops, consider that at the time of the Fitchburg takeover in 1890 the Cheshire had thirty-four locomotives in service. In contrast, by April 1896 the Fitchburg had in service about 215 locomotives. Except for about fifty engines on the Western Division, all repair work was being performed at Keene. At any given time, twenty to thirty engines were at the Keene Shops, receiving or awaiting repairs (*Sentinel* April 22, 1896). Due to the increase in the number of engines being cared for in Keene, Fitchburg management created a new position—roundhouse foreman—to direct operations at the house formerly handled by the machine shop foreman.

Other Fitchburg Improvements. In 1893 the Fitchburg replaced the former Monadnock's roundhouse at

An inward passenger train stretches out across Main Street as it departs Keene's original Cheshire train shed station built in 1847. As business increased and passenger trains grew longer, the public was often inconvenienced by trains blocking Main Street, 1886. J. A. French photo; Hist. Soc. Cheshire Cty.

Winchendon with a wood-frame, three-stall structure. In the summer of 1895, Fitchburg crews extended the Keene station's platform and canopy westward and moved a standpipe further west to allow westbound passenger trains to take water without having their rear cars stand on the Main Street crossing. In addition, water pressure was increased and larger pipes installed, allowing locomotives to take water more quickly. The heavy stone columns supporting the station's arches were replaced with wrought iron posts to improve clearances. Painting crews repainted the station's waiting rooms and painted the new canopy extension and the remodeled buildings at the shops.

In their 1895 Annual Report, New Hampshire's railroad commissioners, decrying the woeful condition of many of the stations about the state (including all the stations along the former Cheshire), declared ". . . they are half a century behind the times and should be demolished to make room for much better ones." Thus it was not surprising that throughout the Fitchburg years

there was constant agitation in Keene to replace the old Cheshire station. A petition filed by Dr. George B. Twitchell and 245 citizens calling for a new union station to be built brought the state railroad commissioners to Keene for a hearing of the matter December 15, 1896 (*Sentinel* Dec. 16, 1896 and Jan. 4, 1897).

Counsel for the Fitchburg and for the B&M (then a tenant in the station) objected to erecting a new station owing to prevailing economic conditions and argued the station—ugly though it might be—was functional and not in the disreputable state portrayed by the petitioners. The commissioners had no power to order a union station to be built, and dismissed the petition with no action. However, while siding with the railroads that conditions in the station were not dire, the commissioners did draw attention to the need to raise the elevation of Main Street about eighteen inches at the crossing. This meant that the station—with its low arches—would ultimately have to be replaced before the crossing could be elevated. The low arches were

In this downstream view, a train is crossing the Fitchburg's granite arch bridge from N. Walpole, NH, to Bellows Falls, VT, ca. 1905. This bridge is said to be unique in having the longest arches with the least rise of any bridge in the country. The spans are each 140 feet long with a rise of only twenty feet. Postcard; Brent S. Michiels coll.

a danger to railroad crews. In 1879 a brakeman riding atop a car was killed instantly when he struck his head on the arch.

In April 1896, the Fitchburg's air-brake instruction car was brought to Keene on the *Flyer*. Every employee who had anything to do with air brakes was required to take instruction and pass an examination given by the men on this car (*Sentinel* April 24, 1896).

In the fall of 1899, the Fitchburg, on the eve of its lease to the B&M, replaced the Cheshire's original bridge over the Connecticut River with the present double-arch granite bridge (B113.60).

The Boston and Maine Years, 1900–1984

The Boston & Maine Railroad (B&M) leased the Fitchburg for ninety-nine years on July 1, 1900, and it became the road's Fitchburg Division. The following year, under terms of the lease, the B&M purchased, for $5,000,000 dollars, the 50,000 shares of Fitchburg common stock held by the Commonwealth of Massachusetts. Five thousand shares were still held by minority interests and the Fitchburg continued as a corporate entity. Its annual meetings continued for

another eighteen years and, under terms of the lease, the B&M was required to continue the Fitchburg's long-standing practice of providing free passage for shareholders traveling to Boston for the meeting. The road was not fully merged into the B&M until December 1, 1919, after all minority interests and bonded indebtedness had finally been extinguished.

The B&M had first entered Keene in 1887 when it leased the Boston and Lowell system, securing for itself the Manchester and Keene Branch. Next the Ashuelot Branch was secured when it leased the Connecticut River Railroad in 1893. And now, upon the lease of the Fitchburg in 1900, the Cheshire Branch fell under the B&M flag. Keene became an all-B&M city.

Boston & Maine Improvements and Other Changes. In 1903 the B&M undertook a large menu of long-overdue improvements to increase safety and efficiency. The original stone walls on the sides of the Joslin Arch were removed and iron railings substituted to allow an increase in the separation of the two tracks to B&M standards. At Winchendon, where the Fitchburg had continued to operate the track plants of all three of its predecessor roads (the BB&G, the Monadnock, and the Cheshire), the B&M chose to reorganize the track layout into a more efficient plan. The Cheshire Branch and Peterboro Branch tracks in the center of town were moved closer together and the Winchendon station was moved to the east side of the Peterboro Branch tracks. In connection with this project, a work train transported workers out from Fitchburg each day. On November 10, engine 1043, while returning to Fitchburg with the train, blew an injector pipe between North and South Ashburnham. The engineer was scalded but made it to South Ashburnham. Tragically, he returned to work only days before he was killed in the Wachusett Wreck of July 5, 1905.

In 1910 Keene finally got its long-sought new station and it was dedicated January 24, 1911, with railroad officials arriving in a private car from Boston. It was a beautiful building, done in yellow brick with red sandstone trim. The interior featured yellow brick walls, polished ash wood trim, and gleaming white marble floors (*Sentinel* Dec. 15, 1910). Heating was by hot water radiators (B&M Valuation Survey 1914, sec. 39.1). The following year an American Express Building was added to the west end of the new station complex and the Main Street crossing was rebuilt, raising the track about two feet.

Orderboards were installed at all Cheshire Branch stations in 1908–1909. Type B Double Arm, Lower Quadrant Block Signals were installed on the branch in 1910–1911 and the system was activated on May 5, 1911. The blocks were a half-mile long. In his letters, B&M historian Bill Fletcher often related how—on the very day the new system was turned on—a big thunderstorm knocked down the whole system between South Ashburnham and Walpole.

In 1925, the old Cheshire engine house at South Ashburnham was removed. In 1926–1929, the railroad made system-wide capital investments to strengthen the track structure and raise speeds on the main lines—heavier rail, deep rock ballasting, bridges strengthened, and so on—for increasingly heavy rail traffic. At this time the Cheshire Branch received mostly 100-pound and some 85-pound relay rail (Spofford Feb. 19, 1962), as the main lines were upgraded to 120-pound rail. The branch was never deep-rock-ballasted. Nevertheless, from 1931 through the mid-1950s, sectionmen maintained track to high standards that allowed maximum permitted speeds of 50/35 miles per hour for passenger and freight trains, respectively, except for streamline train 6000 which was allowed 55 miles per hour.

The B&M retained the Keene Shops, and they remained the road's main engine maintenance and repair facility right up until the Billerica (Massachusetts) Shops opened in February 1914. Wilber (1937) reported that before Billerica opened, normal employment was about 375 "with a peak of 487 reached at one time." Work was sent to Keene from all over the system and the yards were often full of engines awaiting repairs. The springs from electric motor 5004, which had burned in a wreck inside Hoosac Tunnel February 21, 1912, were sent to the Spring Shop at Keene. The springs had been completely flattened by the heat of the fire and had to be retempered (*Sentinel* May 23, 1912).

After Billerica opened, the B&M shifted all engine repair work there. To compensate for the jobs lost in Keene, the Nashua Frog Shop—which specialized in the manufacture and repair of frogs and other track fittings—was moved to the city as were maintenance responsibilities for work and wreck equipment such as steam shovels and cranes (*Sentinel* Feb. 3–7, 1914). By 1928, however, the Frog Shop had become obsolete and work which could be turned out there with existing equipment was declining. At this time the Keene Shops were repurposed as the maintenance headquarters for the road's then-new fleet of gasoline rail motorcars. The Wood Shop continued in operation, repairing baggage carts, hand trucks, crossing gates, and other fixtures (*EM* May28:13).

Fire at the Keene Shops! This fire was confined to a wooden building that housed the Spring Shop. That's the east leg of the wye in the foreground. The Stores Department has a good stock of engine pilots/cowcatchers on hand (right). Keene, March 30, 1912. Bion H. Whitehouse photo; Hist. Soc. Cheshire Cty.

Left to right: "Bert" Isham, engineer; P. J. "Patty" Ryan, fireman; and an unidentified person pose with Ten-Wheeler 175, Keene Shops, Spring 1907. The 175 was new from Schenectady on July 1, 1904 and was scrapped in April 1935 (Frye 1982). Marium E. Foster coll., Hist. Soc. Cheshire Cty.

(below) Left to right: Ryan, Isham, and "Joe" Maloux, road gang foreman, with the 175 at the Keene Shops, Spring 1907. Ryan and Isham were the regular enginemen on the "break-in job" that tested newly repaired engines released from the Shops. Depending on traffic conditions, they would run either to the Falls or to Winchendon and back. Sometimes they would have to stop to work on the engines. It was dangerous work—block protection did not come to the Cheshire Branch until 1911. On August 1, 1908, they tied the 1174 on behind an eastbound freight to push up the hill to Fitzwilliam and cut off at Winchendon. Isham would often walk out along the running boards while an engine was underway to inspect its running gear, and on this particular trip it was found he had leaned out too far to look at something and had struck a carload of lumber on a siding at Marlboro (Fletcher letter, July 13, 1968). As the train continued up the grade, Ryan discovered that Isham was not on the engine and thought he was probably riding in the caboose ahead. But when the freight stopped at Troy, he was not there. Soon Marlboro telegraphed to report that a following train had found him lying by the tracks. He was rushed to Winchendon Hospital, where he died. He was a valuable man, familiar with all the different engine classes. Marium E. Foster coll., Hist. Soc. Cheshire Cty.

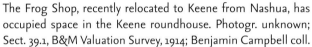

The Frog Shop, recently relocated to Keene from Nashua, has occupied space in the Keene roundhouse. Photogr. unknown; Sect. 39.1, B&M Valuation Survey, 1914; Benjamin Campbell coll.

Maintenance forces are all over Brill gasoline-mechanical car 122 at the Keene Shops. The car, delivered to the B&M in Dec. 1925, still looks shiny new, 1929. Photogr. unknown; Brent S. Michiels coll.

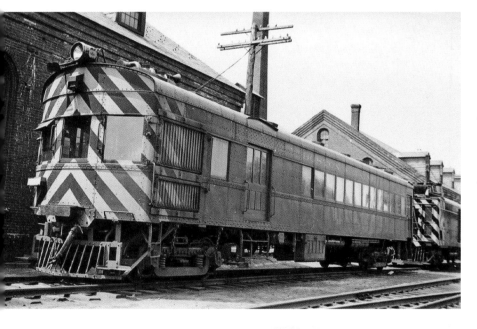

Brill gasoline-electric motorcar 1190 at the Keene Shops (below). This was a unique all-coach car with a second vestibule behind the engine room (Patton 1974). One of the bigger cars—73 feet long with seating for eighty-four passengers—it spent most of its career shuttling passengers between Springfield and Northampton. It was purchased in 1926 and scrapped in Dec. 1947. All the road's motorcars cycled through the fleet maintenance center at the Keene Shops, 1928–1938. S. J. Whitney coll.

Brill gasoline-electric motorcar 1171 (above) and an Osgood Bradley car keep company at the Keene Shops, 1938; Photogr. unknown; Brent S. Michiels coll.

This bird's eye image shows the Keene Shops complex near the end of operations, 1940. The only signs of life are automobiles parked at the main shop building. Note how the shops and roundhouse were completely enclosed in the wye, the east leg of which swings right, the west leg left. Photogr. unknown; Hist. Soc. Cheshire Cty.

The old Keene Shops and the roundhouse, gutted and for sale, ca. 1982. Photogr. unknown; Hist. Soc. Cheshire Cty.

Despite the entreaties of city officials, the B&M closed the shops September 20, 1938, on the very eve of the Hurricane of 1938. Many of the laid-off men were called back to work the next day as flood waters began to create emergency conditions along the road, and within about a week most of the laid-off workers were back (*Sentinel* Sept. 28, 1938). The entire crew at the carpenter shop was busy making crossing gates and other equipment. Unfortunately, the call back did not last and the shops closed for good June 19, 1940.

Remaining work and many of the seventy-six employees still working were transferred to Concord Shops.

The wood-frame, three-stall roundhouse in Winchendon, built in 1893 to replace the Monadnock's old house there, was ravaged by the Hurricane of 1938. No longer needed for railroad purposes, the building was given to L. A. LaRochelle in Winchendon for the cost of salvage in 1939. The turntable was retired April 20, 1942 (B&M Approval for Expenditure, courtesy Richard E. Miller).

Passenger Service. Over the following three chapters, you will find numerous images of Cheshire passenger trains and the infrastructure that supported them. Service was remarkably stable over the years. The Cheshire enjoyed considerable vacation trade of people traveling to and from summer camps. High school students from surrounding towns rode trains to and from Keene. Many railroad employees did not own cars and rode the trains to and from their work.

The Cheshire once hosted two through, named passenger trains between Boston and Montreal in partnership with the Rutland Railroad and Canadian National Railway. The first train over this 321-mile route—an overnight train—ran January 1, 1901. The B&M provided power and 113 miles of track as far as Bellows Falls, where the Rutland took over. Pullman parlor cars and sleepers were added in 1906. Soon, a day train over the route was added. These trains were the forerunners of what in the spring of 1926 became Trains 5511/5502/*Mount Royal* and 5503/5510/*Green Mountain Flyer* (Goodwin 1976; Tobey 1982). Both had New York and Boston sections that met in Rutland, Vermont. The trains carried diner-café cars and the *Mount Royal* carried Pullman sleepers.

The Boston section of the *Mount Royal* carried two sleepers, one for Montreal, the other for Ogdensburg, New York. The Montreal sleeper was eliminated in September 1940. At the same time, the Ogdensburg sleeper was cut back to Alburgh, Vermont, and it was eliminated altogether by the end of January 1948. The *Flyer* made its last through run to Montreal in 1951, after which it terminated in Burlington. All service beyond Bellows Falls ended in June 1953 when the Rutland suspended all passenger service on its lines. The B&M continued to run remnants of these once-proud trains between Boston and Bellows Falls for a few more years.

About 1935, the Boston & Maine Transportation Co., B&M's bus and truck subsidiary, began operating bus service that roughly paralleled the Bellows Falls-Keene-Peterboro-Boston route. The buses snaked their way through the hill towns east of Keene that had lost their rail service due to flood damage.

Lack of automobile ownership, primitive roads, and World War II had all helped support passenger traffic through the 1940s, but after 1950 rapid improvement of roads and soaring automobile ownership spelled the end of passenger rail service on the Cheshire Branch. In the late evening of Saturday, May 31, 1958, the last scheduled passenger train whistled off into the night, closing out 110 years of passenger service to the Elm City. Westbound for Bellows Falls, the last train consisted of E7 3807, E8 3820, nine empty milk cars, a baggage car, and a combine with twenty-three passengers aboard.

Almost ten months after passenger service had ended on the Cheshire, derailments on the Connecticut River Route Main Line brought several detouring passenger trains into Keene on March 20, 1959. At 2:20 a.m. that day, two empty milk cars on a northbound B&M freight had split the switch at the south end of the Bellows Falls Tunnel and derailed, blocking the tracks. Train 70/*Washingtonian*, a Montreal-to-Washington train, was sent to East Northfield via Keene and Dole Junction, adding about twelve miles to the normal trip to Greenfield. However, the train never reached Greenfield! Shortly after regaining the main line at East Northfield, the train only got as far as Mount Herman where it derailed four sleepers and two coaches, thus blocking the line at a second point.

A second southbound passenger train, Train 72, a local between White River Junction and Springfield, was also detoured over the Cheshire, but this train, owing to the derailment at Mount Herman, faced a much longer detour. Passengers were taken off the train and sent by bus to Springfield to make their connections, while the train took on a seventy-two-mile detour over the Cheshire to South Ashburnham, the Fitchburg Route Main Line to Fitchburg and, finally—after its power was turned there—back west to Greenfield. The train never left B&M iron. The two detouring southbounds passed through Keene at about 5:30 and 8:30 a.m. and a northbound (probably Train 73) over the Cheshire from South Ashburnham was expected about noontime (*Sentinel* March 20, 1959; *Times* March 26, 1959). All the detoured trains ran four to six hours late.

As of April 1, 1959, the B&M had dropped speeds on the branch to thirty miles per hour for both freight and passenger trains, and shortly thereafter sought and obtained ICC permission to deactivate the block signals on the branch. Traffic had become so light there were concerns that rust on the rails could interfere with reliable shunting.

CHESHIRE BRANCH.   27

OUTWARD TRAINS (WESTWARD) — FIRST-CLASS.

Passing Sidings. Capacity Cars.	STATIONS.	5501	8107	8219	5503	8111	7301	8113	5507	7305	8225	5511	SECOND CLASS 5509
		Ex. Sun.	Ex. Sun.	Ex. Sun.	Ex. Sun.	Ex. Sun.	Ex. Sun.	Ex. Sun.	Ex. Sun.	Ex. Sun.	Ex. Sun.	Ex. Sun.	Ex. Sun.
		Rut. R.R.	Sou. Div.	Sou. Div.	Rut. R.R.	Sou. Div.	C. R. Div.	Sou. Div.	Rut. R.R.	C. R. Div.	Sou. Div.	Rut. R.R.	Milk
	Boston N	A M L 3.00	A M	A M	A M L 8.45	A M	P M	P M	P M L 2.30	P M	P M	P M L 7.30	P M L 4.15
32	South Ashburnham W N	5.13			s10.35				s 4.17			9.16	s 6.34
18	Naukeag	5.19			10.41				4.24			9.22	6.41
34	Winchendon W N	s 5.25^{5502} / 5.12	L 6.10		s10.48 / 10.54	10.46 / 10.57	s 3.01 / 3.05		s 4.31 / 4.36			s 9.28 / 9.31	s 6.49 / 7.06
26	State Line	5.50			11.00				f 4.43			9.37	7.12
68	Fitzwilliam D	s 6.00			s11.09				s 4.53			f 9.45	7.21
	Putnam												
65	Rockwood Siding	6.06			11.14				4.58			9.50	7.27
46	Troy W D	s 6.12			s11.19				s 5.02			f 9.54^{9554}	7.32
25	Webb D	s 6.18			11.25				s 5.09			10.00	7.39
28	Joslin D	f 6.25			11.31				5.18^{5510}			10.06	7.46
Yard	Keene W N	s 6.29 / 6.39		A11.30	s11.35 / 11.40		A12.26		s 5.23 / 5.28	A 6.46	A 7.36	s10.10 / 10.15	s 7.51
34	Summit	6.52			11.53				5.40			10.27	8.06
50	Tenth Section	6.55			11.56				5.43			10.30	8.10
68	Gilboa	7.02^{5504}			11.58				s 5.46			10.32	8.13^{9554}
35	Westmoreland W N	s 7.10			f12.04				s 5.54			M10.37	s 8.27
30	Walpole D	s 7.26			s12.14				s 6.04			f10.45	8.37
29	Riverside Siding												
26	Cold River	7.31			12.18				6.09			10.50	8.41
Yard	Bellows Falls Frt. Yard	7.33			12.20				6.11			10.51	8.43
	Bellows Falls W N	A 7.35			A12.22				A 6.13			A10.53	A 8.45
	Connects with Rutland R.R. Train No.	A M 157	A M	A M	P M 153	A M	P M	P M	P M 159	P M	P M	P M 143	P M 143

INWARD TRAINS (EASTWARD). — FIRST-CLASS.

Passing Sidings. Capacity Cars.	STATIONS.	5502	8218	8114	5504	7300	8122	5508	7302	5510	SECOND CLASS 5500	THIRD CLASS. 9554
		Daily	Ex. Sun	Ex. Sun	Ex. Sun	Ex. Sun	Ex. Sun	Ex. Sun	Ex. Sun	Ex. Sun	Ex. Sun	Ex. Sun
		Boston	Sou. Div.	Sou. Div.	Fitchburg	C. R. Div.	So. Div.	Boston	C. R. Div.	Boston	Milk	X B 2
	Bellows Falls W N	A M L 3.44	A M	A M	A M L 6.30	A M	A M	P M L 1.15	P M	P M L 4.25	P M L11.10	P M
Yard	Bellows Falls Frt. Yard	3.46			6.32			1.17		4.27	11.12	L 7.15
26	Cold River	3.47			6.33			1.18		4.28	11.14	7.18
29	Riverside Siding											
30	Walpole D	3.52			s 6.39			s 1.25½		s 4.34	11.18	7.25
35	Westmoreland W D	4.04			s 6.53			s 1.39		f 4.47	11.37	7.50
68	Gilboa	4.12			s 7.02^{5501}			1.47		4.55	11.48	s 8.07^{5509} / s 8.18
50	Tenth Section	4.15			7.05			1.50		4.58	11.52	8.23
34	Summit	4.19			7.09			1.54		5.02	11.57	8.30
Yard	Keene W N	s 4.27 / 4.32	L 6.30		s 7.17 / 7.22	L 6.30	L 8.30	s 2.02 / 2.07	L 3.50	s 5.10 / 5.14	s12.11 / 12.15	s 8.47 / 9.07
23	Joslin D	4.36			f 7.27			2.11		5.18^{5507}	12.21	9.17
25	Webb D	4.45			s 7.37			2.20		5.27	12.35	9.35
46	Troy W D	(X)4.55			s 7.47			s 2.31		s 5.37	12.47	9.48^{5511} / 10.00
65	Rockwood Siding	4.59			7.51			2.35		5.41	12.53	10.15
	Putnam											
68	Fitzwilliam D	f 5.05			s 7.58			s 2.42		s 5.48	12.58	10.30
26	State Line	5.14			f 8.07			2.51		5.56	1.05	10.50
75	Winchendon W N	s 5.21^{5501} / 5.35		s 6.56 / 7.00	s 8.14 / 8.19		s11.35 / 11.38	s 2.58 / 3.04		s 6.02 / 6.06	s 1.12 / 1.24	s11.00 / 11.15
18	Naukeag	5.32			8.26			3.11		6.13	1.31	11.40
32	South Ashburnham W N	s 5.40			s 8.34			s 3.19		s 6.21	s 1.43	A11.55
	Boston N	A 7.20			A10.35			A 5.12		A 8.05	A 4.23	
	Connects with Rutland R.R. Train No.	A M 146	A M	A M	A M	A M	A M	P M 150	P M	P M 164	P M 156	P M 120

Cheshire Branch timetable. B&M/Fitchburg Div., ETT No. 61, Sept. 25, 1927. B&MRRHS Archives.

Monadnock Region
79   Cheshire Branch: Boston-Keene-BellowsFalls-White River Jct.

Miles	Northbound		51-5501 exSun A M	5551 Sun A M	Bus Sat. A M	Green Mt 5503 Daily A M	5507 exSun P M	Cheshire ⊛5505u Mon-Fri P M	Monad-nock 5509 Daily P M	Cheshire ⊛5555u Sun P M	Mount Royal 5511 exSun P M	5557 Sun P M
0.0	BOSTON (No. Sta.)......Mass. ...Lv		2 15	...	a8 00	9 00	3 00	4 10 Mon	5 10	6 15	7 45	8 05	...
3.4	Cambridge	...	...	...	b8 08	9 08	3 08	to	v5 18	....	7 53	8 13	...
9.9	Waltham........................ ..	...	2 33	...	...	9 19	3 19	Fri	....	....	8 02	8 23	...
36.1	Ayer	...	3 23	...	9 20	9 53	3 57	inc.	5 57	....	8 40	8 58	...
49.6	Fitchburg........................ { Ar		3 50			10 13	4 19	v5 06	6 15	....	8 58	9 16	...
	{ Lv		4 25	5 05	9 50	10 17	4 25		6 20	v7 11	9 05	9 20	...
59.9	South Ashburnham	...	4 44	5 23	δ10 10	f10 36	4 44	....	....	....	....	...	...
67.9	WINCHENDON............ .. { Ar		4 54	5 33		10 46	4 54	5 29	....	....	9 35	9 50	...
	{ Lv		5 10	5 45	10 30	10 50	4 58	5 34	e6 52	7 35	9 40	9 55	...
70.9	State Line................N.H.		f5 15	f5 50				stream-line train					
76.3	Fitzwilliam	...	5 24	5 57	c10 46	11 03	5 11	f7 05	f7 05	....	e9 52	e10 07	...
81.6	Troy............................ ..	...	5 33	6 11	d10 55	11 12	5 28	f7 14	f7 14	....	10 01	f10 16	...
85.3	Webb	...	f5 38	f6 17	...	...	f5 34						
91.3	KEENE........................ ..	...	6 03	6 35	11 20	11 32	5 50	6 06	7 33	8 08	10 25	10 40	...
100.4	Gilboa	...	f6 20	f6 52	...	...	f6 07						
103.7	Westmoreland	...	6 26	6 58	g11 43								
109.8	Walpole	...	6 36	7 08	g11 55	12 02	6 36	....	e8 03	....	e10 57	....	...
113.8	Bellows Falls.................. Vt. ..Ar		6 45	7 17	12 05	12 10	6 45	6 37	8 10	8 40	11 05	11 20	...
			7 03 exSun			73 exSun	77 Sun	717 exSun			79 exSun	7059 Sun	
113.8	BELLOWS FALLS........ Vt. ...Lv		7 08	....	....	12 48	2 48	7 00	6 37	....	11 32	11 33	...
120.9	Charlestown ... ...N.H. Ar		7 20	...	...	1 01	3 01	7 14	6 51	...	11 44	11 44	...
	Springfield(Vt.Trans.Co.)Vt. Ar						4 40	7 45	7 45				
131.0	Claremont Jct. ... ...N.H. Ar		7 33	...	...	1 16	3 16	7 29	7 03	...	9 08	11 59	11 59	...
138.9	Windsor.................... Vt. ..		7 48	...	...	1 34	3 28	7 46	7 13	...	9 18	12 15	12 16	...
153.0	WHITE RIVER JCT. ... .. Ar		8 10	...	...	2 05	3 50	8 25	7 35	...	9 40	12 45	12 45	...
			A M	A M	P M	P M	P M	P M	P M	P M	P M	A M	A M

	Southbound			A M	78 exSun A M	⊛5506u exSun A M		A M	A M	72 exSun P M	74 Sun P M	74 exSun P M			
	WHITE RIVER JCT............. Vt. Lv			....	4 00	7 00		....	....	12 15	2 50	2 50			
	Windsor			....	4 23	7 22		....	....	12 41	3 12	3 12			
	Claremont Jct. ....N. H.			....	4 40	7 32		....	....	12 55	3 33	3 33			
	Springfield (Vt. Trans. Co.) Vt. Lv			....	....	7 15		....	....	11 30	...	...			
	Charlestown...............N. H.			....	f4 54	7 45		....	....	1 11	3 46	3 46			
	Bellows Falls ... ... Vt. Ar			....	5 06	8 00		....	....	1 22	3 57	3 57			
				Mt Royal 5502 Daily A M	5504 exSun A M	Cheshire ⊛5506u A M	5550 Sun A M	Bus Sat. A M	5508 exSun P M	5512 Sun P M	Green Mt 5510 exSun P M			
	BELLOWS FALLS ... ... Vt. Lv			4 50	6 55	8 00 streamline train	9 40	12 45	1 35	4 05	4 05	...	...
	Walpole.........................N. H.			....	v7 02		9 47	g12 58	f1 42	...	4 12	...	...
	Westmoreland			....	7 12		...	g1 10	...	...	...	...	...
	Gilboa			....	....		...	...	...	...	...	...	...
	KEENE			5 31	7 38	8 31	10 18	1 34	2 15	4 44	4 46	...	...
	Webb..............................			....	....		...	...	...	...	...	...	...
	Troy			v5 50	7 55	... ...	f10 35	d1 51	2 34	f5 01	5 05	...	...
	Fitzwilliam			6 00	8 05	... ...	10 44	c2 01	2 44	f5 11	5 15	...	...
	State Line			....	f8 13	... ...	...	...	...	...	...	...	...
	WINCHENDON...............Mass. { Ar			6 14	8 23	9 03	11 05	2 20	2 56	5 25	5 27	...	...
	{ Lv								3 00	5 25	5 31		
	South Ashburnham ... ... Ar			f6 27	8 35		11 15	δ2 40	3 13	....	....	...	...
	Fitchburg . ... { Ar			6 42	8 48	e9 27	11 28	2 55	3 26	5 51	5 55	...	...
	{ Lv			7 06	8 55		11 42		3 32	5 51	6 01	...	...
	Ayer			7 30	9 16		12 00	3 25	3 57	...	6 18	...	...
	Waltham........................... ..			8 27	9 57		12 37		4 54	6 37	6 52	...	...
	Cambridge			8 37	10 07	e10 17	12 47	b4 40	5 07	6 47	7 06	...	...
	BOSTON (No. Sta.)............... .. Ar			8 45	10 15	10 25	12 55	a4 50	5 15	6 55	7 15	...	...
				A M	A M	A M	P M	P M	P M	P M	P M		

a   Bus stop Park Square.
b   Bus stop Kendall Square.
c   Bus stop Highway.
d   Bus stop Square.
e   Stops to discharge passengers.
f   Stops on signal to discharge or receive.
g   Bus stop Post Office.
k   Saturdays only.
t   Coach passengers change on arrival at New Haven and Springfield.
u   No checked baggage handled on this train.
v   Stops only to receive passengers.
⊛   "The Cheshire" Streamline train is limited in equipment and will receive passengers only to the extent of its capacity. All seats are reserved and assigned in advance. All coach class tickets honored except that those for restricted excursions will not be valid. No checked baggage handled on this train. No skis or other winter sports equipment will be accepted. Buffet service.
‡   Except Saturdays.
✠   Will not run on any holidays listed below.
☐   Will not run Nov. 27, Dec. 25, Jan. 1.
δ   This time is at Ashburnham.
...   Bus Motor Coach.
Holidays: Oct. 13, Nov. 11, Nov. 27, Dec. 25, Jan. 1, Feb. 23, April 19.

Cheshire Branch passenger train service, B&M PTT, Sept. 1947.

Milk Trains. Milk was an important commodity that moved on the Cheshire Branch. The B&M was the crucial third leg that enabled the Bellows Falls Co-operative Creamery (BFCC)/First National Stores (Finast) partnership to work. The BFCC was located on the Bellows Falls Island within the switching limits of the Rutland. While the B&M's main yard was across the river in North Walpole, New Hampshire, the road also owned several yard tracks on the Bellows Falls Island that were used for holding milk cars. Loaded milk cars from the BFCC were handled on Train 5500/the Bellows Falls Milk Train, which departed the Falls every night at 10:30–11:30 p.m. It ran the Cheshire Branch to South Ashburnham and then the Fitchburg Route Main Line to Finast's warehouse in Somerville, Massachusetts. Since the Milk Train moved at night, few people along the route ever glimpsed it, but it was a familiar sound in the Cheshire County night for years. Occasionally loaded milk cars also moved east on scheduled passenger trains. In the 1940s, a BFCC milk car for Providence, Rhode Island sometimes moved on train 5508 and was dropped at Winchendon for 8118—the Peterboro to Worcester local. Milk cars returning to the Falls were handled on scheduled passenger trains, including Trains 5503/*Green Mountain Flyer*, 5507 (unnamed), 5509/*Monadnock*, and 5511/*Mount Royal*. The power and crew for 5500 turned on 5511.

After the cessation of passenger service on the Cheshire Branch on May 31, 1958, the Milk Train continued to run. On July 1, 1958, the Milk Train's run

The westbound White River Milk Train, drawn by F2s 4256 and 4258, passes the Steamtown excursion train in Keene, July 15, 1962. Note the Steamtown ticket kiosk down the tracks at left. Photogr. unknown; Zach Knutsen coll.

After milk traffic ended on the B&M in the mid-1960s, idled milk cars ended up at various locations around the system, some of them used for storage. Among the idled cars were thirty-five relatively new insulated, steel cars delivered in the new McGinnis-era livery in 1957. These cars really stood out in a train's consist! Twenty of the cars were two-door cars for handling milk in ice-protected cans, and the other fifteen were four-door, Thermo-King mechanically refrigerated cars intended for handling bottled milk between Bellows Falls and Somerville. (*EM* JanFeb58, 15). Here are two survivors, one of each type, rusting away on a siding in Gardner, 1988. B. G. Blodget photo.

was extended north to White River Junction, where it would handle Canadian Pacific and Central Vermont milk cars in addition to Rutland and BFCC/Finast milk traffic at Bellows Falls. As a result of this change, the train became the White River Milk Train, and the manifest grew to twenty to thirty-five cars nightly.

This arrangement persisted until the White River Milk Train, in what Cowan (1978) called "the last major compression of milk traffic on the B&M," was canceled on November 3, 1962, and milk traffic over the Cheshire Branch ended. Remaining White River Junction milk business moved on New Hampshire Division freights JB-3/JB-4 via Concord, and remaining milk business from BFCC/Finast moved on freight JE-2 from Bellows Falls to East Deerfield and from there on the main line to Boston (ICC Docket Nos. 22455 and 22457). The BFCC/Finast traffic lasted only a little more than another year; The last carloads of milk left Bellows Falls on July 17, 1964 (*Times* July 23, 1964).

Freight Service. From at least as early as 1915, through freight service on the Cheshire Branch was handled by named freights BX-1/*Frontier* and XB-2/*Champlain*, opposite sides of the job that ran nights between

Boston and Bellows Falls. The names were applied in the early 1930s. Locals 561 and 528 were opposing daytime jobs that operated between East Fitchburg and Bellows Falls. In addition to passing tracks at stations, there were other passing tracks at Summit, Tenth Section, and Rockwood that allowed for ample meeting points for trains. The following are descriptions of work performed by BX-1 and 561 in B&M Symbol Book No. 3, January 1, 1915:

> *B-X 1–Daily (No. 503).* Handles from Boston, merchandise cars for Cheshire Branch including way car for Cheshire Branch stations, same to be dropped at East Fitchburg for 561; Winchendon and Peterboro Branch way car to be dropped at Winchendon; Keene and Bellows Falls house cars, National Despatch and R. W. & O. Line, and proper cars of high-class freight for C. and P. Division and Rutland R. R. or via those lines; Boston Dairy and Alden Brothers milk cars. Mondays, handle packing house cars Boston to Bellows Falls. Fill out as directed with important loads at East Fitchburg, South Ashburnham, Winchendon, and Keene.

> *No. 561–Ex. Sun.* Handles from East Fitchburg, local and merchandise cars for Cheshire Branch. At Fitzwilliam loads granite at different derricks. Makes straight car for Troy, NH. Loads and unloads L. C. L. freight, drop and pick up, and does necessary work on Cheshire Branch. At Keene, freight house men will do unloading while crew is dropping and picking up cars.

Goodwin (1976) explained (without providing a date) how BX-1/XB-2 were abolished to help relieve traffic congestion between Boston and South Ashburnham. The jobs were still listed in the *B&M Railroad Employees Magazine* in 1946 (*EM* Aug46, 15), and Nimke (1991) states they came off during the coal strike in February 1948. In their place, trains WX-1/XW-2 were established between Worcester and Bellows Falls via Gardner, where the Boston cars were interchanged with main line trains. Then early in 1958 the line between Heywood and Winchendon was taken out of service (abandoned in 1959) and trains FX-1/XF-2 between

Fitchburg and Bellows Falls replaced WX-1/XW-2.

The main reason for these through freights—in their various iterations—to and from the Falls was to interchange traffic there with the Rutland. At one time there was enough traffic to warrant a freight each way, six days per week. With a gradual decline in business, service dropped to one freight a day, running three days west and three days east. Through traffic handled with the Rutland abruptly ended September 25, 1961, when Rutland workers walked out on strike and the road summarily closed down and went out of business! Even before this shock to the system, interchange traffic had dwindled to the extent that in June 1961, FX-1/XF-2 was annulled. EK-1/KE-2, the Ashuelot Branch local, East Deerfield–Keene and return was annulled at the same time. Replacing both jobs was EX-1/XE-2, a six-day, two-sided job that ran between East Deerfield and Bellows Falls via Keene using the Ashuelot and Cheshire Branches. In October 1962 this job was extended to White River Junction and resymboled EJ-1/JE-2. EJ-1 ran East Deerfield to White River via Keene; JE-2 ran White River to East Deerfield via Brattleboro.

At the same time EJ-1 was established, F-7/F-8, a Monday/Wednesday/Friday (M-W-F) local turn from Fitchburg was established. It ran to Winchendon and Peterboro and would make a side trip to Troy if required. The October 1966 schedule shows that the EJ-1/JE-2 job has been dropped, but three local jobs are listed: (1) F-7/F-8 M-W-F Fitchburg–Keene and return, (2) EK-1/KE-2 six days, E. Deerfield–Keene and return, and (3) X-4/X-3 weekdays, Bellows Falls–Winchendon and return (Nimke 1991, photo 2-388). The X-4/X-3 job was dropped by the October 1967 schedule, but F-7/F-8 and EK-1/KE-2 continued. In 1968 a side trip to Waterville was added to F-7/F-8's duties and it made a through trip out to North Walpole (for over-dimension cars only) on Saturdays. FX-1/XF-2 was reinstated in the fall of 1967 and ran off-and-on to handle salt traffic into the summer of 1968. When running, it replaced F-7/F-8.

By 1970 it was clear that the era of branch line railroading in New England was ending. F-7/F-8 was eliminated altogether February 1, 1970. As the 1970s unfolded, the duties and working limits of remaining locals out of Fitchburg (F-1, F-3, F-5, and others) underwent constant rearrangement as the road struggled to maintain service to an ever-dwindling number of customers. Some jobs

RS3 1508 with X-4, the Bellows Falls–Winchendon freight, is at the west end of the former passenger platform. The former station building has been gone almost nine years; note the old canopy support bases. Parking meters show that the site has become a parking lot. Keene, Sept. 3, 1967. Richard B. Sanborn photo; Brent S. Michiels coll.

were changed to cover more than one branch or to alternately work different branches on different days. For example, F-1, the so-called "Hill Switcher," for many years worked Fitchburg–South Ashburnham–Gardner, but in the 1970s its working limits were extended to include Winchendon and Peterboro. In 1970, F-5/F-6 took over the Saturday-only trip out to Walpole and return for over-dimension cars once handled by F-7/F-8. Nimke (1991, photo 2-83) shows what is probably F-6—or the Bellows Falls Switcher with cars for F-6—on the Mountain Track (see Chapter 5) en route to Fitchburg Yard with OD cars in October 1970.

Abandonment. As early as 1962, the B&M began to weigh the prospect of abandoning certain sections of the Cheshire Branch (Spofford Sept. 19, 1962) and, on February 6, 1963, filed applications with the ICC seeking permission to abandon track between Winchendon and Troy and between the Keene Yard Limits and Cold River (ICC Docket Nos. 22455 and 22457). While these applications were subsequently withdrawn, by early 1970, it was clear the end for the Cheshire Branch was imminent. The road was cannabalizing unused passing tracks and spurs for relay rail. In the spring of that year,

for example, the 1,936-foot passing track at Gilboa and 550 feet of spur track at Westmoreland were retired (B&M Approval for Expenditure 39753, March 27, 1970) and the rails salvaged.

In late 1970, the last through moves were made over the Cheshire (see Chapter 7). Local freight service was still running from the east end out as far as Troy April 26, 1971 (Nimke 1991). But when heavy snows blocked the line Thanksgiving week of 1971—and there was no call for service—the line went unplowed. The following year, the road between Winchendon and Swanzey and between Keene and Cold River were formally abandoned (ICC Docket Nos. 25991 and 25992).

With the Cheshire Branch thus broken, the Ashuelot Branch became the last route into Keene. Freight service continued on the Cheshire's east end between South Ashburnham and Winchendon until 1984 when, except for a stub remnant at South Ashburnham, it too was given up. Out at the west end, the remaining segment of the main line between Cold River and the New Hampshire/Vermont state line (including the granite arch bridge) was formally abandoned in 1984 (ICC Docket No. AB-32 [Sub-No. 28]) and sold to the Green Mountain Railroad.

Troy, NH, station, (above) Feb. 25, 1970, almost twelve years after passenger service ended. Freight service would end here by mid-1971. The railroad had already sold the station building and it was being used as a residence. The granite landing at lower right was once used for unloading new automobiles destined for local dealerships. Skip Clark photo; Collection of Bob's Photo.

Its work in Winchendon completed, (below) local F-2 departs for Fitchburg with a short consist, typical for the times, May 27, 1975. Frederick G. Bailey photo.

CHAPTER THREE

THE CHESHIRE: EAST END

South Ashburnham, Massachusetts (MP B59.90)
to Joslin, New Hampshire (MP B89.22)

In this chapter we embark on a pictorial trip over the Cheshire, beginning at its connection with the Vermont & Masachusetts Railroad (V&M) in South Ashburnham, Massachusetts, and working outward in station order to Joslin (South Keene), New Hampshire. Bear in mind that the V&M was leased by the Fitchburg Railroad in 1874, the Cheshire was acquired by the Fitchburg in 1890, and the Fitchburg itself was leased by the Boston & Maine Railroad (B&M) in 1900.

There is a lot to see in this aerial view of S. Ashburnham in B&M days and it is worth getting out a good magnifying lens. The Fitchburg Route Main Line is at the bottom, the Cheshire Branch curves across the image from the lower right to the upper left, and the Ashburnham Branch leaves the old Cheshire Yard, crosses Rte. 101, and swings off behind the W. F. Whitney & Co. plant. Note the two-story station with its small detached baggage building (lower right), freight house (left center), and the old Cheshire Yard tracks. The old Cheshire turntable pit and ruins of the engine house are discernible above Rte. 101 at left, ca. 1935. Photogr. unknown.

South Ashburnham—MP B59.90

South Ashburnham was best known for its chairmakers. Three chairmakers—F. W. Lombard, C. A. Whitney & Co., and W. F. Whitney & Co.—used B&M rail service here in 1915.

Fitchburg American 23 with Train 14 at S. Ashburnham, March 23, 1896. Marium E. Foster coll., Hist. Soc. Cheshire Cty.

S. Ashburnham station as it appeared approaching from the east. The Fitchburg Route Main Line curves off to the left, the Cheshire Branch to the right. Beyond, the freight house on the Cheshire Branch and the section house on the main line are visible. The station had two orderboard masts, one for the main and one for the branch, ca. 1942. Marium E. Foster photo; Hist. Soc. Cheshire Cty.

In the hurricane of Sept. 20–21, 1938, the Cheshire Branch suffered considerably less damage than the main line and was released for operation Sept. 30, much sooner than the main line, which was not reopened between Boston and Greenfield until Oct. 23 (*EM* Fall38, 19). The result was a parade of detouring main-line freights, which, coupled with storm-related equipment disarrangements, made for some unusual sights at S. Ashburnham. Here Pacifics 3701 and sister 3705, normally in passenger service, are bringing a detouring freight off the branch, Oct. 1, 1938. Charles A. Brown photo; B&MRRHS Archives.

What's this, a mixed train on the Cheshire Branch? No, it's a detoured train with a riding coach on the end instead of the usual buggy. That's probably the conductor catching the rear end, as everyone looks on at S. Ashburnham, Oct. 1, 1938. Charles A. Brown photo; B&MRRHS Archives.

Train 5507 approaching S. Ashburnham station, the first stop on the Cheshire Branch, Aug. 9, 1941. Marium E. Foster photo; Hist. Soc. Cheshire Cty.

F-1, the "Hill Switcher" crew is busy switching a Santa Fe boxcar with Consolidation 2649 at S. Ashburnham. The tracks in the foreground are the Fitchburg Route Main Line. Photographer Stan Bolton is at right recording his version of this long-ago moment, April 7, 1951. George C. Corey photo.

Two young boys hope for a wave from the engineer as the 2649 goes about her duties switching out the S. Ashburnham freight house. April 7, 1951. George C. Corey photo.

Its work completed, the "Hill Switcher" has its train together and is about to return—tender-first—to Fitchburg. Beyond is the W. F. Whitney & Co. power plant. The station (left) was built in 1874 and razed in 1951, shortly after this image was captured, April 7, 1951. George C. Corey photo.

What was once the little detached baggage building became the final passenger station after the old station was razed in 1951, S. Ashburnham, ca. 1952. Photogr. unknown; B&MRRHS Archives.

Another aerial of S. Ashburnham shows the scene there in the mid-1950s. The view is inward along the Cheshire Branch, with the Rte. 101 crossing just out of the image at bottom, the sweeping main line curve at upper right. The old station is gone, but its footprint remains just east of the "new" station. Reaching the station required a 500-foot drive through the rail yard. Photogr. unknown; Robert N. Phelps coll., Stevens Public Library, Ashburnham, MA.

"Blue-dipped" B&M Alco RS3 1506—with a respectable hitch this day—enters the Cheshire Branch with Fitchburg to Keene local F-7. Close inspection reveals there are several "high-wide" cars, possibly military equipment, on the rear of the train. F-7 will leave these at Keene for E. Deerfield to White River Jct. freight EJ-1 before returning to Fitchburg as F-8. S. Ashburnham, ca. 1966. George C. Corey photo.

Naukeag (North Ashburnham) —MP B64.03

The original name of this station, North Ashburnham, was changed to Naukeag in 1909. The station was located just east of the Winchendon line at the corner of Depot Road and the old Keene–Fitchburg Turnpike (today's Route 12) in Burrageville, North Ashburnham. The station also housed the Burrageville Post Office. From the 1830s, several chair shops, including that of the Burrage Brothers, were located here. Summer vacationers would have used this station traveling to/from the Naukeag Lakes, but a short carriage ride from the station.

On a curve east of the station was the Astor House, a railroad landmark where the railroad and turnpike crossed at grade. Astor House, an old coaching days tavern, was "owned for many years by the Cheshire Railroad" (Stearns 1887, 392). It was apparently never used for railroad purposes, but was leased to others. A grade separation project in 1930 placed Route 12 on an overhead bridge—the Astor House Bridge (B63.42). After the railroad's abandonment, the bridge was entombed in the highway embankment. The Astor House, now a private residence, still stands in its original location.

Naukeag, MA, station, ca. 1930. The station building was removed in the mid-1930s to State Line, NH, to replace the station there, which had burned. Louis Benton photo; Brent S. Michiels coll.

Shot from Depot Rd. crossing, westbound Pacific 3711 hustles past MP64 at Naukeag, April 7, 1951. George C. Corey photo.

Winchendon—MP B67.92

Approximately one and a half miles west of Naukeag, the Walker (1886) and Richards (1898) atlases show a location on the railroad in Winchendon known as Pequoig. We believe it very likely the railroad made a stop here to accommodate workers at the nearby N. D. White & Sons' Pequoig Mills. In Cheshire Railroad days Pequoig was an important wood stop. On September 23, 1870, a fire took out the road's woodsheds here, destroying 300 cords of wood (*Transcript* Oct. 8, 1870).

The B&M and the Boston and Albany Railroad (B&A) competed for business at Winchendon and each road operated its own station and freight house. In 1918, the two roads' station forces were consolidated. The B&A station buildings were closed (and later rented to others) and the B&M's station and freight house were turned over for joint use under Federal Control General Order No. 31 effective September 14, 1918. To reach the B&M station, the B&A used the B&M's Worcester & Contoocook tracks and B&A passenger trains arrived at and departed from the B&M station. The joint payrolls of the station, freight house, yard forces, and operators were charged 84 percent to the B&M and 16 percent to the B&A. This arrangement ended in 1932. Anyone who's seen an image of a B&A train at the B&M station in Winchendon, please raise your hand!

Winchendon's industrial base was centered on woodenware. William Brown & Sons, O. L. Mann & Son, and E. Murdock & Co. were all important cooperage manufacturers, turning out millions of wooden pails, tubs, and barrels that were shipped all over the country. E. Murdock & Co. later became New England Woodenware. Carter & Campbell and Desmond & Brown Cos. were engaged in chairmaking. E. Loud Manufacturing Co. made wooden faucets. M. E. Converse & Son and the Mason & Parker Manufacturing Co. were wooden toymakers, shipping hundreds of carloads of toys from town every year in the "Christmas Toy Rushes" (*EM* Dec29, 13–14). Other important rail customers at Winchendon included N. D. White & Co. (textiles, denim), Baxter D. Whitney & Sons (woodworking machinery), Alaska Freezer Co. (ice cream freezers), Goodspeed Machine Co. (foundry), General Box Co., and J. H. Davenport & Son and G. G. Townsend (coal dealers).

This view is looking east on the Cheshire to its girder bridge ("Black Bridge") over the Millers River. Beyond the bridge (not visible), the B&A Ware River Branch and the B&M Peterboro Branch crossed the Cheshire on a diamond (see Chapter 11 for pictures of the diamond). The ball signal rigging at left governed movements over the diamond—one ball for the Cheshire Branch (normal), two for the Peterboro Branch, and three for the B&A. Trains approaching the diamond were required to stop and send a trainman ahead to set the ball signal to protect against conflicting trains and then normalize the signal after the train had crossed the diamond. The ball signal here was dismantled Dec. 28, 1945 and replaced by color light signals, one of which is visible in the center background. Winchendon, Dec. 1945 (*EM* Feb46, 6). George H. Hill photo.

Consolidation 2728 is arriving at Winchendon with WX-1, the Worcester–Bellows Falls freight. That is the B&A section house at left, Sept. 29, 1951. Stanwood K. Bolton photo.

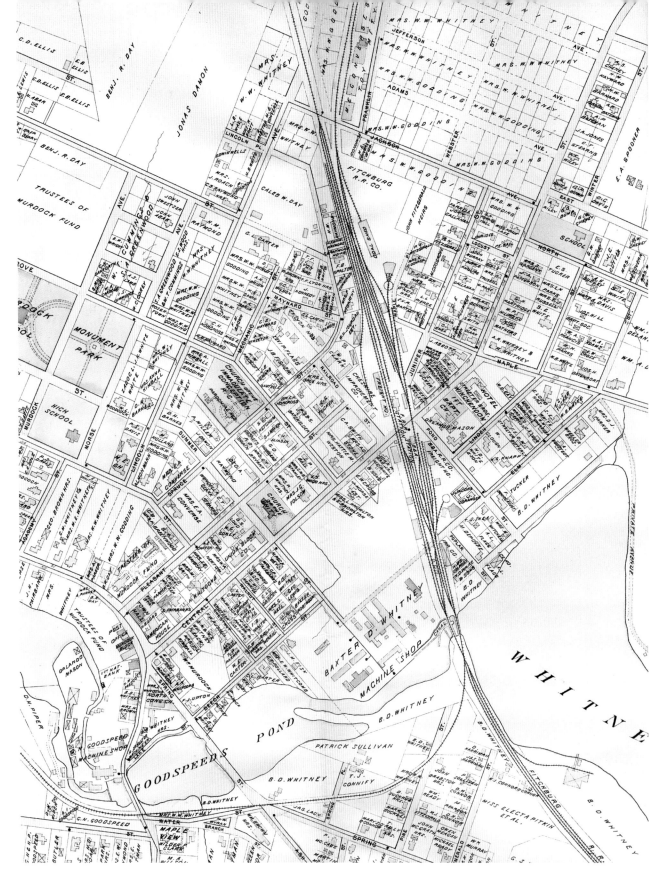

Richards (1898) atlas map of (pre-B&M) Winchendon, showing the railroad track plant of the Boston & Albany's Ware River Branch and the Fitchburg's Cheshire, Worcester, and Monadnock Branches. The Worcester and Monadnock Branches were components of the Worcester and Contoocook (see Chapter 11). It was always a peculiarity here that the Cheshire and the parallel Worcester and Contoocook—while both Time Table east–west routes—were directionally reversed! Note the rail-served icehouse at Whitney Pond, the crossing diamond, and the B&A and Fitchburg turntables, roundhouses, stations, and freight houses.

An outward Peterboro Branch train in the Winchendon station, ca. 1901. This station was built by the Cheshire in 1877 to replace an earlier station. In 1903 the B&M picked up and moved the station across the Peterboro tracks so that all trains would arrive and depart on the same side of the station. Postcard; B. G. Blodget coll.

Winchendon station and freight house viewed from Central St., ca. 1910. Photogr. unknown; S. J. Whitney coll.

In its glory days, the *Green Mountain Flyer (left)*, Montreal-bound, stands in the Winchendon station, ca. 1910. The middle car in the image is one of the six wooden, steel-underframed dining-café cars built in 1906 for the B&M by Pullman Car Co. (Hutchinson 1977). Note that the town's famous wooden horse has not yet taken up residence on the station's lawn. Anderson photo postcard; Dale O. Russell coll.

Winchendon's famous wooden hobby horse was built by the M. E. Converse & Son Co. and presented to the town in 1914. It stood by the railroad station, welcoming visitors to "the Toy Town" until 1934 when it was moved to the grounds of the Toy Town Tavern. It remained there for thirty years. After undergoing repairs, it made its last appearance during the nation's bicentennial in 1976, after which it fell into ruins. Postcard; B. G. Blodget coll.

The east end of the freight house has been removed to make room for this "modern station" at Winchendon, ca. 1957. Photogr. unknown; B&MRRHS Archives.

B&M freight house at Winchendon, ca. 1952. Marium E. Foster photo; Hist. Soc. Cheshire Cty.

For many years one could witness the spectacle of clockwork morning-outward and afternoon-inward meets of Cheshire and Peterboro Branch trains at Winchendon. These daily-except-Sunday meets provided convenient cross-platform transfers. Many rail photographers made the trip to Winchendon to shoot these famous meets in their last years (1949–1953), a time when diesels were fast supplanting steam. On the page opposite is a sampling of these images.

Streamline train 6000 is in the station at Winchendon with Train 5506/*Cheshire*, ca. 1950. Donald S. Robinson photo; B&MRRHS Archives.

On her morning run to Boston, streamline train 6000, running as the *Cheshire*, slides into Winchendon on the heels of a snowstorm. Unlike the freight house dock (left), the passenger concourse (right) has been cleared of snow, ca. 1948. Marium E. Foster photo; Hist. Soc. Cheshire Cty.

Streamline train 6000 making its regular morning stop at Winchendon as viewed from the east end of the freight house, ca. 1949. Marium E. Foster photo; Hist. Soc. Cheshire Cty.

At Winchendon, Mogul 1468 on Train 8111/the Worcester–Peterboro local, awaits the arrival of Boston–Montreal Train 5503/*Green Mountain* from Boston. The B&M's Sept. 30, 1951 PTT gives 8111's leisurely schedule as arriving Winchendon at 10:15, out at 10:53; and 5503's much faster schedule arriving at 10:46, out at 10:50. The view is from a point just west of the station. The track in the foreground is the section house track. The *Green Mountain* will pull in on the Cheshire Branch track on the fireman's side of 8111, ca. 1951. Stanwood K. Bolton photo.

Big meets small. On this day's morning meet, big Pacific 3711 is in charge of 5503 and Mogul 1403 is on 8111. Train 8111 usually ran coach first with the baggage-RPO trailing. The edge of the station roof is at left, the roof of the freight house beyond the trains, Winchendon, Jan. 22, 1952. Berton G. Towle photo; Brent S. Michiels coll.

This day Mogul 1448 is on 8111 and is picking up a few passengers for Peterboro off of 5503 powered by RS3 1538. Winchendon, April 30, 1952. Philip R. Hastings photo; B&MRRHS Archives.

Same meet, different day at Winchendon, July 26, 1952. Richard R. Wallin photo; R. R. Richards Jr. coll.

The gates have been dropped at Jackson Ave. and friendly waves are exchanged as Pacific 3710/*Peter Cooper* departs town with 5503/*Green Mountain*, Winchendon, July 18, 1949. Donald S. Robinson photo; Brent S. Michiels coll. and Winchendon Hist. Soc.

And now for the afternoon meet of inward Trains 5508 and 8118. The view is through the windshield of 5508's F7 diesel approaching Winchendon station. Ahead, 8118 is already in the station awaiting 5508, Feb. 25, 1951. Photogr. unknown; Collection of Bob's Photo.

RS3 1545 on 5508 (left) and leased New Haven RS3 561 on 8118 are side-by-side for their inward meet at Winchendon, Feb. 17, 1953. Berton G. Towle photo; B. G. Blodget coll.

Train 5508 was scheduled out of Winchendon a few minutes ahead of Train 8118. In this fireman's view from 8118 standing on the B&A's bridge, he can see that the Boston train has cleared the diamond and his train can now cross the Cheshire Branch and head for Worcester, Feb. 17, 1953. Berton G. Towle photo; Brent S. Michiels coll.

State Line—MP B70.93

Here at State Line, the Damon Family had a long-running relationship with the railroad, dating back to the Cheshire Railroad days of wood-burning locomotives. There was a large woodshed at State Line where engines stopped to "wood-up." The Damon timberlands supplied the railroad with immense quantities of wood and also shipped wood. The Damon Mill produced dimension lumber and manufactured wood turnings. Another business at State Line cut and shipped ice from a siding at Sip Pond.

The original Cheshire Railroad-built station (and post office) at State Line, NH, as it appeared looking from Rte. 12. Note the orderboards (added about 1908) above the roofline and the flag stop signal. That is the section house at right, which was across the tracks from the station, ca. 1910. Photogr. unknown; Hist. Soc. Cheshire Cty.

State Line station and section house, ca. 1930. Louis Benton photo; Dale O. Russell coll.

The original State Line station burned to the ground Nov. 23, 1930. Three thousand table legs delivered to the station from the Damon Mill the previous day all burned (*Monadnock Breeze*, Nov. 28, 1930). This little station, the former Naukeag station, was moved to the site as a replacement. An old boxcar was brought in to serve as a baggage room. Photogr. unknown.

The second State Line station, ca. 1950. State Line was discontinued as a passenger station Feb. 7, 1949 (*EM* Mar49, 20). Train 5504 continued to stop for mail into mid-1954. The little building survives today–in ruins–on Maple Street in Winchendon Springs, MA. Photogr. unknown.

Pacific 3628, with all-coach Rutland-to-Boston Train 5510/*Green Mountain*, blows past MP71 at State Line, April 8, 1950. Stanwood K. Bolton photo.

Fitzwilliam—MP B76.28

Fitzwilliam's station was located about a mile south of the center of town in an area that came to be known as Fitzwilliam Depot—or, as the locals referred to it, just "the Depot." After the Cheshire Railroad was built through Fitzwilliam, the Depot soon became an important area for commerce and by 1890 had developed into a thriving industrial village based on granite quarrying and associated businesses. In 1915 there were seven granite shippers (see Chapter 15) and six shippers of wood and dimension lumber. Other B&M customers included Mason & Co. (hay and grain), J. M. Parker & Co. (operator of a twelve-car capacity grain elevator), and the E. L. Taft Co. (brooms). Though only a mile apart, Fitzwilliam Center and the Depot were culturally very different places and it became a matter of some importance whether you lived in one or the other.

A shipment of blueberries awaits the train to Boston at the east end of the Fitzwilliam station platform. Although other Monadnock Region towns might challenge it, Fitzwilliam was sometimes called "The Blueberry Capital of the World," 1917. Photo from *Fitzwilliam: Profile of a New Hampshire Town* (1985:77), courtesy Town of Fitzwilliam.

Fitzwilliam, NH, station. East of the station, Enos Blodgett's granite cutting shed is visible, ca. 1915. Photogr. unknown.

Train 5507 has just dropped passengers at Fitzwilliam, as the scene appeared looking from the train's rear platform. Note the gray- and white-striped B&M wayside telephone box at the corner of the station, and the freight house across the tracks, 1945. Marium E. Foster photo; Hist. Soc. Cheshire Cty.

Fitzwilliam Depot near the end, October 17, 1970. George Morrison photo; Brent S. Michiels coll.

Troy—MP B81.55

In the nineteenth century, Troy was a destination of choice for people seeking to climb Mount Monadnock, and the railroad brought a great deal of business to the town. For accommodations, the Kimball House was just across the street from the station. The Monadnock Hotel, known for its grand view of the mountain, was located on the town's common, a short walk from the station.

In 1867 the Cheshire Railroad, for some reason, was considering changing the name of the station from Troy to "Troyville." Upon getting wind of this, several dozen citizens of Troy petitioned the railroad to adopt the name "Monadnock Station" instead (petition dated Oct. 3, 1867, B&MRRHS Archives). The Cheshire dropped the idea and the name was never changed.

Industrially, Troy seems to have been best known

as the home of the Troy Blanket Mills, famed for their horse blankets, and the Troy White Granite Co. (see Chapter 15). Other railroad customers in 1915 included Platts Box Co., Carl Howe (lumber), Farrar Bros. (cooperage), H. F. Holtham and O. P. Whitcomb (apples), and A. I. Watson (dressed squabs).

Starting in 1900, the Troy Granite Railway (TGRy) delivered loads of granite to the B&M at the Troy station until the quarry closed and operations ceased in late 1916. (See Chapter 15 for more about this little-known operation.)

The once thriving business at the Troy freight house, as was the case at stations everywhere, dried up in the 1950s, and the house track was spiked out of service to be retired in December 1959.

Troy, NH, station, April 3, 1954. This station did a tremendous summer business. Henry David Thoreau arrived at this station for at least one of his treks to Mount Monadnock on June 2, 1858 (journal entry). L. S. Twombly photo; Brent S. Michiels and Dale O. Russell colls.

At Troy, the Troy Granite Railway's tracks (left foreground) passed close to the station, crossed Depot St., and ran out Water St. The catenary for this little electric industrial road is visible in the image. Across the street from the station is the Kimball House, 1910. Hist. Soc. Cheshire Cty.

Troy station, looking down Depot Street. A way-freight is in town. The freight house is across the tracks at right, the team track full of cars at left, ca. 1910. Hist. Soc. Cheshire Cty.

Troy freight house and adjacent section house with the "putt-putt," undated. Photogr. unknown; Hist. Soc. Cheshire Cty.

The rugged country north of Troy is evident in this image showing Gulf Bridge (B83.88) crossing both the deep gorge of the Ashuelot River's South Branch and the primitive, Keene–Troy Road, ca. 1920. Postcard; Brent S. Michiels coll.

Gulf Bridge and Troy Ledges, looking west, Troy, ca. 1947. The earlier truss bridge here was replaced by this girder bridge during a system-wide bridge strengthening program in 1929–1930. Stanley H. Smith photo; Collection of Bob's Photo.

Pacific 3635 with Train 5510/*Green Mountain*, at Gulf Bridge, Troy Ledges, Troy, Sept. 8, 1950. Albert G. Hale photo; Dale O. Russell coll.

(Above left) E7 3814 with Train 5553, the Sunday *Green Mountain*, is at Troy Ledges, crossing Gulf Bridge. Rte. 12 is just visible at extreme upper right, Troy, Nov. 11, 1951. George C. Corey photo.

(Above right) GP7 1563 is passing through Troy Ledges, with Bellows Falls–Fitchburg freight XF-2. Note how vegetation is starting to take control of the right-of-way, Troy, June 20, 1968. H. Bentley Crouch photo; Walker Transportation Coll., Beverly Hist. Soc.

(Left) Vegetation is already well on its way to reclaiming the Cheshire's right-of-way in this post-abandonment image at Troy Ledges, Oct. 19, 1973. H. Bentley Crouch photo; Walker Transportation Coll., Beverly Hist. Soc.

Webb (Marlboro)—MP B85.30

Webb was one of two stations in Marlborough. Originally called "Marlboro," it was built when the Cheshire came through town in 1847. Its location in the remote southwest corner of town, over two miles distant from the village, is indicative of the importance the town attached to having its own station on the new railroad. Little did the town know that thirty years later the Manchester and Keene Railroad would build through town and open a station—Marlboro Village— only a half mile north of the village. In 1909, in order to avoid confusion between the two stations, the B&M changed their names. Marlboro station became "Webb" and Marlboro Village became Marlboro.

Woodenware and stone were the important commodities shipped from Webb. After 1890, the Webb Granite & Construction Co. became a very large customer here, shipping carloads of granite and paving stone (see Chapter 15). In 1915, woodenware makers G. E. and A. J. Fuller, C. L. Lane, and Nelson Manufacturing were also listed as active shippers here.

Webb was discontinued as a passenger stop in 1948 or 1949 and the passing siding here was spiked out of service January 3, 1957.

This is the sweeping view looking down the valley of the Ashuelot River's South Branch from the steep—and then treeless— hill above the Marlboro depot area. Between the station and the freight house is the Cheshire Branch main line and passing track. The main line right-of-way can be discerned running down the valley to the right. A westbound train stands in the station, and just uphill from the octagonal brick water tank building, one rail of the sand bank spur is visible (see next image). The Granite Railway of New Hampshire's line to the Webb Quarry shows at bottom right. This quarry road interchanged with the B&M by a switchback 1,000 feet east of the station. The late Bill Fletcher could recall how the station agent's daughter would provide flag protection for the quarry switcher when it would come down to the depot for water, ca. 1905. Photogr. unknown; Marlborough Hist. Soc.

A Cheshire gravel train has backed into the sandbank spur just east of Marlboro, where a dozen workmen are loading flatcars with hand shovels, July 1, 1878. The remains of this old gravel bank are visible even today. J. A. French photo; Hist. Soc. Cheshire Cty.

Marlboro station and freight house in Cheshire Railroad days. Note the Marlboro Depot Post Office in the freight house, July 1, 1878. Teamsters must have done a thriving business hauling freight up the steep hill from here to the village. J. A. French photo; Hist. Soc. Cheshire County.

Webb depot area showing the passenger station (center), freight house (left), and brick water tank house—all original Cheshire Railroad structures. Note, however, that the station now sports a signal mast with orderboards, something unknown in Cheshire or Fitchburg Railroad days, ca. 1910. Marlborough Hist. Soc.

Webb station (below) was located on the steep side of a hill in the western part of Marlborough, NH; Keene is to the left. At right, Webb Depot Road comes down the hill, cuts right at the station, and then parallels the tracks for a short distance before resuming its steep downward course, cutting left beneath the high Webb granite arch bridge (B85.34; see photo on page 56 in Chapter 2), ca. 1930. Louis Benton photo; Hist. Soc. Cheshire Cty

The seldom-photographed street side of Webb station. As was typical in the day, the station had separate sides for men and women, ca. 1917. Photogr. unknown; Marlborough Hist. Soc.

East Swanzey

Here comes E7 3820 attacking the ruling eastward grade with Train 5504/*Mount Royal*. She is passing the Golding-Keene Company's truck-rail transload facility at Siding 0757 in East Swanzey, NH, about halfway between Webb and Joslin, March 25, 1950. Golding-Keene mined and milled feldspar at its plant in Keene. The 3820, delivered in April 1949, was the twenty-first and final E7 to be rostered by the B&M. She would be lost in the terrible wreck of the *Redwing-New Englander* on the New Hampshire Division at Nashua, Nov. 12, 1954. George C. Corey photo.

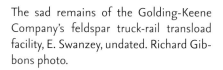

The sad remains of the Golding-Keene Company's feldspar truck-rail transload facility, E. Swanzey, undated. Richard Gibbons photo.

Joslin (Swanzey, South Keene)—MP B89.22

Early railroad customers here included Keene (Bodwell) Granite Co. and J. B. Elliot & Sons/Clipper Mowing & Reaper Works. Keene Granite moved stone over a haulage road from its quarry in Roxbury to the plant here until 1878, when the company connected itself to a rail spur off the M&K in Marlborough and the plant at South Keene was sold. The haulage road was later given to the Fitchburg Railroad, which used a portion of it when it built the South Keene Spur to reach customers down along the Ashuelot River in 1890. In 1900–1909, carloads of coal were delivered to the Keene Electric Railway in South Keene.

The station's name was changed from South Keene to Joslin in 1909. In 1915, the B&M listed Keene Chair Co. (porch chairs), Fred B. Pierce & Co. (handles and spokes), and D. R. and F. A. Cole Co. (grain dealer/grist mill and elevator operator) as customers at Joslin.

In 1953, the New Hampshire (formerly Keene) Chair Co. went out of business and the Joslin Spur was retired except for a ten-car-length stub that was retained as a siding. WX-1 used the siding to clear for Train 5503 (the Joslin passing track had already been removed). In the 1960s, carloads of salt were spotted on the siding for unloading and it became known as the "salt track."

Joslin, NH, station, another original Cheshire-built structure, ca. 1930. Louis Benton photo.

Built about 1878, all that remains of the Clipper Mowing & Reaper Works at South Keene is the smokestack after a fire June 15, 1891 (Wadsworth 1932). In the foreground is the switch for the South Keene Spur. The station is just out of the picture to the right. Ahead, the road swings left and will cross three bridges in quick succession—a stone arch bridge over Swanzey Factory Road (B89.34), the Joslin Arch (B89.41), and the Marlborough Street (Rte. 101) Bridge (B89.47). Undated., Hist. Soc. Cheshire Cty.

Keene (Bodwell) Granite Company workers at the company's cutting plant located across the tracks from the South Keene station, ca. 1878. J. A. French photo; Hist. Soc. Cheshire Cty.

A Pacific engine, its tender heaped with coal, steps across Joslin Arch with an eastbound passenger train, Feb. 22, 1934. Note the two milk cars behind the engine. Photogr. unknown; R. R. Richards Jr. coll.

Streamline train 6000, Train 5505/*Cheshire* on the Joslin Arch, ca. 1950. The 6000 was taken off the *Cheshire* at the end of April 1952 and replaced with conventional equipment. Photogr. unknown; Hist. Soc. Cheshire Cty.

E7 3802, with Train 5506/*Cheshire*, crosses the Joslin Arch, April 18, 1953. Stanwood K. Bolton photo.

CHAPTER FOUR

THE CHESHIRE: AT KEENE

Keene, New Hampshire (MP B91.28)

Keene's first railroad station, a three-portal, shed-style station built in 1847 by the Cheshire Railroad, as it appeared ca. 1890. Only the left and middle portals of this station had tracks; the passenger concourse was inside the right portal. Passenger trains of the Ashuelot and Manchester & Keene Railroads also used the station. A bypass track, which ran along the south side of the station, was used by freight trains. The Cheshire's offices were located on the second floor. Photogr. unknown; R. R. Richards Jr. coll.

After the Boston and Maine Railroad (B&M) leased the Fitchburg Railroad in 1900, Keene became an all-B&M city, a division point in fact for three B&M divisions: the Connecticut and Passumpsic Division (Ashuelot Branch), the Worcester, Nashua & Portland Division (Keene Branch), and the Fitchburg Division (Cheshire Branch).

In this chapter—in roughly chronological order—we look at railroad scenes and happenings along the Cheshire

(and its successors) in Keene. In its pre-1890 days of independence, the Cheshire always maintained its headquarters and shops in Keene. After local control ended, the general offices were removed to Fitchburg. However, as we saw in Chapter 2, the Keene Shops were greatly expanded in the Fitchburg years and would continue as an important facility until the B&M opened the Billerica Shops in November 1914. There is little doubt that between 1880 and 1920, the Cheshire and its successor

Keene's first station and adjacent buildings on Main St.'s west side, ca. 1905. At left is the Dunbar House, built in 1785. Cynthia Dunbar, mother of Henry David Thoreau, was born here in 1787. Owned by the Cheshire Railroad from 1846, the house was apparently never used for railroad purposes, but was leased by the Cheshire and successor roads to various tenants. After 101 years in railroad ownership, the B&M sold the property to the Houpises, owners of the Crystal Restaurant, in 1947. At right is the Sentinel Building, built in 1893. From their strategic location, the *Sentinel* staff kept a watchful eye on the railroad, and by their diligent reporting left a treasure trove of railroad history. American Express maintained offices in the Sentinel Building for twenty years before their own building was built in 1912. Note the Keene Electric Railway tracks in the foreground. Bion H. Whitehouse photo; Hist. Soc. Cheshire Cty.

En route back to Boston after a 30-day transcontinental excursion to San Francisco, a group of Knights Templar poses in front of Burlington Route's Pullman drawing room/sleeping car *Modena*, stopped on the Main St. crossing in Keene, Sept. 4, 1883. The special train consisted of six brand-new Pullmans (including the *Modena*), Chicago, Burlington & Quincy coach number 99, and a baggage car (Roberts 1884). J. A. French photo; Hist. Soc. Cheshire Cty.

East Yards and downtown in the Cheshire's last summer before the Fitchburg takeover. At extreme left can be seen the Ashuelot's roundhouse and freight house and the Cheshire's passenger station. On this day, the yard appears to be full of stock cars. Note the stock pen at left center where animals were held for their trains, Keene, 1890. J. A. French photo; Hist. Soc. Cheshire Cty.

Beech Hill looms above the East Yards, busy with many cars spotted at consignees. The view is from the Newbury Building. Over the flat-roofed C. A. Jones Building can be seen Swift's Western Dressed Beef warehouse and the Cheshire Chair Co. in the Beaver Mills complex beyond. The stock pen is gone. Across the tracks at lower right is the old Ashuelot freight house. Keene, ca. 1910. Postcard; Hist. Soc. Cheshire Cty.

owners ranked among Keene's largest employers. From their beginnings in the 1840s through the mid-twentieth century, the roads employed thousands of residents of the city and surrounding towns. Today, many area residents boast of family members who were employed in various capacities by the roads.

By the turn of the century, Keene was already an important rail center. Atkins' list of active B&M customers at Keene in 1915 shows the flourishing railroad- and industrial-based economy nearing its peak in the early twentieth century. Some customers had private sidings, while others were offline and drayed materials between their plants and a B&M team track. Atkins' list does not break down the customers by division territories in the Keene Yards.

A sampling of the B&M's 1915 customers in Keene includes dealers in coal (Spencer Hardware Co. and three others), grain (J. Cushing & Co. and George H. Eames & Son), building materials (Pearson Bros. and Knowlton & Stone), and wagons and sleighs (F. C. & L. A. Nims, J. L. Perry, H. A. Pierce, and H. M. Wilder). There were three

Fitchburg Train 17/*Green Mountain Flyer* has just crossed the Joslin Arch and is starting across the bridge over Marlborough St., Keene, ca. 1895. The Keene Electric Railway tracks along the street were not laid until 1900. A. A. Clough photo; Hist. Soc. Cheshire Cty.

Another westbound passenger train with the usual American-type engine passes over the steel Marlborough St. Bridge. Now we see the Keene Electric Railway tracks along the right side of the road, ca. 1910. Hist. Soc. Cheshire Cty.

Keene's first railroad station has been skeletonized in the demolition process, 1910. It is evident that the right-hand (north) portal never had a track. The track at left crossed Main Street to reach the engine house built there by the Ashuelot Railroad in 1885. It saw less and less use after the Ashuelot's lessee, the Connecticut River Railroad, was taken over by the B&M in 1893. Postcard; Dale O. Russell coll.

The north wall of the old station performed its last service as a wall for temporary baggage quarters during construction of the new station, seen rising beyond. Train service continued uninterrupted during the construction of the new station. The J. Cushing & Co. (flour, grain, and hay) buildings are at right, the Crystal Restaurant at left. Keene, 1910. Bion H. Whitehouse photo; Hist. Soc. Cheshire Cty.

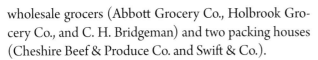

wholesale grocers (Abbott Grocery Co., Holbrook Grocery Co., and C. H. Bridgeman) and two packing houses (Cheshire Beef & Produce Co. and Swift & Co.).

There were manufacturers of boxes (Fowler, Norwood & Greene Co.), bricks (Keene Brick Co.), brush handles (A. A. Ellis), chairs (Burdett Chair Co., Cheshire Chair Co., L. J. Colony, C. L. Russell & Sons, Norwood Calef Co., and Sprague & Carlson Co.), combs for textile

machinery (Wilcox Comb Co.), cooperage (Beaver Mills Co., Impervious Package Co., and Keene Wooden-ware Co.), granite (Victoria White Granite Co.), dimension lumber (Norcross & Parker Co.), glue (Keene Glue Co.), hoops (O. D. Beaverstock Co.), horse medicine (J. G. Lesure), machinery (J. C. Black Co. and Humphrey Machine Co.), mica products (American Insulator & Mica Co. and the Keene Mica Products Co.), pottery (Hamp-

Keene's second station, built by the B&M in 1910 and dedicated Jan. 24, 1911, brought a fresh new look to the neighborhood. A beautiful building of yellow brick and red sandstone trim, it would serve the city well until the end of passenger service in 1958. Postcard. B. G. Blodget coll.

Keene was a vitally important water stop on the Cheshire, as locomotives climbing to either Surry or Fitzwilliam Summit demanded plenty of steam. Sustained periods of subzero cold could freeze water supplies, starve locomotives for steam, and bring the whole railroad to a halt. Pictured at left is an octagonal brick tank house, a holdover from Cheshire Railroad days that stood just east of Main Street on Railroad Ave. across from the C. A. Jones Building. Similar tank houses were located at Winchendon, Fitzwilliam, Troy, Webb, and Westmoreland. The tank houses were warmed by stoves to protect the wooden tanks inside from freezing. At right is a 50,000-gallon tank that stood on the south side of the tracks west of the passenger station. The railroad's water supply at Keene was purchased from the city. Photogr. unknown; Sect. 39.1, B&M Valuation Survey, 1914; Benjamin Campbell coll.

shire Pottery Co.), scrap metal (J. L. Brisk, Louis Tatle-man, and New England Machinery & Metal Co.), shoes (Ashuelot Co. and Monadnock Shoe Co.), silver polish (Greene Mineral Paste Co. and J. A. Wright Co.), soft drinks (N. D. Guernsey & Co.), toys (Wilkins Toy Co./ Kingsbury Manufacturing Co.), wagons (R. C. Jones), woodenware (Robinson-Brett Co.), wood heels (Lynnwood Heel Co.), and woolens (Faulkner & Colony Mills and Gilsum Woolen Co.).

Keene Granite Terra Cotta & Tile Co. was an earlier (1890–1894) industrial customer. Keene Mica Products was bought out and reorganized as the Golding-Keene Co. in 1922. Golding-Keene acquired a feldspar mine on the southern edge of Alstead, eleven and a half miles north of the city, and built a feldspar milling plant in Keene, the first such plant in New Hampshire. Feldspar ore was trucked to Keene for milling or to be loaded on railcars and shipped elsewhere (Ladoo 1922). Milled product was trucked to a truck-rail transload facility in East Swanzey to be shipped out. Golding-Keene closed its mine and plant in 1966. Chabott Coal Co., Crocker Metals (scrap dealer), and Wetterau Foods were other important later users of rail.

In Chapters 9 and 13, our discussion of the Ashuelot and the Manchester & Keene Railroads (and their successors) will again bring us into Keene.

A huge send-off crowd surrounds B&M Extra 1008 East, which has stopped at Keene to pick up National Guardsmen from the Monadnock Region answering President Wilson's call to serve on the Mexican border. About seventy, including Mayor Orville E. Cain, were Keene residents, June 20, 1916. Bion H. Whitehouse photo; Hist. Soc. Cheshire Cty.

Images like this exemplify the central role the railroads played in America in the first part of the twentieth century. Keene, June 20, 1916. Hist. Soc. Cheshire Cty.

As a sea of people crowd Railroad Square, Extra 1008 East departs Keene after Guardsmen from the Monadnock Region have boarded the train. Note the early motorcycle with side seat at lower left and the interesting variety of automobiles mixed with horse-drawn conveyances. June 20, 1916. Postcard; B. G. Blodget coll.

There appears to be a lot of excitement—we're not sure what about—in the city on this day as B&M 0-6-0 switcher 174 is going about its work. The switcher has just crossed to the east side of Main St. and is about to pass Perley Safford's Garage on the engineer's side. A northbound Keene Electric Railway open car—with many empty seats—will now be free to cross the B&M tracks. The three-story balconied building visible southward on Main St. is the Ellis Hotel, Keene, 1917–1920. Photogr. unknown; R. R. Richards Jr. coll.

Another 0-6-0 switcher, with a brakeman doing a balancing act on the tender, clatters across the Keene Electric Railway diamond as it backs across the street on Track Three. Visible beyond is the fourth track across Main Street that was used by Ashuelot Branch trains. Perley Safford's Garage (the old Ashuelot engine house) is at left, the station out of view to the right. Keene, ca. 1920. Hist. Soc. Cheshire Cty.

Ten-Wheeler 2126 and a sister are double-heading an inward passenger train on the Marlborough Street Bridge (B89.47). It would appear from the condition of the tracks (right) that the Keene Electric Railway has given up. Keene, ca. 1926. Photogr. unknown; B&MRRHS Archives, *B&M Bull.* 4(4):29, 5(2): 4.

The B&M streamline train 6000.
In the early afternoon of March 22, 1935, the first full day of spring, a strange blatting horn was heard at the Island Street crossing. It was the B&M's brand-new stainless steel streamliner, on its week-long demonstration tour of the system, announcing her arrival in the city. Its visit had been well publicized in advance. Even while automobiles were already starting to erode the passenger business, the pictures of the crowds that came out to see the train show there was still much public interest in the railroad. The train had departed this day from White River Junction and had shown at Windsor, Claremont Junction, and Bellows Falls before arriving in Keene. The road estimated 2,200 visitors had gone through the train at the Falls, and that at Keene an amazing 7,359 residents of Keene and surrounding towns inspected the train. Large crowds gathered at crossings and stations all along the route to see the train pass.

The 6000, arriving from Bellows Falls, makes her debut in Keene, March 22, 1935.

Long lines are cued up at the station for a chance to go through the train, the first streamline train in the East. Note the *Flying Yankee* nameplate, under which name she would enter service April 1, 1935, between Boston, Portland, and Bangor.

Schoolboys look over the 6000's less-photographed boattail. This was such a big event that we suspect school was probably let out for the afternoon. Keene, March 22, 1935.

Her exhibition visit at Keene completed, the "tin fish" slips across the Marlborough Street Bridge as she leaves for Boston, Friday evening, March 22, 1935. Arrival in Boston was delayed because the crowd at Fitchburg was so huge that the road authorized an unscheduled stop there. Postcard; Hist. Soc. Cheshire Cty.

The 6000 was a diesel-powered, three-car, articulated streamliner with fluted stainless steel car bodies. No one had ever seen anything like it. It was filled with many "firsts," including all-sealed windows and modern mechanical air-conditioning. There was a galley for light meals and 132 comfortable seats. The rear car's solarium featured wrap-around windows and even a speedometer the passengers could watch to see how fast the train was moving.

It entered revenue service as the *Flying Yankee* April 1, 1935, covering the run between Boston, Portland, and Bangor. It came off this run and ran as the *Cheshire* between Boston, Keene, Bellows Falls, and White River Junction from November 1944 through April 1952. For its final assignment—except in the summer of 1955 when it operated as the *Businessman* between Boston and Portland and a brief reprieve as the *Cheshire* from December 1956 to April 1957—it ran as the *Minute Man* between Boston and Troy, New York. On May 7, 1957, it made its last run from Troy to Boston and was retired. In its 22-year career, the 6000 had streaked through the Monadnock Region twice daily for almost thirteen years.

The 6000, given its popularity and limited seating, always ran on an "all seats reserved in advance" basis. In the years it operated as the *Cheshire*, timetables would show minor year-to-year variation, but the basic pattern remained unchanged. Looking just at the service between Keene and Boston shown in the B&M's October 15, 1945 PTT, Train 5506 departed Keene at 8:36 a.m., made no stops at Troy, Fitzwilliam or State Line,

left Winchendon at 9:08, stopped only to discharge passengers at Fitchburg at 9:34, and arrived at North Station in Boston at 10:30 a.m. Train 5505 departed Boston at 4:10 p.m., stopped only to receive passengers at Fitchburg at 5:07, departed Winchendon at 5:32, and arrived in Keene at 6:04 p.m. The 91.3 miles from Boston to Keene was covered in one hour and fifty-four minutes. The 23.4-mile dash between Winchendon and Keene was covered in thirty-two minutes in both directions. At Troy, the station agent would always clear everyone off the station platform when the *Cheshire* was due. It was a safety measure, especially for small children. The streamliner would pass the station so fast it could create a suction effect (John Marrotte, retired B&M signalman, pers. comm.).

East end of the Keene Shops. That's the Ashuelot Branch curving to the left, ca. 1937. Marium E. Foster photo; Hist. Soc. Cheshire Cty.

Shipped directly from the factory, Plymouth ML-8 101, a 30-ton, 225-horsepower gasoline industrial switcher, has arrived in Keene, May 28, 1938. Photogr. unknown; Brent S. Michiels coll.

Crew members pose with brand new Plymouth ML-8 101, which was delivered to Keene and immediately placed into service to help eliminate coal smoke and dust downtown, 1938. Marium E. Foster photo; Hist. Soc. Cheshire Cty.

In busy times, an eastbound train is in the station at Keene. It appears passengers and their baggage are all on board as a trainman (right) watches for the conductor's "go-ahead," ca. 1940. Photogr. unknown; Peter Hayward coll.

As World War II loomed, these General Motors coaches from the Boston and Maine Transportation Co., the railroad's rubber-tired subsidiary, have come to Keene to pick up armed forces draftees after a send-off at City Hall, April 21, 1942. Photogr. unknown; Hist. Soc. Cheshire Cty.

THE CHESHIRE: AT KEENE

Looking west down the freight house platform, ca. 1945. Marium E. Foster photo; Hist. Soc. Cheshire Cty.

The 6000 (below) running as Train 5506/*Cheshire* with her full crew pose at Keene station, Nov. 10, 1945. Scotty's Photo; R. R. Richards Jr. coll.

A B&M boxcar being unloaded at the J. A. Wright & Co. (silver polish manufacturer) siding. Keene, ca. 1945. Photogr. unknown; Hist. Soc. Cheshire Cty.

Unusual: two eastbound passenger trains side-by-side in the station at Keene. Train 5504 with Pacific 3677 in charge is running late this day and the streamliner, running as Train 5506/*Cheshire*, appears to have caught up with it. You guess which gets out of the station first, 1946. Marium E. Foster photo; Hist. Soc. Cheshire Cty.

The westbound, streamline train 6000, running as Train 5505/*Cheshire*, crosses Main St. as it arrives for its evening stop at Keene, 1944–1952. Marium E. Foster photo; Hist. Soc. Cheshire Cty.

Consolidation 2728 (below left) stopped at the Keene station with XW-2, takes water as the engineer oils around, 1948–1951. Victor M. Zolinsky photo.

XW-2 (below right) is at Water St., departing Keene, 1948–1951. Victor M. Zolinsky photo.

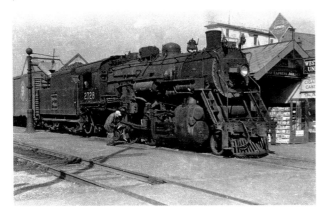

E7 3800 in the station with a westbound train. Keene, ca. 1948. R. R. Richards Jr. coll.

E7 3817 in the station with Train 5508. Keene, May 21, 1949. Stanwood K. Bolton photo.

Maine Central E7 708 in the station with Train 5503/*Green Mountain*, a daily train carrying through coaches to Rutland, Vermont. Why the Maine Central locomotive in Keene? The B&M and Maine Central Railroads maintained an unusual relationship for many years: sharing a common management, yet remaining operationally unconsolidated. From time to time they experimented with pooling power, and Maine Central power could turn up anywhere on the B&M system. Keene, ca. 1950. Victor M. Zolinsky photo.

GE 44-T switcher 115 rests on the turntable lead at the engine house. The shops were shuttered in 1940. At the time this picture was taken, New England Screw Company had occupied the former main shop building. The turntable and three stalls in the 16-stall engine house—one for the switcher, one for the gas-electric, and one for a spare—were still in use. The two tracks behind the switcher are the Cheshire Branch main line. It is west (left) to Island St. and east to Main St. Looking eastward, boxcars are visible on the freight house leads. Keene, ca. 1950. Victor M. Zolinsky photo.

GE 44-T switcher 115 rests at the freight office, Keene, ca. 1950. Stanwood K. Bolton photo.

The B&M operated a spectacular, twilight-of-steam *Rural New England Excursion* for the Railroad Enthusiasts-New England Division on June 10, 1951. With Mogul 1415 and Atlantic 3235, plus ten coaches and a diner, the 16-hour trip carried 550 passengers and ran 257 miles, traversing parts of several Fitchburg Division branches. The fare? $4.25. Here in Keene, after dropping the train in the East Yard, the power has run across Main St. to the station for water, the lifeblood of all steam locomotives. Robert A. Buck photo.

With a long day's run ahead, crews are wasting no time tending to their engines' needs as a boy takes in the happenings from the gangway of the 1415. The last of her class, Atlantic 3235 is being watered by her fireman at the standpipe. With complete dieselization of the B&M only five years away, Mogul 1415 and Atlantic 3235, built in 1906 and 1909, respectively, were on the eve of their retirement. Both would be cut up for scrap by the end of 1952. In but a few years after this excursion, the railroad infrastructure necessary to support such a steam operation would be gone forever. Keene, June 10, 1951. Robert A. Buck photo.

Trackside view of Keene's second station, looking west, showing its impressive 375-foot platform canopy, ca. 1953. Marium E. Foster photo; Hist. Soc. Cheshire Cty.

The newsstand building under construction (by the MacMillin Co. of Keene) at the Main St. end of the platform canopy. Keene, 1953. Marium E. Foster photo; Hist. Soc. Cheshire Cty.

A school group and other passengers are boarding RDC-1 6100/ *Cheshire*, for a trip east in the last month of passenger service in Keene, May 1958. Marium E. Foster photo; Hist. Soc. Cheshire Cty.

Keene's second station, as it appeared just after passenger service to the Elm City ended in June 1958. The B&M sold the station to the city, which wasted no time in razing it. Demolition began in December and the station was history by the end of Jan. 1959. Hist. Soc. Cheshire Cty.

Railroad Square, Keene, at the end of passenger service, June 1958. The newsstand building in the foreground houses The Armstrong Company's Fountain News. It, along with a small section of the passenger canopy, is the only remnant of the station that has survived. Today, the city leases the building to the Corner News. Hist. Soc. Cheshire Cty.

As a final good-bye to the station, we share this seldom-photographed view of the station complex, captured from the street side looking east. The station had four sections, from west to east, the American (Railway) Express Building, Baggage Department, Passenger Department, and, not visible at the Main Street end, the newsstand building. The passenger and baggage facilities were built in 1910, the express building in 1912, and the newsstand building in 1953. June 1958. Hist. Soc. Cheshire Cty.

STEAMTOWN, U.S.A.

IT & PIERCE ENGINEERS   MOREHOUSE & CHESLEY ARCHITECTS

In June 1961, Steamtown proposed to develop an operating museum that would house F. Nelson Blount's steam locomotive collection in the B&M's former roundhouse and shops in Keene. However, the plans—reflected in this architect's rendering—later shifted to a site on the Cheshire about two miles northwest of Keene. This dream was never realized and Steamtown's home base remained in N. Walpole until its move to Riverside in Rockingham, VT, in 1966. Hist. Soc. Cheshire Cty.

In the summer of 1962, there was a brief recrudescence of passenger trains in Keene. Steam-powered, tourist train operator Monadnock, Steamtown & Northern Amusement Corporation (MS&N) began running excursion trains over the Cheshire Branch from the city nine miles out to Gilboa and back. MS&N operations out of Keene would only last the 1962 season. We will have much more to say about the MS&N in the following chapter.

It's inauguration day for MS&N's 1962 excursion train operation in Keene. Left to right in the top row is an unidentified young girl, Governor's Councilor Harold Weeks, Keene Mayor Robert L. Mallat Jr., Steamtown founder F. Nelson Blount, and an unidentified man. Standing on the footboards are an unknown (left) and Robert Clark, July 13, 1962. Photogr. unknown; Hist. Soc. Cheshire Cty.

MS&N 2-8-0 15 at Keene with the 1962 excursion train. For these trips, the engine would pull the train up to Gilboa where it would run around the train and, running backwards, return to Keene. The trains were dispatched by the B&M, which owned the tracks and was still using them every day. John Krause photo; Frederick G. Bailey coll.

MS&N 15 at the West Street crossing, Aug. 26, 1962. Donald S. Robinson photo; Dale O. Russell coll.

MS&N 15 on the granite arch over Chesterfield Rd., W. Keene, Aug. 26, 1962. Donald S. Robinson photo; Dale O. Russell coll.

MS&N 15 and her train in W. Keene, Sept. 8, 1962, with Mount Monadnock in the distance. David K. Johnson photo; B&MRRHS Archives, *B&M Bull.* 17(1):18.

The 60-foot gallows turntable at the Keene roundhouse, April 1963. The B&M sold the property to the New England Screw Co., which, in 1974, donated all the remaining rail on the property to Steamtown. The turntable was donated to the Wolfeboro Railroad, which moved it to Sanbornville, NH. Photogr. unknown; Collection of Bob's Photo.

Led by RS3 1508, FX-1 has a respectable hitch this day, approaching Main St., Keene, 1967–1968. Larry Kemp photo.

The B&M often assigned EMD SW1 switchers to the Keene Switcher job. Here (left) we see the 1117 in her original paint scheme, ca. 1950, and (right) "blue-dipped" 1120, ca. 1970. Photogrs. unknown.

The "Transportation Center" (left), was built on the site of the second Keene station in 1976. At the Main St. crossing beyond, the Corner News building and a vestige of the station canopy are all that remain of the old station. Keene, 1982. S. J. Whitney photo.

After no trains in the city since early Jan. 1983, Keene residents were surprised to hear the sound of a locomotive's air chime horns the morning of May 15, 1984. It was bright-blue B&M GP9 1714, in her bold Dustin-era livery, delivering empty gondolas to be loaded with lifted rail. Track conditions were such that management decided to pull the loaded cars at a later date with a trackmobile, a highway vehicle that can also run on rails. Photo by *Keene Sentinel* photographer Martin Frank.

GP9 1744 rests at the "Transportation Center," on the site formerly occupied by Keene's railroad station (1848–1958), after dropping off another string of gondolas for the rail salvage work. We would bet the crew is on lunch break in Lindy's Diner, Keene, May 1984. David Kruschwitz photo.

CHAPTER FIVE

THE CHESHIRE: WEST END

Summit (MP B97.08) to Bellows Falls, Vermont (MP B113.83)

Starting at Summit Cut in Surry, we will now continue our journey outward along the Cheshire, passing stations at East Westmoreland (Gilboa), Westmoreland, Walpole, and Cold River, to the road's terminal facilities at Fitchburg Yard, North Walpole and across the river on the Bellows Falls Island.

At the end of this chapter, we will look at Monadnock, Steamtown and Northern Amusement Corp., Green Mountain Railroad, and Vermont Railway operations on the west end of the old Cheshire.

Summit—MP B97.08

Though barely touched by the railroad and with less than a mile of track, Surry, NH enjoyed the distinction of having the highest elevation on the railroad between Keene and Walpole. The high point (830 feet) was reached here at Summit Cut, where Rte. 12 bridges the railroad. Prior to its rebuilding in the early 1940s, Rte. 12 passed beneath the railroad in West Keene. Photogr. unknown; Hist. Soc. Cheshire Cty.

We are not sure if the fallen rock in this picture is a natural rockslide or ledge removal work in progress. Either way, the track in Summit Cut will be out of service while the steam derrick and crew work to clear the tracks, 1912. Postcard; Photogr. unknown, Hist. Soc. Cheshire Cty.

Handling WX-1, Consolidation 2728 has worked its way up the grade through West Keene and is about to pass beneath the Rte. 12 Bridge at Summit Cut in Surry, April 8, 1950. Stanwood K. Bolton photo.

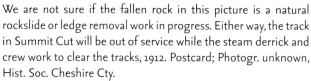

Flanked by snow-covered ledges at Summit Cut in West Keene, streamline train 6000, running as Train 5506/ *Cheshire*, is leaving the Rte. 12 Bridge in Surry behind her. Bound for Boston from White River Jct., she is just starting her descent into Keene down the Cheshire Branch's steepest (1.42 percent) eastward grade at 8:20 a.m. on an overcast February day in 1952 (*EM* Feb52, 1). George H. Hill photo.

BOSTON and MAINE
RAIL • BUS
RAILROAD
"MINUTE MAN SERVICE"

BOSTON AND MAINE
RAILROAD
MAGAZINE

Volume 20   February 1952   Number 2

Gilboa (East Westmoreland)—MP B100.36

The Boston and Maine Railroad (B&M) changed the name of the East Westmoreland station to Gilboa about 1909. Gilboa along with State Line were the only "left-handed" stations (i.e., on the fireman's side outward) between South Ashburnham and Bellows Falls. Rail users at Gilboa in 1915 included F. W. Aldrich (headings), O. G. Thompson (shingles & lumber), and E. E. Rhodes (shipper of eggs and fruit).

Fitchburg train and engine crewmen pose with American 27 (ex-V&M 15) on Train 22 at E. Westmoreland, 1896. Marium E. Foster coll., Hist. Soc. Cheshire Cty.

This is probably the station agent, enjoying a quiet moment at E. Westmoreland, NH, in Fitchburg Railroad days. The view is looking west, ca. 1895. Photogr. unknown; Hist. Soc. Cheshire Cty.

Westward (left) and eastward views of the E. Westmoreland (now Gilboa) combination passenger and freight station, now equipped with a signal mast and orderboards. The treeless countryside at the time made it worth a visit here just to enjoy the spectacular view of the Connecticut Valley below the station, ca. 1909. Randall photo postcards; B. G. Blodget and Jim Dufour colls.

Bellows Falls to Worcester freight XW-2 blasts past Gilboa Siding. Only the automobile and a distant railroad telephone box mark where the station once stood. The B&M agency here closed in 1927 and the station building was sold and removed from the site in 1936. However, one could still board a train here and purchase a ticket from the conductor right up to the end of service in 1958. This image was captured by twelve-year-old Victor M. Zolinsky who, with signal maintainer George Converse, was waiting in the clear for the train to pass, 1948.

F3 4255A with Train 5508 passing Gilboa Siding. Most of the F3s were not steam boiler equipped and thus could only be used on passenger trains in the warmer months. Notice the milk car on the head pin, ca. 1948–1952. Victor M. Zolinsky photo.

The original Westmoreland, NH, station and adjacent brick water tank house. Note the signal mast with orderboards, newly installed about this time, ca. 1910. Postcard, photogr. unknown; B. G. Blodget coll.

Westmoreland—MP B103.66

This station served the Park Hill area of town and the County Farm and Home. The station building burned March 1, 1918 after an oil lamp tipped over. Two railroad employees who rushed in to save mail and baggage were seriously burned and were transported by train to Elliot Hospital in Keene. The B&M sent out an old coach to serve as the agent's office and a waiting room for passengers while a replacement station was being built later the same year.

Railroad customers here in 1915 included George H. Aldrich (eggs), Arthur Chickering and E. C. Clough (livestock dealers), and Earl Warren (coal, grain, and hay). In 1960–1961, the County Home was receiving its coal supply here, and four grain and feed dealers were using rail service. Carloads received in 1960 and 1961 numbered 103 and 94 respectively (Spofford Feb. 19, 1962). A farm supply business here was the last customer using rail between Keene and Cold River at the time the line was abandoned in 1972.

The second Westmoreland station, built in 1918. Note the station sign's reversed color scheme with dark lettering on a white background and the post office sign. Today, the only remnant of this station is an embedded line of granite slabs that once marked the edge of the station platform, April 3, 1954. L. S. Twombly photo; Brent S. Michiels coll.

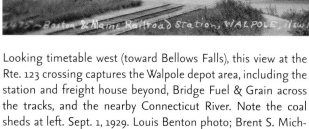

Looking timetable west (toward Bellows Falls), this view at the Rte. 123 crossing captures the Walpole depot area, including the station and freight house beyond, Bridge Fuel & Grain across the tracks, and the nearby Connecticut River. Note the coal sheds at left. Sept. 1, 1929. Louis Benton photo; Brent S. Michiels coll.

Under a full head of steam, Pacific 3669 is Boston-bound with Train 5508 at Westmoreland, March 16, 1949. Hopefully nobody was hoping to board at Westmoreland; 5508 made no stops between Walpole and Keene. Stanwood K. Bolton photo.

Walpole—MP B109.82

This station, built in 1905, was located on Route 123, about a mile from the center of town. Across the river in Vermont, not even a mile from this station, was the Westminster station on the Connecticut River Route Main Line. Residents of the two towns, connected by the Route 123 Bridge, were well-fixed when it came to transportation! The Walpole station was closed in 1959 and it became a carload-only freight station under the agent at Bellows Falls. In 1961–1962, the station and adjacent hillside were obliterated by a Route 12 realignment project.

Customers here in 1915 included N. W. Holland (coal) and the Walpole Ice and Lumber Co. Hubbard Farms, founded in 1921, became an important customer that received poultry feed and express-shipped poultry breeding stock all over the country. In 1960 and 1961 there were 202 and 187 carloads received at Walpole. At that time, there were four receivers of poultry feed and grain, the largest being Hubbard Farms (Spofford Feb. 19, 1962). The railroad's last customers here included Bridge Fuel & Grain and R. N. Johnson (farm machinery). After service to Walpole ended in 1972, both took rail delivery at either Cold River or Bellows Falls.

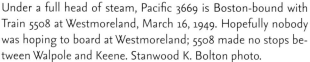

Another view of the depot area, looking down the steep Rte. 123 hill. Note the two hopper cars spotted on the Bridge Fuel & Grain siding. Undated. Photogr. unknown; Brent S. Michiels coll.

A Hubbard Farms truck delivering a shipment of pullets at Walpole station, ca. 1950. Hubbard also shipped through the Westminster, VT, station across the river. Photogr. unknown; Walpole Hist. Soc.

Cold River—MP B112.57

Cold River Stock Yards, an important railroad customer in Cheshire Railroad days, opened for business at Cold River in 1872. The company maintained yards and facilities for loading and unloading stock east of the station. The company also advertised comfortable hotel quarters for drovers traveling with their stock. Also at Cold River, a spur left the main line west of the station and ran up the Cold River Valley about a mile to reach the Bellows Falls Brewing Co., a beermaker in business under various trade names in 1877–1907.

In 1915 customers doing business with the B&M through its station at Cold River included J. H. Byrnes (coal) and A. B. Lufkin, a plow manufacturer in Alstead that drayed its products to the team track here. During World War I the Whitcomb Manufac-turing Co. produced gunpowder in the former brewery building. In 1930, the American Mineral Products Co. of New York built a milling plant on the spur, on the site presently occupied by Aubuchon Hardware. B&M delivered gondola loads of lithium ore here, and lifted carloads of ground product. Also, locally mined feldspar ore was trucked to the plant, ground, and shipped out by rail. Foote Mineral Co., the last operator of the plant, shipped its last loads in April 1962. After the B&M abandoned the Cheshire Branch east of Cold River in 1972, carloads for remaining consignees at Walpole and Westmoreland were spotted by the Bellows Falls Switcher on the team track at Cold River, to be transloaded and trucked to the consignees' facilities (Spofford Feb. 19, 1962).

The Bellows Falls Brewing Co. operated this self-propelled steam car, believed to be a Woodbury car (White 1985, 583), for switching cars at its brewery in Walpole. Here the car is shown at the brewery with a Cheshire boxcar. The car may have also been used for transporting employees. A 1906 Sanborn Map shows an "enginehouse"—where we presume the steam car was kept—just beyond the brewery at the end of the Cold River Spur, Walpole, ca. 1890. Blake photo; Brent S. Michiels coll.

This is the Rte. 12 crossing in Cold River, NH, looking east. The Cold River Spur runs off to the left of the station where several boxcars sit on the team track, 1915. Postcard; Brent S. Michiels coll.

Looking west at the Cold River combination flag station and freight house. The N. Walpole engine house is about a mile ahead. Note the span boards (used for bridging the gap between a freight car and the dock) leaning up against the wall and the flag stop signal at the corner of the platform, ca. 1915. Postcard; B. G. Blodget coll.

Mount Kilburn rises dramatically behind Cold River station in this westward view, ca. 1930. Cars visible in this image are running along Rte. 12, which passes behind the station. Though not visible, the Cold River Spur would have also passed behind the station. While the station is long-gone, the building across Rte. 12 (at left) is still standing. Louis Benton photo; Brent S. Michiels coll.

North Walpole—
MP B113.50 and Bellows Falls—
MP B113.83

Yard Limits at North Walpole, New Hampshire, began at the Cold River Bridge (MP112.33). There were actually two yards in North Walpole, the Cheshire Railroad Yard squeezed between the Connecticut River and Mount Kilburn and the Sullivan Railroad Yard about a mile further north on the Connecticut River Route Main Line (see Chapter 8). In B&M years these two yards came to be referred to as the Fitchburg and Conn River Yards, respectively, and in the interest of consistency we will use these names to distinguish them.

Linking the two yards was a connecting track. Originally about a mile in length, it was built by the Sullivan in 1848 to link up with the Cheshire. In the B&M years it was extended to skirt Fitchburg Yard almost to Cold River. Officially yard track, it achieved some importance as a freight bypass, allowing continuous operation between the Connecticut River Route Main Line and the Cheshire without the necessity of crossing the river to Bellows Falls and passing through the Rutland Railroad Yard. One train that used the bypass was EJ-1, the East Deerfield to White River Junction freight, which operated via Keene. The track was variously called the Cold River Bypass or (at least as early as 1906) the Mountain Track, referring to its path along the foot of Mount Kilburn. Though the original one-mile section of the Mountain Track—that connecting the two yards—was not used after 1972, it was not formally abandoned until 1982 (ICC Docket AB-32 [Sub-No. 13F]; US District Court for the District of Massachusetts, No. 70-250-M).

Across the river in Bellows Falls, the railroad facilities were all located on an island ("the Island") formed by the Connecticut River and a power canal. The Fitchburg Yard was originally connected to the Island by a covered wooden bridge built by the Cheshire Railroad in 1849. The Fitchburg Railroad replaced this bridge with the double-arched granite bridge in 1899. The Conn River Yard was connected to the Island by another wooden bridge similar in all respects to the Cheshire's bridge and located just upriver, almost over the Connecticut River Dam. This bridge was built by the Sullivan Railroad in

Looking downstream, the Great Falls of the Connecticut are aboil this day with mountain snowmelt beneath the Cheshire Railroad's 280-foot covered wooden truss bridge. The bridge's siding was designed to reflect the huge trusses inside. The granite piers visible left and right of the bridge's center are actually those of the Tucker Toll Bridge, which is eclipsed in this image by the Cheshire's bridge. N. Walpole, May 1, 1888. J. A. French photo; Hist. Soc. Cheshire Cty.

A rare interior view of the Cheshire's covered wooden bridge showing its arched trusses. Undated. J. A. French photo; Hist. Soc. Cheshire Cty.

This handsome machine is the Cheshire's American second 9/*Keene*, built in 1880—the last engine built in the road's home shops. It became Fitchburg's 209 in 1890, B&M's 935 in 1900, and was scrapped in 1904. Note the light rail and sand ballast, ca. 1885. Rutland Yard, Bellows Falls. Photogr. unknown; Brent S. Michiels coll.

1851 (see Chapter 8). Since the New Hampshire-Vermont border follows the west bank of the Connecticut River, all these bridges are in Walpole, New Hampshire.

After the Fitchburg's consolidation with the B&M in 1900, the B&M controlled all the trackage in North Walpole. The Rutland owned most of the trackage on the Island—the Rutland Yard—with the notable exception of the B&M's Connecticut River Route Main Line that sliced right across the Rutland Yard on a series of crossing diamonds (at one time as many as six of them). The B&M also owned several tracks on the Island that were used for holding milk cars.

The crossing diamonds were governed by a ball signal system. A ball tender, using a pulley rigging, could move the balls in and out of a metal sleeve. Three balls displayed (normal) gave Connecticut River Route

trains the right-of-way; two balls, Cheshire trains; and one ball, Rutland trains. The balls were replaced by oil lanterns at night. The ball signal system here was no longer required after CTC was installed in 1964, and it was dismantled May 1, 1965.

In the B&M era, the Fitchburg, Conn River, and Rutland Yards were sometimes lumped together and referred to as "the Bellows Falls Yard." Switching duties here, at one time twenty-four hours a day, were shared under various agreements over the years between the Rutland and the B&M. The Bellows Falls Switcher job roamed among the three yards. At the end of World War II, there were four switcher jobs in the yard—the Rutland's switcher and first, second, and third trick B&M switchers. As traffic declined in the postwar era, these jobs were slowly eliminated until only the first trick

On the eve of its takeover by the B&M, the Fitchburg Railroad, preparing for heavier traffic, replaced the Cheshire's bridge with the double-arched granite bridge (B113.60) that is still in service today. Here we see the new granite arch bridge under construction, even as the Cheshire's old covered bridge—just downstream and alongside it—is being dismantled. Note that the wooden sides have been removed, exposing the old bridge's huge wooden arches. The view is toward Bellows Falls at the Great Falls of the Connecticut, N. Walpole, 1899. Herbert F. and Walter S. Pierce photo; Vermont Hist. Soc., Barre, VT.

The double-arched granite bridge built by the Fitchburg in 1899 and the Tucker Toll Bridge built in 1840 were both located over the Great Falls of the Connecticut. Tolls ended Nov. 1, 1904. The toll bridge was razed and replaced by the Charles N. Vilas Bridge in 1931. Beyond, the original Sullivan (left) and Cheshire engine houses are visible, side-by-side at the base of Mount Kilburn, N. Walpole, ca. 1900–1910. Rockingham Public Library's Catalogued Photograph Coll.

B&M switcher job remained—and it was abolished in June 1972 (Patalano 1997, 29).

We would be remiss to neglect the Bellows Falls and Saxtons River Street Railway (BF&SR), an electric operation (1900–1924) which ran in Bridge Street onto the Island and then northerly on a private right-of-way to reach the depot. In addition to handling passenger traffic to/from the depot, the road also interchanged freight traffic with the B&M—notably textile business, inbound coal, and outbound pulpwood (Cook 1977). The BF&SR was built to be a feeder line to the B&M and was constructed using fifty-six-pound relay rail supplied by the B&M.

At the turn of the century, the Bellows Falls Island was a dense industrial mecca. Railroad tracks ran almost completely around the Island. Atkins' (1915) compilation of B&M consignees shows that manufacturing here was dominated by six papermakers: International, Liberty, Moore & Thompson, Robinson, J. T. Moore and Son, and Standard. The B&M served the first four partly or wholly via interchange with the Rutland Railroad and the last two at B&M team tracks. Other manufacturing concerns served by the B&M included Bogart & Hopper (boxes), S. J. Cray (packing house), Sidney Gage (baskets), Bellows Falls Hide & Tallow Co. (hides), Vermont Farm Machine Co./US Cream Separator Co., and—through interchange with the BF&SR—the Saxtons River Woolen Co. The B&M had accounts with many commodity dealers in Bellows Falls, including coal (5), wood (1), lumber (2), vehicles (2), flour, grain, feed and hay (2), wholesale liquors (2), scrap metal (3), and ice (1).

Another important B&M customer at Bellows Falls was the Bellows Falls Co-operative Creamery, which opened its plant on the Island in November 1921. The plant was located on Rutland rails. Carloads of bottled milk consigned to First National Stores (Finast) in Somerville, Massachusetts, were interchanged with the B&M, which moved the milk over the Cheshire Branch every night for early morning delivery in Somerville. The last rail shipment of packaged milk and cream to Finast left the Falls on July 17, 1964, ending forty-two years, seven months, and seventeen days of unbroken service.

The original side-by-side engine houses of the Cheshire and Sullivan Railroads, both occupied by Fitchburg locomotives, stand next to their shared turntable, near the end of the Fitchburg years, N. Walpole, ca. 1898. In 1899, the Fitchburg would replace the double-portaled, wooden covered bridge over the Connecticut River (extreme left) with a granite arch bridge, and in 1900, the Fitchburg would be swallowed by the B&M. Photogr. unknown; Brent S. Michiels coll.

This view, looking southward across Depot St. from Bellows Falls Union Station, shows the Vermont Farm Machinery Co. building. At right is the southern extension of the station's passenger canopy showing the B&M Connecticut River main line tracks on the west side of the canopy and those of the BF&SR on the east side. The absence of catenary indicates this image was probably captured after the BF&SR had ceased operations in 1924. Postcard; B. G. Blodget coll.

In its ninety-one years, the Tucker Toll Bridge withstood many a flood. Note how the bridge's middle granite pillar is armored with wooden or iron beams to protect it from debris thrown against it by the river. The Fitchburg's bridge and the coaling tower in the Fitchburg Yard are visible beyond. Note the double-arm automatic block signal visible over the top of the bridge (at right). N. Walpole, Nov. 4, 1927. James Studio photo; Rockingham Public Library's Catalogued Photograph Coll.

An uncommon view showing the Mountain Track's Rte. 12 crossing at the entrance to Fitchburg Yard. The Connecticut River is at right with the Fitchburg's bridge and the Tucker Toll Bridge just beyond, N. Walpole, Nov. 28, 1928. Photogr. unknown; B&MRRHS Archives.

(opposite page) In 1943 the B&M—starved for power during the war years—purchased four Pacifics from the Delaware, Lackawanna & Western Railroad. After extensive repair work, they were assigned to their own class as P5a's and numbered 3696–3699. They were used mostly in passenger service on the Connecticut River Route. Here we find the 3698, which has just made a visit to the coaling tower at N. Walpole, June 1947. George C. Corey photo.

Covering an assignment as the Bellows Falls Switcher is Class G11a 413 at the coaling tower in Fitchburg Yard, N. Walpole, June 1947. Rte. 12 is visible behind the engine. The Mountain Track is at the far right. George C. Corey photo.

The Bellows Falls Switcher, this day B&M Class G11b 434, steps lightly over the Fitchburg Bridge, N. Walpole, NH. At different times, both the B&M and the Rutland supplied the power and crews for this job, which covered switching duties in Bellows Falls and N. Walpole, Oct. 31, 1948.

On this day, Pacific 3703 has arrived Bellows Falls with a train from Boston. Two balls on the signal mast give Cheshire Branch trains permission across the diamond, May 1948. This and the following two photos by Dwight A. Smith.

The Bellows Falls Switcher is backing over the Fitchburg Bridge with a transfer move from the Fitchburg Yard in N. Walpole to the Rutland Yard in Bellows Falls. The sign "Signal Territory Starts" refers to the B&M's Type B double-arm, lower quadrant block signal system that was used on the Cheshire Branch in 1911–1959. That's the B&M's coaling tower across the river in N. Walpole, Oct. 31, 1948.

The *Cheshire*, which traversed the Monadnock Region between Bellows Falls and South Ashburnham on its daily
round trip between White River Junction and Boston, was
truly the region's signature train. In 1944–1952, the 6000 was
covering the run as Trains 5506/5505. The turning of the train
at the Bellows Falls diamond was a clockwork, twice-daily
ritual. Let's watch the morning action at Bellows Falls, captured in some timeless images from November 5, 1949 by
Dwight A. Smith.

The streamliner (right), arriving Bellows Falls from White
River Jct., clatters across the Rutland Yard diamonds. Finding
three balls on the signal mast, she will proceed across the
Rutland main line diamond, then back over the connecting
track (foreground) onto the Rutland main line, and finally,
pull forward across the diamond again and into the station.

Crossing the Rutland main line on the diamond (below).
The side of the Rutland's roundhouse and the Rutland canal
bridge are at left.

Backing over the connecting track to the Rutland main line, the 6000 will back all the way out onto the canal bridge and then make her final move into the station. Note the ball tender has already changed the ball signal to show two balls, which allowed Cheshire Branch trains to cross the diamond.

After all those moves—which really only took a few minutes—the *Cheshire* (below) sits in the station, ready to depart for North Station–Boston with stops at Keene, Winchendon, Fitchburg, and Ayer. *All Aboard!* Those were the days, my friends.

The Rutland's four Class L1 Mountains (4-8-2, numbers 90–93), built by Alco in 1946, were the most advanced steam power the road ever owned. Too big to fit on the road's turntable in Bellows Falls, they would be sent across the river to be turned on the B&M's table. On this day, Dwight Smith caught the 92 in Fitchburg Yard. The Mountains led a glorious but short life—sidelined in 1952 when the road dieselized, and scrapped three years later. N. Walpole, June 10, 1950.

Here comes RS3 1545 with Train 5503/*Green Mountain*, crossing the Fitchburg Bridge. Note the B&M engine house (right) and coaling tower (left) beyond, at the base of Mount Kilburn, N. Walpole, Sept. 1950. Dwight A. Smith photo.

RS3 1535 has arrived at Bellows Falls with a Cheshire Branch train. At left, an engine stands at the Rutland's coaling tower. Undated, Nash-Ludlow photo; S. J. Whitney coll.

The Rutland's turntable and four-stall roundhouse. At right, one of the two "armstrong bars" used to manually turn the table is visible, Bellows Falls, June 10, 1950. This and the next, Dwight A. Smith photos.

Pacific 3628 has been turned and will soon tie onto a train and head east. In the foreground is Signal C1135 with its battery tub. The block signal system was battery powered and did not rely on an outside power source. N. Walpole, Sept. 8, 1951.

The 6000 was taken off the *Cheshire* and replaced by conventional steam and diesel-powered trains in April 1952. Then from 1954 to the end of service May 31, 1958, brand-new Budd self-propelled RDCs were assigned to handle the *Cheshire*, except for a brief reappearance of the 6000 from Dec. 1956 to April 1957. Effective with the April 28, 1957 PTT, the *Cheshire* terminated at Bellows Falls. Here an RDC-1 stands at the ready in the Bellows Falls station, ca. 1955. Nash-Ludlow photo; S. J. Whitney coll.

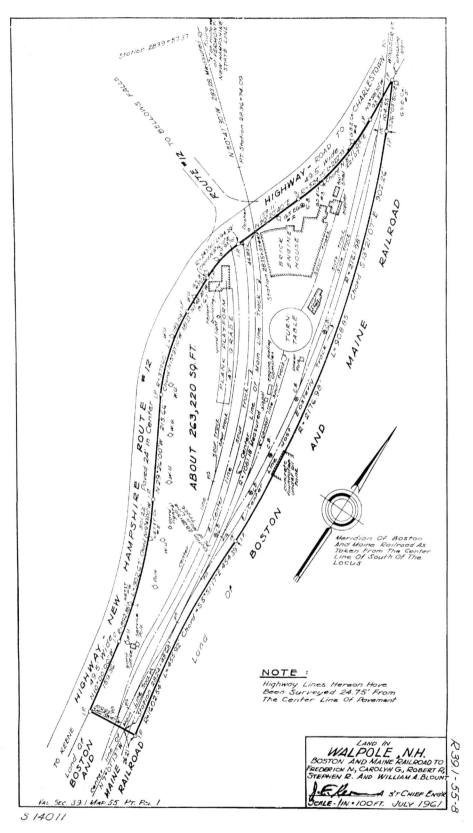

Deed survey map of Fitchburg Yard land and facilities in N. Walpole transferred by the B&M to the F. Nelson Blount interests in 1961. The B&M retained ownership of its main line through the yard and certain trackage rights in the yard. July 1961, S. J. Whitney coll.

Looking west into Fitchburg Yard we see the Bellows Falls Switcher, RS2 1500, laying over in the yard. To the right of the engine house are the coaling tower and sand house. The block signal system was discontinued in 1959 and the semaphore blade has been removed from signal C1135. It appears a good crop of weeds is starting to grow on the main line. N. Walpole, Sept. 1963. Dwight A. Smith photo.

Alco S4 1274, covering the Bellows Falls Switcher job, is in Fitchburg Yard, ca. 1963. She was the only unit in her class to ever wear the McGinnis-inspired "Bluebird" paint scheme. Originally delivered from Alco in 1950 as S3 1174, she was burned in an engine house fire in Springfield, MA, on March 23, 1957. Later in the same year she was returned to Alco, rebuilt as an S4, made a "Bluebird," and renumbered 1274. About 1973 she received the economical "blue-dip" paint job, which she wore until her scrapping in 2005 at age 55. Photogr. unknown.

The Bellows Falls Switcher, SW1 1121, trundles over the Fitchburg Bridge from Bellows Falls with two boxcars and four trailers on flatcars, N. Walpole, April 1965. Dwight A. Smith photos.

SW1 1117 in Fitchburg Yard, N. Walpole, ca. 1965. Frederick G. Bailey photo.

SW9 1231 in Fitchburg Yard, N. Walpole, ca. 1965. Photogr. unknown.

SW9 1224, the Bellows Falls Switcher, is all bundled up with her radiator cover on this winter's day at Fitchburg Yard. Two Steamtown behemoths—Union Pacific Big Boy X4012 and B&M Pacific 3713—keep company in storage at left. N. Walpole, March 1967. Dwight A. Smith photo.

RS2 1500 in Fitchburg Yard, N. Walpole, date and photogr. unknown.

RS2 1500 (above) in Fitchburg Yard, N. Walpole, July 1967. Frederick G. Bailey photo.

GP7 1574 keeps company with MS&N 15 in Fitchburg Yard, N. Walpole, 1967. Dwight A. Smith photo.

The Monadnock, Steamtown and Northern Amusement Corporation

As railroads all over the country were scrapping the last of their steam power in the 1950s, millionaire F. Nelson Blount became interested in collecting steam locomotives for preservation and operation. In need of a place to store his collection, Blount purchased the Fitchburg Yard and locomotive facilities in N. Walpole from the B&M in 1961. As it was still running milk trains between Bellows Falls and Somerville, the B&M held out of the sale its Cheshire Branch main line that ran through the yard and also reserved the right to store an engine in the yard. Steam locomotives purchased by Blount soon began to arrive in N. Walpole. In 1961 Blount established the Monadnock, Steamtown and Northern Amusement Corporation (MS&N) to hold and operate historic steam locomotives. It was not an ICC-regulated railroad. It began operations April 26, 1961 and ended operations December 31, 1967.

In order to operate steam excursions, MS&N leased track from the B&M between Cold River and Keene and commenced Steamtown excursions between Keene and Gilboa in the summer of 1962. This would be the only season Steamtown excursions ever ran from Keene. Blount's dream to locate his Steamtown museum and live steam operation in Keene broke down amid politics and squabbling among the city, the State of New Hampshire, and the B&M.

With eight coaches this day, the MS&N excursion train is ready to depart for Keene as soon as the trainman finishes relining the east switch for the main line. The B&M wayside telephone box reminds us this was still an active B&M line. Gilboa, Fall 1962. Photogr. unknown.

The engineer on MS&N 15 is watching the conductor's signals as the train of equipment is being assembled to move to Keene for the startup of the 1962 season. The car on the headpin is ex-B&M diner *Mountaineer*, which was included in the trainset used by President Roosevelt on his trips to Campobello Island, New Brunswick. This would be the only year Steamtown ran a diner on its trains. Fitchburg Yard, N. Walpole. Photogr. unknown; Hist. Soc. Cheshire Cty.

MS&N 15 has brought her train up from Keene and is now running around the train at Gilboa and will run tender-first back to Keene, 1962. This was F. Nelson Blount's first Steamtown season running on the Cheshire Branch and the only one that ever ran from Keene. Photogr. unknown.

Gilboa-bound MS&N 15 blasts through Summit Cut in Surry, NH, Sept. 2, 1962. It doesn't appear the B&M was spending heavily on weed control. Donald S. Robinson photo; Dale O. Russell coll.

Defeated at Keene, Blount operated Steamtown excursions between its operations base in N. Walpole and Westmoreland during the 1963 season. Then in 1964, although the base of operations remained in N. Walpole, MS&N leased former Rutland Railway track (then in limbo and owned by the State of Vermont) between Bellows Falls and Chester for Steamtown excursion trains. The boarding point for the excursions was about two miles north of the Bellows Falls station at a site known as the NEPCO Farm property (Riverside). In 1965, the Green Mountain Railroad, another Blount-controlled company, took over Steamtown's passenger excursion operation from the MS&N, and the following year Steamtown relocated its headquarters and steam locomotive collection to Riverside.

Two famous locomotives in the Steamtown collection are Union Pacific Big Boy X4012 and B&M Class P4 Pacific 3713/The Constitution, looking sharp side-by-side in Fitchburg Yard, N. Walpole, April 1965. Today these locomotives are at Steamtown National Historic Site in Scranton, PA. Dwight A. Smith photo.

Now it is 1963 and Steamtown excursions are running from these makeshift station facilities in Fitchburg Yard, N. Walpole, out to Westmoreland and back. In this view, MS&N 15 has just returned from Westmoreland with the train, Aug. 1963. Alan Thomas photo; Frederick G. Bailey coll.

If you've ever been frustrated trying to locate where Walpole station once stood, here's why! The station and all nearby buildings, including Bridge Fuel & Grain, were obliterated and the surrounding area radically transformed when Rte. 12 was rebuilt in 1963. Here the Steamtown excursion train passes the work area, Aug. 1963. Alan Thomas photo; Frederick G. Bailey coll.

The Green Mountain Railroad and the Vermont Railway System

The Green Mountain Railroad (Green Mountain), founded by F. Nelson Blount, was chartered by the State of Vermont April 3, 1964, and became ICC-certificated March 19, 1965 to operate on track of the former Rutland Railway between Bellows Falls and Rutland, Vermont, now owned by the State of Vermont. Operations began April 4, 1965. In its first year the Green Mountain assumed responsibility for the passenger excursion operations at Riverside from the MS&N. Between the end of November and early December 1966, the Green Mountain moved the Steamtown Museum engines from Fitchburg Yard in N. Walpole to Riverside (Nimke 1985, 128).

Though Steamtown's headquarters and collection had moved to Riverside in 1966, the operations and maintenance base for operator Green Mountain remained, of course, in Fitchburg Yard, N. Walpole. Green Mountain power for the Steamtown excursion train would make a light move from Fitchburg Yard to Riverside at the start of each operating day, and a light move back to Fitchburg Yard at the end of the day. Here, Green Mountain 89, an ex-CN Mogul, has just crossed the Bellows Falls diamond on her way to Riverside. Ahead of her is the late Rutland road's canal bridge. North of the diamond is B&M's Conn River main line bridge, ca. 1967. John Krause photo; Frederick G. Bailey coll.

Green Mountain 89 is on the main line at the Bellows Falls station in the former Rutland Railway's now grass-filled yard. B&M Alco S3 1185, the Bellows Falls Switcher, is tied up on the station track. In the last years before the job was abolished, it became standard practice for the switcher to tie up here instead of across the river in Fitchburg Yard. Note the old BF&SR freight house beyond, occupied at the time by Wayne Feed Supply, 1966. John Krause photo; Frederick G. Bailey coll.

A bird's eye view of the north end of Fitchburg Yard with its centerpiece five-stall roundhouse. The one-mile section of the Mountain Track (upper right) that connected the Fitchburg and Conn River Yards is out-of-service, its Rte. 12 crossing paved over. Further north on the Mountain Track, the building and smokestack of the former Whiting Milk Co. creamery are visible (top center). The Cheshire Branch main line swings off to the left, crossing the granite arch bridge to the Bellows Falls Island. 1978. Frederick G. Bailey photo.

Blount died tragically on August 31, 1967, while flying from Riverside to his home in Dublin, New Hampshire, when his plane ran out of fuel and crashed in Chesham, New Hampshire (Nimke 1985, 26, 129). The Blount Estate sold the Green Mountain on December 30, 1969 and the road became employee-owned. As a part of the purchase and sale agreement, the Green Mountain inherited the North Walpole yard and engine house property. Green Mountain continued running the passenger excursions through August 27, 1971, after which Steamtown Museum began running its own trains with Pacific 1246 leased from the Green Mountain. In 1983-85 Steamtown made yet another move—this time to Scranton, Pennsylvania— where it has been developed into a National Historic Site.

Today, Fitchburg Yard is the only remnant of original Cheshire Railroad trackage still in service. Importantly, Fitchburg Yard includes the only surviving roundhouse and turntable still in daily use by an operating freight railroad in New Hampshire and—other than the short stretch of the Conn River main line further north in North Walpole—it is the only remaining active trackage anywhere in Cheshire County.

Fitchburg Yard would not exist today had it not been for F. Nelson Blount. Blount purchased Fitchburg Yard and the accompanying locomotive facilities there from the B&M in 1961. The B&M, which at the time was still running trains on the Cheshire Branch, retained ownership of its main line through the yard (between Cold River and the New Hampshire/Vermont border) and granted the Green Mountain trackage rights to use the track. The B&M finally relinquished its interest in the track, formally abandoning the track (ICC Docket No. AB-32 [Sub-No. 28]) and selling it to the Green Mountain Railroad in 1984.

For over three decades, Green Mountain operations were based at Fitchburg Yard. The road's signature freight train between Bellows Falls and Rutland (XR-1) was made up in the yard. In 1997, the Vermont Railway (VTR) purchased a controlling interest in the Green Mountain and it was consolidated into the VTR system. The operating base for trains on the Green Mountain was transferred from Fitchburg Yard to Rutland. Today, VTR subleases the Fitchburg Yard facilities to a subsidiary which performs freight car repair work in the roundhouse. The yard continues to serve as the storage and maintenance base for the road's fleet of passenger cars and as a locomotive layover and fueling station.

Green Mountain RS1 401, shot through the Vilas Bridge, is heading for Bellows Falls with a DOT/FRA track geometry car, N. Walpole, late 1970s. Frederick G. Bailey photo.

Green Mountain's handsome fleet of Alco diesels rest in the N. Walpole roundhouse, ca. 1979. RS1 405, a vintage Rutland diesel, remains on the roster today. Frederick G. Bailey photo.

Looking downstream, Green Mountain 405 is crossing the granite arch bridge from N. Walpole to Bellows Falls with a passenger train, Sept. 1995. Note the bridge has been "strapped up" with steel beams and rods—work probably done in the 1929–1931 bridge strengthening program—"to restrain movement in the spandrel walls and separations between voussoirs in the arch ring" (Spofford Feb. 19, 1962). The road was preparing for heavier locomotives and traffic. Frederick G. Bailey photo.

B&M GP40 303 on the turntable at the N. Walpole engine house. The Vermont Railway had purchased the unit and it became VTR's 308. Fitchburg Yard, N. Walpole, ca. 1985. S. J. Whitney photo.

Green Mountain RS1 405 switching cars of US Army tanks being unloaded in Bellows Falls. The former BF&SR freight house (left), last used by Sunshine Feeds, collapsed in ruins shortly after this image was captured, July 1994. Frederick G. Bailey photo.

The Bellows Falls Switcher, VTR GP38-2 201, has come across the canal bridge and is crossing the diamond en route to Fitchburg Yard with a car, Bellows Falls, April 2014. B. G. Blodget photo.

Fitchburg Yard crowded with VTR equipment, N. Walpole, April 2014. B. G. Blodget photo.

Clarendon & Pittsford GP38-2 204 and VTR GP40-2 307 on the stone arch bridge heading to Fitchburg Yard, N. Walpole, Jan. 2013. Frederick G. Bailey photo.

CHAPTER SIX

THE CHESHIRE: WRECKS AND MISADVENTURES

No 517 Green Mt Flyer on Cheshire Br. collided with the Local No 561 at Troy N.H. The engine of the flyer no 1053 was overturned and the buggy of the local and 4 cars were badly wrecked. but no one was hurt. The cause of the accident was an open switch on the main line

The Flyer was on time and it is supposed the local was in to clear There is a ½ mile of straight track east of the station and the wreck occurred at the east end of the long passing siding

The Flyer was approaching the station quite fast. the Engineer had just started to put on the brakes so as to stop at Troy.

The Engineer saw the rear end and at the same time saw the open switch both he and the fireman jumped.

The wreck cars took fire from the overturned buggy stove

Train wrecks do not rank among the most popular railroad topics and categorically seem to be passed over lightly or dismissed altogether by many authors. However, wrecks—and there were many—are an important part of railroad history. Particularly in the early years of railroading through 1920, wrecks were a terrible plague upon the roads. One person who appreciated this was the late B&M railroad historian emeritus William J. Fletcher of Worcester, Massachusetts, who took a keen interest in wrecks. We encountered handwritten Fletcher letters and notes on railroad history—especially wrecks—in the files of many libraries and historical societies in the Monadnock Region. Fletcher, a former B&M fireman, and his friend Chester Smith, a former B&M engineer, traveled around the region for years, researching old newspaper accounts of wrecks. Smith would read the stories aloud as Fletcher took copious notes.

The accounts of wrecks provide interesting insights not only into their causes, but also how the roads responded to them. In the day, railroad service was essential and the roads were remarkably adept at cleaning up wrecks. Wreck gangs—often a hundred or more men—would descend upon a wreck scene and have the road reopened within twenty-four hours. In this chapter we present a sampling of some of the more notable wrecks experienced by the original Cheshire Railroad and its successors. Bear in mind that for the earliest mishaps and for those that happened at night, images are lacking. We will get into wrecks on other roads in the Monadnock Region in the appropriate chapters.

The Cheshire's Annual Report for 1859 reported "no passenger has been injured by accident to the trains since the opening of the road." For a single iron road, the Cheshire had a relatively good safety record, but the road did experience some horrific accidents before block signalization went into effect in 1911. Possibly the first recorded wreck on the Cheshire occurred on December 21, 1864. The following account of this wreck (Wilber Aug. 7, 1935), as reported in the press at the time, reveals the ghastly details:

Three persons were killed and a few others injured in a rear-end collision about 4 miles west of Keene. Three trains—two freight and a passenger/mail—were moving toward Keene. The first freight, dispatched in time to reach Keene with ample clearance, was delayed by a heavy snowstorm then prevailing and a shortage of water, and it had come to a stop. Following the freight, the passenger/mail, which was signaled, came up slowly with the intention of pushing the freight ahead of it into Keene. But before this could be done, the second freight, pushing a snowplow, struck the rear car of the passenger/mail, the plow lifting and splitting it for about half its length. A correspondent of the *Boston Journal* who was aboard said, "The terror and excitement after the collision no one could describe." Although the passengers, at the approach of the engine, fled toward the end of the car furthest from it, no escape was possible, and the car was crushed to splinters. The two stoves were upset with the danger of the debris taking fire, while the smokestack of the engine had been broken off and emitted a dense volume of smoke which made the situation still more fearful. The car struck by the engine was telescoped into the car ahead about five feet, its passengers being thrown into a panic and attempting to escape through windows. On the last mentioned car, Joseph Howerth and wife of Keene and John Moore, a boy about six years old, of Walpole, were killed by being crushed between the cars. It required about half an hour to chop away the wreckage sufficiently to release Mr. Howerth, during which time he frequently called for his wife, who was lying near him, dead, crushed between the floors of the two cars, and her body nearly severed. Several times the wreck caught fire, but by the well directed efforts of Conductor Stone, all escaped the flames.

On April 22, 1868, "the up freight" (westbound) drawn by the 14/*Fitzwilliam* ran upon a rock slide in the cut west of East Westmoreland, New Hampshire, (probably London Cut) and the engine's boiler exploded. Four tank cars, fortunately containing only residual amounts of petroleum oil and which were coupled in behind the tender, were burned (*Sentinel* April 30, 1868). This wreck is instructive, showing that even with seventeen years remaining before the Cheshire would complete its wood-to-coal fuel conversion program, the commercial petroleum era was already underway in the Monadnock Region.

On September 1, 1876, an express (freight) off the Cheshire road rammed the rear of a Mixed on the V&M Division of the Fitchburg about a third of a mile west of Wachusett Station. (At this time, the Cheshire rented trackage rights on the Fitchburg between South Ashburnham and Fitchburg.) The Mixed had stopped west of Wachusett where the crew cut off the engine and ran rapidly ahead, down the grade to the station in order to get cars out of the station siding to be added to the train.

Meanwhile the train followed, drifting down the grade at seven to ten miles per hour. This risky procedure was customarily followed to save time. As the cars of the Mixed—twenty-six freight cars and one passenger car—were thus following their engine down the grade, the Cheshire Express rounded a curve at speed and, unable to stop in time, smashed into the Mixed's caboose. The caboose was shoved into the passenger car ahead, telescoping the car and killing one passenger.

The accident report cited the "inexcusable" lack of train brake equipment on the Mixed at such a late date in railroading, insufficient provision in the rules of the Company to ensure proper interval of spacing between trains, a "singularly primitive" system of communicating spacing, and carelessness of the Cheshire engineer and conductor for failure to give proper attention to cautions received at both South Ashburnham and Westminster (Mass. Railroad Comm. Report 1877, 25–27, 117).

On October 21, 1876, the locomotive *Bellows Falls,* westbound with a passenger train, collided head-on with a down freight near Summit. The crew of the passenger train escaped serious injury, but engineer Henry M. Staples and his fireman, Lewis Phillips, on the freight were killed, the latter instantly. Staples, crushed between the tender and firebox of his engine, was literally roasted to death, living about an hour and a half and suffering indescribably, as efforts were made to free him. It was reported that he was brave, calm, and rational to the last, enduring the torture heroically (*Sentinel* Oct. 26, 1876). Staples was a Civil War veteran of several battles, among them Winchester and Cedar Creek, and he was also in the party that captured and assisted in escorting Jeff Davis to the Union Army headquarters (*Sentinel* Nov. 2, 1876).

On December 18, 1878, "the down freight" was run into by a Fitchburg V&M Division freight train at South Ashburnham. Both engines were damaged but there were no injuries (*Cheshire Republican* Dec. 21, 1878). On February 5, 1881, The Night Express from Boston slammed into the rear of a freight train just west of Fitzwilliam station near Rockwood Pond. Seconds before the collision, Engineer J. L. Davis jumped from his engine, but then lost his balance in the snow bank, fell under the train, and was dragged a short distance and killed. The engine telescoped the caboose and nosed beneath it, lifting it right up upon the boiler (*Sentinel* Feb. 10, 1881).

On January 6, 1890, On January 6, 1890, Cheshire Local Freight Number 9 Engine 29/Ashburnham met Wild Train E.C. Thayer head-on just west of Summit Cut in Westmoreland on account of a transcribing error by Westmoreland agent operator Harriet L. Cook. The term "wild train" was used for an "extra," a train with no timetable authority that could proceed only on written orders. Timetable trains had to be on. the lookout for wild trains and would receive written orders telling where they were to meet them. Cook had given orders to Number 9 to meet the E. C. Thayer at Summit when the order should have been to meet at Tenth Section. The telegraph orders from the dispatcher were found to have been correct, but somehow Cook had copied them wrong. Engineer Sidney W. Slate and Fireman Charles W. Gibson on Number 9 were killed (*Sentinel* Jan. 8, 1890).

Before block signalization there was no margin for error and train orders had to be communicated flawlessly. Imagine how an operator, with no means to communicate with a train after it had departed a station, must

have felt upon discovering an error had been made in the orders. At that terrible moment it became just a matter of waiting for word of the collision.

About 6:30 Monday evening, July 6, 1891, two Fitchburg freights were wrecked in Troy near "Farrar's Crossing" (Marlborough Road), about a mile west of the depot. Train 14, a twenty-four-car westbound train drawn by Ten-Wheeler 237, collided with eastbound Extra 13. Extra 13 was a stock train with twenty carloads of hogs, drawn by Ten-Wheeler 233, and running on Train 13's time as a second section. Train 14 met the first section of Train 13, according to orders, at Fitzwilliam. But the crew on Train 14 failed to notice Train 13 was displaying red flags, which—at that time on the Fitchburg—signaled that another section of the same train was following (*Sentinel* July 8, 1891). To the attentive reader, we note that the train numbers reported in the *Sentinel* are correct; on the Fitchburg system, up until about 1892, inward trains were indeed odd-numbered, outward trains even-numbered (Alden H. Dreyer, pers. comm.).

Fitchburg Ten-Wheelers 233 (ex-Cheshire 33) and 237 (ex-Cheshire 37) appear just about fused together in the smash-up at Troy, July 6, 1891. Miraculously there were no fatalities in this wreck; The engineer and fireman on both engines jumped for their lives. As bad as things often appeared in these wrecks, the engines—some of them veterans of multiple bang-ups—were usually repaired (including these two) and sent back out on the road. The 237, one of the last two engines acquired new by the Cheshire (in March 1890), soldiered on into the B&M years until it was scrapped in 1911 (Edson 1982). Photogr. unknown; Hist. Soc. Cheshire Cty.

Fitchburg Mogul 130, on her side at Jefferies Crossing, W. Keene, July 17, 1897.

Steam is still rising from the lead engine, Fitchburg Mogul 130, after the derailment at Jefferies Crossing, W. Keene, July 17, 1897.

From a safety standpoint, the period 1885 to 1915 was a notoriously dangerous time to be a railroader. Traffic was increasing and, in the absence of block signalization, head-on collisions, usually attributable to human error, occurred with distressing frequency. It wasn't until well into the Boston and Maine Railroad (B&M) era—on May 5, 1911, to be exact—that the block signal system on the Cheshire was finally activated. At first, crews were distrustful of the system because they didn't understand it and doubted it would really work. But it did, and "cornfield meets" were effectively ended.

After the helper, Fitchburg American 15, left the iron, it appears the force of the train shot right past and piled up all around her, Jefferies Crossing, W. Keene, July 17, 1897.

The wreck train from Fitchburg has been backed out to the scene from the Keene Shops as a large crowd looks on, W. Keene, July 17, 1897.

The Hog Train Wreck. Arguably one of the most-recalled wrecks on the Cheshire occurred on July 17, 1897, when Fitchburg Train 246, a Bellows Falls-to-Boston freight with two engines, twenty-three cars of live hogs, and the buggy, left the iron at Jefferies (a.k.a., Pemberton's) Crossing, about a half mile above Bradford Road in West Keene. Both engines—Mogul 130 and helper American 15—and five cars of hogs were derailed. Reporting marks C&CTRR are visible on two of the stock cars. The engineer on the first engine, Milan Curtis, was crushed and killed instantly. The cause of this wreck may have been a track bolt placed upon the outer rail of the curve where the lead engine's wheels first derailed. The wreck occurred about 1:00 p.m. A wreck train was sent out from Fitchburg and arrived in Keene at 3:25 p.m. Fitchburg Train 17/*Green Mountain Flyer*, due out of Keene at 1:50 p.m., was forwarded over the B&M's Ashuelot Branch to reach Bellows Falls via South Vernon. The track was cleared by midnight.

About 450–500 hogs escaped from the cars and ran about the countryside, some as far as two miles away. About sixty injured hogs were immediately killed; most of the remaining hogs were eventually rounded up, placed in a makeshift corral, and reloaded onto cars (*Sentinel* July 17 and 19, 1897). Not recorded was how many of these porkers found their way to local dinner plates! J. A. French photos; Hist. Soc. Cheshire Cty.

On August 22, 1900, shortly after the B&M takeover, Train 517/*Green Mountain Flyer,* collided with three runaway cars of crushed stone between Fitzwilliam and State Line, New Hampshire. The cars had run away from a work train switching cars at Symond's Siding about one and a half miles east of Fitzwilliam. The work train engineer ran after the cars, but could not make a hitch and had to give up when they were almost on 517's time. They got into the clear, knowing an accident was going to happen unless the cars made it beyond curves to a long straightaway where they could be seen by 517's engineer, Frank Hughes. Unfortunately, this was not to be, and in the ensuing accident Engineer Hughes was badly injured. Train 518 came upon the scene and transported Hughes and other injured crewmen back to Keene. Hughes died in Elliot Hospital that evening.

Train 502/the *Green Mountain Flyer,* drawn by American 965, struck a landslide a quarter-mile west of Dickinson's Cut in West Keene about 6:30 the evening of December 22, 1902. The train, which had left Westmoreland at 6:19, was not heard from again until 7:40, when Baggage Master Smith reached the Keene station on foot to report the wreck. The engine turned over down a thirty-five-foot embankment. The engineer and fireman went down with the engine, ending up beneath the engine, partially buried in dirt, but miraculously unhurt. The train consisted of a milk car, baggage/smoker, coach, and two Pullmans. All the cars left the iron and partially overturned, but none of the sixty passengers aboard was seriously injured. A wreck train from Fitchburg and a steam derrick were on the scene shortly after midnight and the road was cleared about 9:30 the next morning (*Sentinel* Dec. 23, 1902).

Milk cans, which were scattered about the land, have been salvaged for pickup and return to their points of origin the morning following the wreck of Train 502, W. Keene, Dec. 22, 1902. The photo, now in the Hist. Soc. of Cheshire County Archives, was originally preserved in the collection of Tommie W. Smithers, the conductor on the train, who survived.

Consolidation 1146 is in trouble at the west end of the Joslin Arch, where it appears the Joslin Siding derail, installed there to protect the main line, has done its duty, ca. 1904–1910. Hist. Soc. Cheshire Cty.

It's another head-on collision, this one between B&M Americans 1097 and 1135 somewhere in E. Westmoreland, Aug. 1910. Before block signalization arrived in 1911, the track through Westmoreland was regarded as the Cheshire's most dangerous stretch due to its deep cuts and curves that reduced visibility. Bion H. Whitehouse photo; Hist. Soc. Cheshire Cty.

American 1138 and her tender on Train 517/*Green Mountain Flyer*, tipped over and almost went down the steep embankment just off the west end of the Joslin Arch, Sept. 27, 1909. The train was running an hour late and had taken the passing track at Joslin to meet 518. As the train crept down the passing track to a point just off the arch, the crew forgot about the derail there and over she went. Luckily, the coupler between the tender and the combine broke and none of the cars derailed. The engineer and fireman jumped to safety. The train, consisting of a combine and three coaches, was pulled back across the arch to Joslin station (*Sentinel* Sept. 27, 1909). Bion H. Whitehouse photo; Hist. Soc. Cheshire Cty.

On January 26, 1912, Train 505, the overnight train to Montreal (known in later years as the *Mount Royal*), operating on this particular day with a helper engine, ran the ball signal at Winchendon and went right through a Gardner-to-Elmwood freight on the diamond. The freight was struck three cars ahead of its caboose. Though there were no injuries, two cars were demolished and lumber strewn about the roadbed. As a consequence of this accident, the road instituted a new rule requiring any regular train with a helper to have the regular crew running the lead engine (Fletcher letter, undated).

Bellows Falls to Boston freight XB-2 piled up just west of State Line station about 7:00 a.m., Sunday, June 29, 1930. In the stillness of the morning it was reported the wreck could be heard for miles. Fifteen cars out of the train's seventy-five cars derailed, with several pitched over the embankment into Damon's Brook and meadow. The derailment tore up 500 feet of track, fouling both tracks, but 100 employees and officials arrived within hours and both tracks were cleared and repaired by Monday night. The cause of the accident was believed to have been a swaying derrick about six cars from the headpin. Damaged merchandise included new Packard and Buick automobiles; a new American LaFrance fire truck being delivered to Belmont, Massachusetts; wooden toys, marble, hay, and grain (*Sentinel* June 30 and July 1, 1930). Photogr. unknown; Brent S. Michiels coll.

The *Mount Royal* wreck, just west of Signal 654, Winchendon. The track has been cleared, allowing trains to pass, Sept. 1938. Laurie Bowman photo; Ashburnham Hist. Soc.

The Mount Royal Wreck. Windswept torrential rains had swept the Monadnock Region most of the day, September 20, 1938. Rivers were rapidly rising and a dark and stormy evening loomed as the Hurricane of 1938 bore down on the Region. At the time—absent radar and satellite imagery—weather forecasting was still relatively primitive, trains were not radio-equipped, and cell phones were unknown. A train out on the road was little different than a ship at sea. After leaving a station, it would not be heard from again until it made its next station stop.

And so it was that Montreal-bound Train 5511/ *Mount Royal*, led by Pacific 3621, was proceeding under a twenty-mile-per-hour emergency slow order received at Fitchburg. The train was running about an hour late. At 10:25 p.m., the train ran into a washout just west of the old Camp Chanrudoma Road crossing in Winchendon (about one and a half miles west of Naukeag) and was wrecked. The 3621 toppled over on her left side, plowed into the roadbed, and slid down an embankment into a swampy area along the Millers River. Three head-end cars—a baggage-RPO and two baggage cars—also derailed and went down the embankment. A coach and two sleepers (Pullmans *Dinant* and an unknown) remained on the tracks. The fireman and baggage master received non-life-threatening injuries. Thirty passengers were shaken up but uninjured (*Worcester Telegram*, Sept. 21, 1938).

In the darkness, Conductor Charles H. Brooks made his way almost a mile to a dwelling to summon help. A rescue train arrived later in the night and pulled the two sleepers off the rear end of the train and took them back to Fitchburg. Coach passengers were accommodated on the *Dinant*. Meat and fish were salvaged and distributed to storm "refugees" in Waterville. Sacks of soaked mail were taken to the Winchendon post office, dried out, and distributed from there (*Sentinel* and *Winchendon Courier*, Sept. 22, 1938).

Pacific 3621 lay on her side for over a month before the B&M, beset by more pressing post-hurricane problems, got around to putting her back on her feet. Here we see a group of men looking her over on Oct. 1, 1938. She was finally hauled to Billerica on Nov. 3, entered the shop Nov. 26, and was out-shopped Dec. 15 after 3,055 man-hours of labor (data from B&M Form LM-2). Dana D. Goodwin photo; B&MRRHS Archives.

Train 5511/*Mount Royal*, gone astray in Winchendon about 1.5 miles west of Naukeag. The train's two sleepers have been taken back to Fitchburg; the coach is standing on the crossing of the old road to Camp Chanrudoma in N. Ashburnham, Sept. 21, 1938. Photo courtesy the *Worcester Telegram & Gazette*.

Another view of the *Mount Royal* wreck with a close-up of the baggage-RPO car, Oct. 1, 1938. Dana D. Goodwin photo; B&MRRHS Archives.

The roadbed has been repaired with sandy fill and an access track laid along the foot of the embankment to reach the engine, Oct. 29, 1938. Photogr. unknown; B. G. Blodget coll.

The Monadnock Wreck of Friday, August 14, 1942. Described as "the worst passenger train accident in the Monadnock Region in a score of years," Train 5509/*Monadnock*, with five or six wooden milk cars on the head pin and two steel passenger cars—a combine and a coach—trailing, came upon a washed-out culvert at Cushing Crossing just west of Rockwood Pond in Fitzwilliam, and the whole train was derailed. The locomotive made it across the washout and did not derail. The wooden milk cars piled up and were smashed to splinters, spilling their loads of empty forty-quart milk cans throughout the woods. One of the passenger cars tipped over on its side, the other at a forty-five-degree angle. There were thirty-five passengers aboard, miraculously none of them seriously injured. About an eighth of a mile of track was torn up and utility poles were sideswiped, knocking out telephone service between Fitzwilliam and Keene. The washout was caused by a freak, localized cloudburst. The washout developed so soon after the cloudburst that sectionmen did not have time to patrol the track before 5509 was due and the train crew had no warning of trouble.

Emergency responders had a difficult time reaching the scene. The road system was still quite primitive. Even Route 12 had not yet been built. The injured were transported to Elliot Hospital in Keene in beachwagon "ambulances" made available by Fitzwilliam residents. Most of the uninjured were forwarded to their destinations by bus. Salvaged milk cans were loaded on trucks and sent to Bellows Falls. The railroad made short work of cleaning up the splintered remains of the milk cars—with a match!

Wrecking trains were sent out from Fitchburg and Greenfield and railroad men worked through the night under floodlights to clear the tracks and replace damaged rail. Eight carloads of cinders were brought to the scene early Saturday for filling material. During the work, Cheshire Branch trains were detoured via Greenfield. Repair work was completed in less than twenty-four hours, and the first trains passed over the iron Saturday afternoon shortly after 4:00 p.m. (*Boston Globe* Aug. 15, 1942; *Sentinel* Aug. 15, 1942).

Streamline train 6000 derailed and wrecked at the Walpole freight house siding. The main line was not fouled or damaged and trains could pass the scene at reduced speed. Notice the stock pens in this image, once a familiar—but rarely photographed—sight at many stations, Jan. 18, 1945. The B&M quickly moved the 6000 to the Concord Shops. Photogr. unknown; B&MRRHS Archives.

The Streamline Train Goes Astray. On the morning of January 18, 1945, the 6000—running as Train 5506/*Cheshire* on the morning run to Boston—derailed just west of Walpole station and went astray. Running at an estimated speed of fifty miles per hour, she veered into the freight house siding, demolished the side of an agricultural warehouse, damaged cattle pens, and nosed about six feet into the freight house. All three cars of the unit remained upright, but all the trucks derailed.

The cause of this derailment was determined to be "a No. 1 traction motor gear case bottom or front half that dropped into the guardrail, broke, got under the wheels and derailed the leading wheels. The derailed No. 1 truck then struck and threw the switch to the freight house track causing the unit to go into the freight house siding while still derailed on the outside of this siding" (B&M Memorandum, D. C. Reid, General Superintendent Motive Power, to F. W. Rourke, General Manager, Jan. 31, 1945). This was the only serious accident in the 6000's history. Fortunately, there were no serious injuries to the sixty people aboard. Some passengers were enjoying breakfast at the time of the accident and food was splattered about the cars. The B&M made up a steam train in the Falls that picked up the stranded passengers and continued on to Boston (*Sentinel* Jan. 18–19, 1945). Until the 6000 returned to service in the fall, Train 5506 was suspended due to a national coal shortage and a federal emergency order that prohibited railroads from adding any new coal-fired trains.

Wreck damage to the 6000 is evident in this image taken at Concord Shops, Jan. 1945. The Budd Company dispatched personnel from their Philadelphia plant to assist with repair work. Photo by V. Hrubant of the Budd Company; B&MRRHS Archives.

Alco RS2 1500 Reaches the End of Her Career. In the late afternoon of January 21, 1975, Alco RS2 1500, en route to Winchendon with local freight F-5, encountered ice buildup on the Old County Road crossing in Ashburnham (about two miles above South Ashburnham) and derailed. The result was a wrenched frame that would end her twenty-seven-year career on the B&M. At the time, she was the last RS2 still in service.

If ever there was a diesel most associated with the Monadnock Region, it was the 1500. You'll find her going about her work in several places in our book. This unit began life as Alco's RS2 demonstrator, its assigned number 1500 corresponding to its horsepower rating. It was delivered to the B&M in May 1948, the first of only ten RS2s ever purchased by the road. As the only Alco road switcher on the road that lacked multi-unit capability, her usefulness in main-line freight service, except for occasional pusher duty, was limited. However, like her sisters, she had a steam boiler (inside her short hood) for use in passenger service. She spent much of her life in passenger service on the Connecticut River Route and in branch line freight service throughout the Monadnock Region.

The 1500 was the only RS delivered in the black switcher livery. She would never wear the maroon and gold paint of her sisters (1501-04 and 1530-34), but was "Blue-dipped" in 1969. She carried her original Alco demo number to the end.

B&M crews rerailing the 1500, Ashburnham, Jan. 22, 1975. Norman Bingham photo; Brian Roy coll.

CHAPTER SEVEN

THE CHESHIRE: SPECIAL, LATE, AND LAST MOVES

When it came to road power in the early diesel era (through the 1950s)—with the notable exceptions of EMD E7 passenger diesels, the streamline train 6000, and RDCs—Alco RS2 and RS3 road switchers ruled the Cheshire Branch. The photographic record shows that it was not until the final years of the branch's operation (after 1965) that EMD GP7 and GP9 road switchers began to make appearances with any degree of regularity. By 1969, through trains had become a rare event. Yet even still, old soldiers from B&M's dwindling fleet of Alcos put in appearances on some of these last moves.

In its twilight years, the Cheshire, having no restrictions on over-dimension cars, was used chiefly as a detour route for those loads that the road didn't want to try squeezing through the Bellows Falls Tunnel. The Cheshire and Ashuelot Branches were also used on various occasions as a detour route for Connecticut River or Fitchburg main line trains.

In this chapter, we will "chase" a sampling of these moves in the twilight years of the old Cheshire, beginning with the move of Union Pacific Big Boy (Alco 4-8-8-4) X4012, one of the largest steam locomotives in the world, over the road in 1964. The big engine was being moved to North Walpole to join the Steamtown collection.

At 8:00 a.m. the morning of September 23, 1964, Gardner Tower issued the following advisory message (from original carbon copy, courtesy of Richard E. Miller) over the initials of Fitchburg Division Superintendent I. W. Clifford, to the conductor and engineer of F-7 at Fitchburg Tower: "PB-2 will reach South Ashburnham this am about 1010 A. M. and will have for F-7 local U. P. eng 4012 for Bellows Falls with 2 idler cars slow speed of 15 M. P. H. use caution passing cars on adjacent tracks. X-4 Bellows Falls local will pickup this equipment at Winchendon this P. M. for move to Bellows Falls all concerned protect."

Alco S4 1267 is pulling into the East Yards with X-3, the Winchendon–Bellows Falls local, with Union Pacific Big Boy X4012 in the consist. The Big Boy's passage though Keene had been advertised in advance and it was held in the West Yards for a short time to allow a crowd of several hundred people to view it. Keene, Sept. 23, 1964. Richard E. Miller photo.

Big Boy X4012, of course, in the East Yards, Keene. B&M boxcar 1124 was being used as an idler on account of the locomotive's weight. Sept. 23, 1964. Richard E. Miller photo.

GP7 1563 leads XF-2, the Bellows Falls–Fitchburg freight, at Signal 1082, Walpole, NH, June 20, 1968. This and the following three photos by H. Bentley Crouch; Walker Transportation Coll., Beverly Hist. Soc.

At Signal 1002, Gilboa, NH.

In Summit Cut, about to pass beneath the Rte. 12 Bridge, Surry, NH.

At Signal 772 in Fitzwilliam, NH.

B&M 4265 and two Alcos lead a train of forty-four vats destined for a new Anheuser-Busch Brewery under construction in Merrimack, NH, at Signal 1002, Gilboa, Jan. 4, 1969. H. Bentley Crouch photo; Walker Transportation Coll., Beverly Hist. Soc.

Pulling through the East Yard and approaching Eastern Ave., Keene.

Same train crossing the Ashuelot River trestle, Keene. This and the following four photos by Frederick G. Bailey.

At the Troy Ledges.

The late afternoon shadows have lengthened as the train approaches the Rte. 12 Bridge in Troy. This view is nonexistent today, after a half-century of forest growth.

Pulling across Island St. near the Colony Mill, Keene. It's been thirteen years since Patrick B. McGinnis took the reins at the B&M and clearly none of the battle-weary units on this train has ever worn blue paint. The girder bridge just ahead of the lead engine spans the Colony Mill's old power canal.

On the straightaway 1.5 miles west of Westmoreland, NH.

In all, there were seven of these special vat train moves and here comes another one: Extra 1564 with OD cars, carrying twenty-six more vats for the new brewery in Merrimack, coming over the Mountain Track to Fitchburg Yard. Mountain Road (Rte. 12) is at right. The building and smokestack seen above the train is the Whiting Milk Co. creamery, N. Walpole, Feb. 16, 1969. This and the following three photos by H. Bentley Crouch; Walker Transportation Coll., Beverly Hist. Soc.

As viewed from atop one of the old Manchester & Keene bridge abutments, X1564 is crossing Eastern Ave., Keene.

At Summit Cut, Surry.

A train with OD cars, probably headed for Fitchburg, has just come off the Mountain Track and is entering Fitchburg Yard, N. Walpole, April 1969. The sand house burned Oct. 15, 1969. The big coaling tower, retired in 1958, stood until Oct. 4, 1972, when it was dismantled, its timbers salvaged for other uses (Nimke 1984). Frederick G. Bailey photo.

Alco RS2 1500 in the "blue-dip" livery inward at Cold River, with retired Pacific 3713/*The Constitution*, Aug. 1969. Steamtown had lent the 3713 for outdoor display to the Museum of Science in Boston. There she would remain until Feb. 21, 1985, when she left the city for Scranton, PA, to rejoin the Steamtown collection that had relocated there from Bellows Falls a year earlier. This and the following four photos by Frederick G. Bailey.

Passing the former station site, Westmoreland.

At Gilboa. Still proudly worn, the "speed lettering" on the 3713's tender is a flash-back to the engine's glory days when she could be found on any of the B&M's crack passenger trains, including the *Mount Royal* and the *Green Mountain Flyer* that once sped over these same rails.

Viewed from the Rte. 12 Bridge at Summit Cut, Surry.

Approaching Island St., Keene.

B&M's GP9 "Bluebirds" were held mostly on the main lines and made infrequent appearances on the Cheshire Branch, but this was one of them. Class engine 1700 is tied in behind GP7 1573 on the same military move at Gilboa pictured below.

Extra 1573 passing under the Rte. 12 Bridge in Walpole with a mostly military OD train, Sept. 1969. This and the following two photos by Frederick G. Bailey.

A "Bluebird" buggy brings up the rear of Extra 1573 with a crewman up in the monitor keeping a watchful eye on all those tanks. The country was involved in the Vietnam War at this time, and the B&M was doing its part. Gilboa.

In 1970 the Cheshire Branch entered its last year of through operations. The B&M was still actively keeping the line open for traffic—witness snowplow Extra 1573 pushing a Russell snowplow westbound in Walpole after a pretty good snowfall, Jan. 1970. This and the following three photos by Frederick G. Bailey.

Coming (left) and going (right) at Cold River.

On the Mountain Track in N. Walpole.

An SW9 has brought an OD car over the Mountain Track and is just stepping onto Rte. 12 at the north end of Fitchburg Yard, N. Walpole, Jan. 1970. Frederick G. Bailey photo.

In early 1970, a typical OD train, often with SW9 1231 for power, looked like this: one or two of these new P&H (Pawling & Harnischfeger) cranes and a "Bluebird" buggy. Here Extra 1231 East is crossing Rte. 12 into Fitchburg Yard, N. Walpole, late April 1970. This and the following six photos by Frederick G. Bailey.

(left) Approaching Rte. 12 crossing, Cold River, (right) At River Road crossing, Walpole.

At Gilboa.

East of Gilboa.

At Summit Cut, Surry, where the last of winter's ice still lingers. It was not unusual for snow and ice to linger here well into May.

And at the track watchmen's shanty, W. Keene.

The RRE Special, stranded on the Connecticut River Route Main Line because of a derailment at Putney, VT, awaits orders at Riverside, Bellows Falls. Eventually the B&M decided to detour the train of six Budd RDCs, led by RDC-1 6105, over the Cheshire Branch, Oct. 17, 1970. Photogr. unknown; Brent S. Michiels coll.

On Saturday evening, October 17, 1970, an RRE excursion train from Boston, consisting of six Budd RDC cars, became stranded on the Connecticut River Route Main Line in Bellows Falls when a freight derailment at Putney, Vermont, fouled both mains. Four hundred passengers on the train were kept in suspense for three hours, until, with dusk fast approaching, the B&M finally decided to detour the train over the Cheshire Branch to South Ashburnham, where it would join the Fitchburg Route Main Line for the rest of the trip back to Boston. Since most of the move occurred in darkness, pictures were never an option and the last passenger train to traverse the Cheshire Branch slipped away in the night.

The Cheshire Branch was still in use in late 1970. It was still being regularly inspected and crossing flashers were still working. On the morning of October 17, the same day as the RRE Budd car excursion, Local F-5 had made its usual Saturday-only through trip from Fitchburg to North Walpole to pick up OD cars. But while returning from the Conn River Yard, it derailed an OD car (carrying steel for the I-93 Construction Project in Boston) on the Route 12 crossing at the entrance to Fitchburg Yard. Had this derailment occurred at Cold River or further east, the RRE excursion passengers probably would have been "rubber-tired" back to Boston. We also note that Ben English photographed B&M SW9 1230 at Fitzwilliam and Troy with another late F-5 trip November 7, 1970 (see Melvin 2009, 68).

By 1982 nature was making considerable headway reclaiming the old Cheshire Branch right-of-way. The tracks had been abandoned east of Eastern Avenue since 1972, though the rails and crossing flashers remained in place until 1985. The skeletal remains of an old block signal, deactivated in 1959, poke above the lush vegetation. The concrete slab at the center marks the end of a 100-foot granite block abutment (see photos on page 141-142 in Chapter 13), part of the bridgework that once carried the Keene Branch over the Cheshire's grade crossing at Eastern Avenue, Keene, 1982. S. J. Whitney photo.

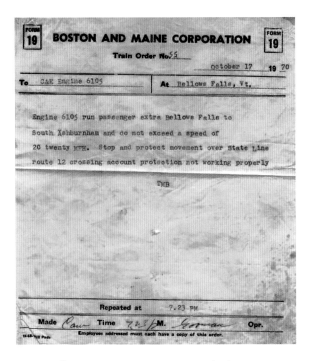

Form 19 for Passenger Extra 6105 East, the last passenger train to ever run over the Cheshire Branch, Oct. 17, 1970.

CHAPTER EIGHT

THE SULLIVAN (COUNTY) RAILROAD

Bellows Falls, Vermont (MP S83.99)
to Charlestown, New Hampshire, Townline (MP S85.50)

This view is looking due west (upstream) at the Sullivan Railroad's covered wooden truss bridge, built almost over the Connecticut River Dam in 1851. Oak Hill in Bellows Falls rises beyond. The Bellows Falls Island is at left, N. Walpole is to the right. The Cheshire Railroad's similar bridge is about 0.4 miles downstream. Note the smoke pipes atop the Rutland engine house just off the bridge on the Island, ca. 1870s. Rockingham Public Library's Catalogued Photograph Coll.

In the far northwestern corner of our defined region, we find the southern end of the Sullivan Railroad, a small road named to honor Revolutionary War hero Brigadier General John Sullivan, and chartered July 10, 1846, to build a line from Windsor to Bellows Falls, Vermont. Except for its termini, the road was entirely in New Hampshire, running along the east side of the Connecticut River. The road was twenty-six miles in length. Only about one and a half miles of main line between Bellows Falls and the Charlestown town line were in our defined area.

When first built, the Sullivan connected itself to the Cheshire Railroad in North Walpole. There, in late 1848, the same contractor building the Cheshire's last section in North Walpole was also building the Sullivan's section "from south of 'Governor's Brook' to its connection with the end of the Cheshire." After delays

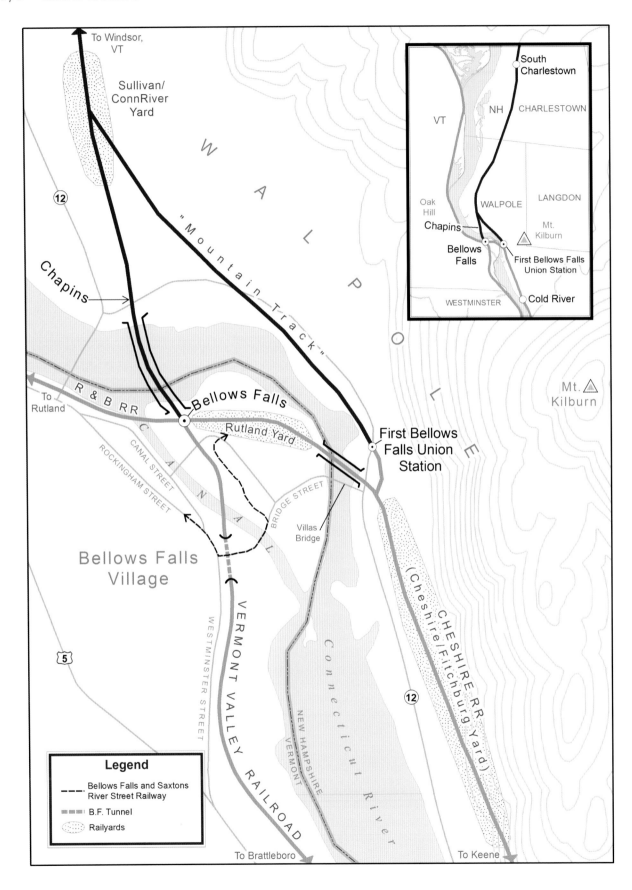

To Windsor, VT

Sullivan/ ConnRiver Yard

W A L P O L E

12

Chapins

"Mountain Track"

R & B RR

To Rutland

Bellows Falls

Rutland Yard

First Bellows Falls Union Station

CANAL STREET

ROCKINGHAM STREET

CANAL

Bellows Falls Village

BRIDGE STREET

Villas Bridge

5

WESTMINSTER STREET

VERMONT VALLEY RAILROAD

Connecticut River

NEW HAMPSHIRE

VERMONT

12

CHESHIRE RR

(Cheshire/Fitchburg Yard)

Mt. Kilburn

To Brattleboro

To Keene

Inset map:

South Charlestown

VT   NH   CHARLESTOWN

Oak Hill

LANGDON

WALPOLE

Mt. Kilburn

Chapins

Bellows Falls

First Bellows Falls Union Station

WESTMINSTER

Cold River

Legend

– – –   Bellows Falls and Saxtons River Street Railway

▪▪▪▪   B.F. Tunnel

▒▒▒   Railyards

Springfield, Mass.	*00.00*	N. Walpole/Charlestown townline*	85.50
Brattleboro, Vt.	*60.32*	N. Walpole Interlocking*	86.01
Bellows Falls, Vt. (*Cheshire,R&B,VV*)	83.99	S. Charlestown	87.18
Chapins, N.H. Interlocking*	84.27	Charlestown, N.H.	91.08
N. Walpole (Sullivan/Conn River Yd.)	Yard[1]	Windsor, Vt. (*CVRy*)	109.11
N. Walpole (Cheshire/Fitchburg Yd.)		*White River Junction, Vt.*	*123.19*

Mileage table for the Sullivan (County) Railroad, Bellows Falls to Windsor, showing stations, junctions with other railroads and distances from Springfield, Mass. (Connecticut River Div., Springfield to Windsor, *B&M ETT No. 1,* April 29, 1928 and *ETT No. 1,* April 27, 1980). The shaded area denotes the section of the Sullivan included in our discussion. Trains on the Sullivan moving *away* from Springfield are northward/outward trains. Trains moving *toward* Springfield are southward/inward trains.
[1]Encompasses the so-called Mountain Track.
*Not a station stop; included for reference only.

caused by a difficult ledge on the Sullivan's section, the two lines finally met on New Year's Day 1849 and "the first train of cars ever seen in this vicinity passed over the Cheshire Road and Sullivan to Charlestown, N. H." (*Bellows Falls Gazette* Jan. 4, 1849). Since neither of the railroads' bridges across the river had been completed, the Cheshire and Sullivan shared a temporary station—the first Bellows Falls Union Station—near the end of the Tucker Toll Bridge in North Walpole. Regular service between North Walpole and Charlestown began February 5, 1849, and the road opened through to Windsor on March 31, 1849.

It would be another two and a half years before the Sullivan entered Bellows Falls on its own rails. The Sullivan's destiny was to become one of the links in the then-forming line between Springfield, Massachusetts, and Wells River, Vermont—the 164-mile Connecticut River main line.

This is the second Bellows Falls Union Station built by the R&B, Cheshire, and Sullivan Railroads in 1851 at the crossing of the R&B and Sullivan main lines. Note the crossing diamonds at right. The station was a two-story brick structure that included passenger facilities, ticketing and telegraph offices, employee quarters, and a restaurant. On the windy, subzero night of Dec. 21, 1921, a fire got started in the basement kitchen of the restaurant and spread through the partitions to the Western Union Telegraph office on the second floor before breaking out in an uncontrollable blaze that destroyed the structure. Postcard; B. G. Blodget coll.

Union Station, Bellows Falls, Vt.

The third Bellows Falls Union Station was built in 1923 as a one-story structure, incorporating salvageable portions of the second station's first-floor brick walls. The ball signal rigging in this and the preceding image governed the diamond crossings. A signal maintainer, using a pulley system, could move the balls in and out of a metal sleeve. Three balls displayed (normal) gave Connecticut River Route trains rights over the crossing; two balls, Cheshire trains; and one ball, Rutland trains. The balls were replaced by oil lanterns by night. Aug. 26, 1956. Benjamin Perry Jr. photo.

In the summer of 1851, the Sullivan built a covered wooden truss bridge (resembling the Cheshire's bridge in every respect) over the Connecticut River Dam in North Walpole and laid rail across to the Bellows Falls Island. There it connected with the Cheshire as well as the Rutland and Burlington Railroad (R&B), which had opened between Bellows Falls and Burlington in December 1849, and the Vermont Valley Railroad (VV) which had opened between Brattleboro and Bellows Falls in 1851. The VV and the Sullivan would become integral parts of the Connecticut River Route Main Line.

The Sullivan's original connection with the Cheshire in North Walpole would continue to be of some importance since it allowed Sullivan-Cheshire freight traffic to bypass Bellows Falls. From at least 1906 this short connecting track was known as the Mountain Track in reference to the way it wrapped around the south end of Fall Mountain.

In addition to its north-south Connecticut Valley traffic, the Sullivan hoped to offer in conjunction with the Cheshire and Fitchburg roads, a competitive route between Boston, Canada, and the Great Lakes. But it became apparent early on that this was not to be. In 1852 the Vermont Central, to prevent diversion of traffic at White River Junction for Boston via the Sullivan-Cheshire-Fitchburg Route, ceased all interchange of east-west traffic with the Sullivan. Baker (1937, 229) describes what happened next:

> . . . The Vermont Central entered into agreements with the Northern (N.H.) Railroad and the Northern (N.Y.) Railroad as to exclusive interchange with those roads of all traffic under their control destined for points within reach of their lines. This contract of 1854 had the practical and premeditated effect of sealing up the Sullivan Railroad as far as western business was concerned. . . .

Eventually the Vermont Central, the two Northern roads, the Concord Railroad, and the Nashua & Lowell and Boston & Lowell roads formed a consortium to protect traffic on what they called their "Great Northern Route." The consortium's actions were keenly felt by both the Sullivan and the Cheshire—but especially by the Cheshire, forced for most of its life to survive on its online business and what overhead western traffic the Rutland could feed it.

By 1858, the Northern (NH) Railroad, as a protective move, had tightened its financial control of the Sullivan, and in September 1861 leased it to J. G. Smith of the Vermont Central. As a hapless captive of the Northern, the Sullivan was a *de facto* member of the consortium, but obviously it had little sway in matters. In danger of defaulting on its bonds, the road was reorganized in 1866 as the Sullivan County Railroad. The Northern, which held the road's bonds, remained in control and continued to lease the road to the Vermont Central—which itself suffered financial reversals and was reorganized as the Central Vermont (CV) in 1872.

In October 1880 the status quo was shaken when the Northern suddenly sold its interest in the Sullivan County to the VV, the twenty-four-mile road connecting Brattleboro and Bellows Falls. The majority of VV stock was held by the Connecticut River and B&M Railroads. The Northern calculated that the Sullivan County, in the hands of VV interests, would pose no more threat to its east-west traffic than the CV had and would be a stronger road for building north-south traffic. By its purchase of the Sullivan County, the VV hoped "to improve its connections in the Connecticut River Line" (VV Annual Reports).

At the time it acquired the Sullivan County, the VV was already being run by the Connecticut River Railroad (CRRR) under an 1877 fifty-year operating agreement, and this agreement was quickly expanded to include the Sullivan County effective June 1, 1881. Thus, under the operating agreement, the CRRR had gained access to forty-nine miles of road from Brattleboro north to Windsor, Vermont.

The CV, humiliated by the Northern's sale of the Sullivan County, expressed its displeasure by breaking away from the consortium and diverting traffic from the Great Northern Route to the Sullivan-Cheshire-Fitchburg

Route for a short period from late 1880 into early 1881. The surge in traffic was apparently first felt December 27, 1880, when it was reported:

> . . . about 200 cars of freight were suddenly thrown into Bellows Falls (by the CV) for transportation over the Cheshire line, and this continued at a rate of about 100 cars a day more than usual through the week. The number of freight trains had to be at once doubled. . . . On Sunday fifteen engines were out with trains, all running entirely by telegraph. . . . It would have been impossible to have done this work without the aid of the telegraph and a perfect system of rules (*Sentinel* Jan. 6, 1880).

The CV also went a step further and actually threatened to build a proprietary line that would circumvent both the Northern and the Concord Railroads. This was essentially a revival of the Windsor and Forest Line Railroad, chartered in 1870 to do the same thing but never built. As now projected, this line would start at Windsor, run south about seven miles along the west bank of the river to Ascutneyville, where it would cross the river and continue southeastward about forty-four miles through Claremont, Unity, Lempster, Marlow, Stoddard, and Antrim to a connection with the Boston and Lowell at Hancock Junction.

By early March 1881 the tempest had cooled. A new contract was negotiated securing the CV trackage rights over the Sullivan County and the CV rejoined the consortium. Talk of a new line ended and things settled back to the way they were before the diversion. In hindsight, had the so-called Forest Line ever been built, it would have achieved little beyond creating another redundant line with which future railroad managements would have had to struggle. Whether this plan was really serious or all bluff remains a subject of some mystery to this day.

In addition to provoking the dust-up between the Northern and the CV, the Northern's sale of the Sullivan County to the VV had another, longer lasting consequence. It set up the makings of an unusual

Sullivan County Atlantic (4-4-0) 9 down the valley at Springfield, MA, ca. 1915. In 1926 this unit was renumbered 3240 in the B&M system and served the road until it was scrapped in April 1946. Photogr. unknown; Brent S. Michiels coll.

arrangement on the seventy-four miles of the Connecticut River Route between East Northfield, Massachusetts, and White River Junction, Vermont, where different sections were owned or controlled by two companies—the CRRR and the CV—each with operating rights over the other's segments. The CRRR (and successor B&M) controlled forty-nine miles from Brattleboro to Windsor, the CV eleven miles from East Northfield to Brattleboro and fourteen miles from Windsor to White River Junction. This division of the pie would last until 1988. We will have more to say about this in Chapter 14.

On January 1, 1893, the B&M leased the CRRR for ninety-nine years, and in 1912 the VV was acquired outright by the CRRR. Later, in the B&M's 1919 Plan of Reorganization, the CRRR was finally consolidated into the B&M (Bradlee 1921; Frye 1997–2000)—and the VV/Sullivan County Operating Agreement came along with the deal.

In its detail the VV/Sullivan County Operating Agreement was unusual in that the roads' corporate identities were not submerged. While the lessees furnished

and operated the roads, all equipment was recorded as VV or Sullivan County property and marked as such. Boxcar numbers 500–789, for example, were nominally reserved for the Sullivan County (B&M Car Service Dept. 1909) and in the B&M's 1911 engine-renumbering scheme, Sullivan County engines were separately numbered (1–13). The lessees had to provide accounting and appropriate division of revenues among the companies. The roads all operated as one system, but in the back offices accountants were kept busy for many years.

A new operating agreement went into effect April 30, 1926. VV and Sullivan County markings and locomotive numbers were converted into the B&M system in early 1926 (Frye 1982). At the B&M's 1930 annual meeting, "shareholders authorized the consolidation of the VV and Sullivan County Railroads with the B&M" (EM May 30, 17). For some arcane reason this did not happen. Shareholders again approved consolidation of the two roads at the 1949 annual meeting and such was finally completed by the end of 1949. Perhaps to explain why the transaction was never a high priority, the company stated that while corporate simplification was achieved,

This is the Sullivan County Railroad's iron lattice truss bridge at the Connecticut River Dam that was erected in 1882, replacing the road's original wooden bridge, N. Walpole, NH, 1890. Across the river in Bellows Falls, note to the left of the white buildings, the Rutland's canal bridge, a boxed pony truss bridge that was in use here at the time. It was replaced by a steel truss bridge around the turn of the century. J. A. French photo; Hist. Soc. Cheshire Cty.

This is the same bridge, now looking from Bellows Falls toward N. Walpole, with the Fall Mountain Range beyond. The Rutland's tracks pass in the foreground; Bellows Falls Union Station is to the right. 1890–1910. Rockingham Public Library's Catalogued Photograph Coll.

financially it merely changed the payment of principal and interest on VV bonds due in 1955 from an indirect to a direct obligation (B&M Annual Report 1949).

The Sullivan was built with fifty-six- to seventy-five-pound iron rail. When the CRRR assumed operation of the road in 1881, it immediately set about upgrading the road from iron to steel rail, which work was completed in 1884. In 1882 it replaced the Sullivan's original wooden bridge over the Connecticut River with an iron lattice truss bridge. The Sullivan County had 8.68 miles of second main by the time the B&M took control in 1893, and 17.4 miles by 1904. In the B&M era, the bridge was replaced yet again—this time by a steel truss bridge—in 1911–1912. The northern approach to the bridge and significant sections of the Mountain Track were lost in the great flood of November 3–4, 1927. The Mountain

Mountain Track washout at the Rte. 12 entrance to Fitchburg Yard, N. Walpole, Nov. 4, 1927. Postcard; Brent S. Michiels coll.

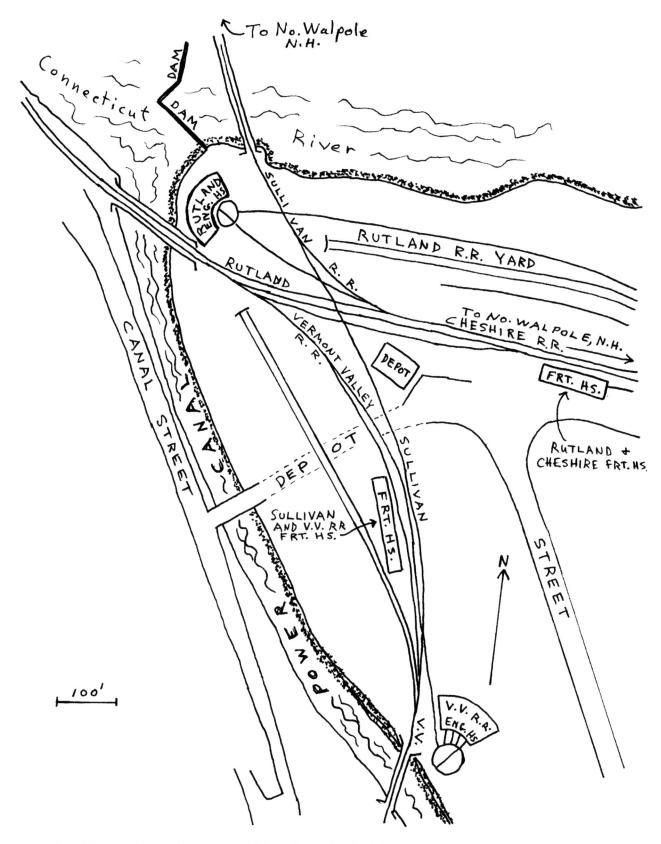

General track layout on the northwestern part of the Bellows Falls Island showing interconnections among the Sullivan, Vermont Valley, Cheshire, and Rutland Railroads, 1885.

Track, however, was quickly restored and served as a detour route to reach Bellows Falls via the Fitchburg Yard.

In its early years, the Sullivan's general offices were in Charlestown. The road had an engine house and a repair shop located on the west side of the tracks just south of the Charlestown station. The Sullivan and the Cheshire had small side-by-side roundhouses with a shared turntable where the two roads connected in North Walpole. In Bellows Falls, Sullivan power turned on the turntable at the VV Enginehouse and Repair Shops, which were located on the Island east of the tracks just north of the Canal Bridge. After the CRRR assumed operation of the VV and the Sullivan County in 1881 and, certainly, after the CRRR came under B&M control in 1893, the roads—by sharing equipment and running through on each other's tracks— had less and less need for turning facilities in Bellows Falls. Then, after the B&M took control of the Fitchburg in 1900, it gained access to the engine facilities and turntable in North Walpole and the VV facilities became totally redundant. As of 1898, a B&M turntable roster still showed the five-pit VV turntable in Bellows Falls (Walker 1987), but it disappeared sometime in 1902–1906 (Sanborn Insurance maps). The B&M replaced the old facilities at North Walpole with a new five-stall, brick roundhouse in 1917.

The section of the Island on the west side of the tracks between the VV's Canal Bridge and the Rutland's Canal Bridge (today's Island Park) was entirely occupied by a freight yard shared by the VV and Sullivan County roads. A freight house jointly owned by the two roads was located approximately where the Waypoint Visitors Center is found today. Before 1900, Depot Street did not cut through this yard area. The B&M enlarged the freight house after 1893 and it stood until about 1975 when it was burned by the Bellows Falls Fire Department.

As an originated commodity, pulpwood was an early mainstay on the Sullivan County, just as granite was on the Cheshire. From about 1880 into the early years of the twentieth century, the Sullivan County benefited from the big business of log driving on the river. The log drives could not pass the dam in North Walpole and booms of logs collected above the dam. A spur was built from the Sullivan County's main line in North Walpole to an International Paper Company (IP) log yard along the river—essentially a river-to-rail intermodal facility—where pulpwood logs were loaded onto IP flatcars and taken to the company's mill on the Bellows Falls Island. The last of the really big, long, log drives occurred in 1915. The IP mill closed and regular pulpwood drives as far south as North Walpole ended completely in 1921. IP was reportedly in the process of selling the log yard in April 1922 (*Times* April 20, 1922, 1; David Deacon, pers. comm., Nov. 13, 2014). Nimke (1991) states that the former IP log yard spur was abandoned in 1944–1946.

Pulpwood logs are being loaded at International Paper's skid-way ramp on the riverfront in N. Walpole. Look closely and you will see some horses' legs at the far end of the car. Horses were used to move pulpwood cars around the yard and spot them at the loading ramp. The Sullivan County would later pick up and move cuts of cars across the river to IP's siding south of the Bellows Falls Tunnel, ca. 1890–1900. Photogr. unknown; photo courtesy *The Vermont Journal/The Shopper.*

In the first half of the twentieth century the Conn River Yard was a busy place. Different consignees came and left over the years. As late as the early 1960s, active consignees still included Connelly Fuels, Cray Oil, Standard Oil of New Jersey, Kerr-McGee (chemicals), the Green Company (wooden boxes), United-Murray Heel Co. (shoe heels), Vermont Packing Co., and Checkerboard Feeds (Whitney 2017). From 1923 to 1955, the Whiting Milk Company operated a creamery on a siding off the Mountain Track, about midway between the Conn River and Fitchburg Yards, where it received and shipped milk (Frizzell 1963, 413).

The short section of the B&M's Connecticut River Route Main Line through North Walpole was always the busiest road in Cheshire County and an excellent place for train watching. For many years, the B&M typically operated two through freights in each direction daily between Springfield and White River Junction. These trains carried not only Canadian traffic, but also paper mill traffic for Berlin and Groveton, New Hampshire.

In addition to the B&M's through freights, the CV, exercising its trackage rights between Brattleboro and Windsor, ran two (sometimes three) through freights daily in both directions in the steam era and beyond into the mid-1960s. The best known of these trains were 430/429 and 490/491, the former often called the *Newsboy* because it carried, among other commodities, newsprint for the *New York Times*. With diesels able to handle heavier trains just by adding extra units as required, the CV combined their freights into Trains 444/447, a daily train in each direction.

In 1970, after a long period of declining business and the insidious effects of deferred maintenance, the B&M entered its second bankruptcy. In the mid-1970s, seeking to reduce costs, the B&M and its interchange partners Canadian Pacific and Central Vermont began the practice of pooling their trains and power. Two through trains—now pool trains—continued to run each way daily. SPCP/CPSP were joint B&M-Canadian Pacific trains between Springfield and Newport, Vermont. SPCV/CVSP were joint B&M-Central Vermont trains between Springfield and St. Albans, Vermont. In the particular case of the Central Vermont, pooling with the B&M to Springfield was forced after newly-formed Conrail refused to interchange with the CV at its traditional Palmer connection. In both cases, the time and expense of changing power and rearranging trains at White River Junction was eliminated.

Of particular interest to train watchers were the power lash-ups on SPCV and CVSP, which varied from day to day and could include all B&M, all CV, or mixed power. Engines from CV sister roads Grand Trunk Western and the Duluth, Winnipeg and Pacific Railroads, as well as from parent Canadian National Railway (CN) could appear in the mix at any time.

Train 42, White River Jct.-to-Springfield, Engine 619, piled up at 3:30 p.m. June 15, 1905, at Chapins in N. Walpole Yard, injuring the engineer and fireman. Note VV's side-door buggy at right. Hist. Soc. Cheshire Cty.

With three balls on the mast, northbound B&M Santa Fe (2-10-2) 2904 shows her stuff at the Bellows Falls diamond, Jan. 5, 1941. The station is obscured behind the engine, the edge of the Rutland's turntable pit visible at lower right. Photogr. unknown; S. J. Whitney coll.

Central Vermont 2-10-4 701 on the B&M main line in N. Walpole, June 10, 1950. Dwight A. Smith photo.

RS2 1502 is carrying New Haven coaches this day on a southbound Connecticut River passenger train. It has just crossed the river and is passing the Rutland's water tank on its approach to Bellows Falls station, ca. 1950. Herman Shaner photo; S. J. Whitney coll.

Blocking Depot St., E7 3800 is stopped at the Bellows Falls station with Train 77/*Day White Mountains*. At right is the joint B&M/Rutland freight house, ca. 1951. Nash-Ludlow photo; S. J. Whitney coll.

Uh oh, here comes the boss! EMD FT 4208, lead unit on a Springfield-bound through freight, has plowed into the rear of a White River Jct.–East Deerfield local, derailing itself and demolishing the wooden caboose. Luckily, when the FT hit, the rear-end crew was on the ground setting off a car. Dense early morning fog, an often-remarked hazard on the Connecticut River line, was blamed for this mishap on the southbound track in N. Walpole, Sept. 19, 1951. Photo reprinted with permission of the *Brattleboro Reformer*.

F2 4224A is paused at the Depot St. crossing just south of the station. Bellows Falls, ca. 1955. Photogr. unknown; S. J. Whitney coll.

In steam's final days in the Monadnock Region, CV 2-10-4 707 with CV Train 430, a through freight Montreal–New London, CT, approaches N. Walpole, where it will cross the Connecticut River to Bellows Falls, Jan. or Feb. 1957. Dwight A. Smith photo.

F2 4226A/B stands on the diamonds at Bellows Falls while making its station stop with the *Ambassador*. Note the joint B&M/Rutland freight house at right and the ball signal and its tender's shanty at center, ca. 1960. B&MRRHS Archives.

RS3 1540 and the buggy is all JE-2, the White River Jct.–E. Deerfield local, amounted to this day at N. Walpole, 1965. Traffic had dwindled and the EJ-1/JE-2 jobs were abolished in Oct. 1966. Note the three-color light signal in this image. CTC was installed in sections on the Connecticut River line in 1963–1965 and reached north as far as Windsor, VT in 1964 (R. Miller, pers. comm.). Now with CTC in place, the main line between Bellows Falls and Claremont was single-tracked in 1965. Dwight A. Smith photo.

The operator hoops up orders to the fireman on southbound F3 4228A. The work train at right, in town this day to remove the ball signal, has completed the task, mid-1960s. Photogr. unknown; S. J. Whitney coll.

F7 4265A on a northbound freight, Bellows Falls, mid-1960s. Photogr. unknown; S. J. Whitney coll.

Springfield to St. Albans pool Train SPCV, this day led by a GTW GP7 with two trailing CV "geeps," is just north of the Charlestown line, ca. 1977. Frederick G. Bailey photo.

The more recent history of the Connecticut River line is a complicated mix of turmoil and change. On June 30, 1983, the B&M was purchased out of bankruptcy by Guilford Transportation Industries. Guilford, which had earlier acquired the Maine Central Railroad in 1981 and would acquire the Delaware & Hudson Railroad in January 1984, swept all three railroads into its Guilford Rail Systems unit. Soon after acquiring the Delaware & Hudson, Guilford chose to shift most of the Canadian through traffic, which had remained a mainstay of the Connecticut River Route, to the Delaware & Hudson's Montreal Route in eastern New York.

Thus downgraded, the Connecticut River Route fell upon hard times. The B&M-CP pool trains were terminated in early 1984, followed by the B&M-CV pool trains in 1985. Local freight business was in serious decline. Guilford strikes in 1986 and 1988 forced many of the road's remaining customers to shift to trucks or go out of business. Nimke (1991) notes that Twin States Fertilizer was the only remaining consignee at North Walpole in 1991.

Train CPSP, with pooled Canadian Pacific and B&M power, passes through N. Walpole, March 1983. Soon, through Canadian traffic would be shifted to the Delaware & Hudson in eastern New York and the era of pool trains on the Connecticut River Route would be over. Frederick G. Bailey photo.

GP40 362 on Guilford local WJED at N. Walpole, 1990. By the late 1980s, B&M (now Guilford Rail Systems) service on the Connecticut River line had dwindled to the extent that just a single GP40 could handle the occasional trip from E. Deerfield to White River Jct. and return to service remaining consignees. Frederick G. Bailey photo.

After the end of pool service in 1985, the CV continued to operate its through freights 444/447 between St. Albans and either Brattleboro or Palmer, MA. In 1992, parent CN replaced 444/447 with trains 324/323, all-CN through freights between Montreal and Brattleboro, using all CN power. In late 1993 Train 324's run was extended to Palmer when the CN began routing intermodal traffic to the Massachusetts Central Railroad.

Three big Canadian National GP40-2LWs led by the 9414 on Train 324 en route to Brattleboro are caught at N. Walpole, 1992. Frederick G. Bailey photo.

(opposite page) This image of a three-way meet at Bellows Falls fairly encapsulates railroading in the old river town in the early 1990s. Guilford GP40 350 is standing on the Green Mountain main line just north of the Canal Bridge with EDWJ. Having completed its interchange with the Green Mountain, it is waiting for a southbound CV work train on the Connecticut River main line to leave town so that it can back off the Green Mountain and continue its northward trip to White River Jct. Meanwhile, Green Mountain XR-1, the Bellows Falls-to-Rutland freight, is waiting to depart for Rutland, but cannot move until EDWJ is out of the way. Frederick G. Bailey photo.

The CV, which had operated Amtrak's *Montrealer* from its inception September 29, 1972, was forced to suspend the train in April 1987 due to deteriorated track conditions between Brattleboro and Windsor. In 1988, the ICC stepped in and ordered Guilford to sell its B&M line between Brattleboro and Windsor to Amtrak, which immediately resold it to the CV. After years of shared ownership, the Connecticut River main line between East Northfield, Massachusetts, and White River Junction was now completely in the hands of the CV. The ICC granted Guilford trackage rights over the line to service their remaining customers and to solicit new business under certain conditions. After making urgent track improvements, the *Montrealer* was reintroduced in 1989, only to be eliminated April 1, 1995 due to budget cuts. The very next day, the popular train was replaced by the *Vermonter*, a state-subsidized Amtrak train that ran only as far as St. Albans and which has continued to operate to the present.

Amtrak 156, dressed in a special fortieth-anniversary livery, southbound on the Connecticut River Route with Train 55/*Vermonter*, Charlestown, NH, just above Walpole, Aug. 2012. Frederick G. Bailey photo.

Amtrak 103 with Train 55/*Vermonter* at Chapins, N. Walpole, Jan. 2013. Frederick G. Bailey photo.

New England Central 9534 on Train 323 meets Guilford 369 on WJED, N. Walpole, 1995. Frederick G. Bailey photo.

Meanwhile, in 1994 parent Canadian National sold the CV to portfolio railroad operator Railtex, Inc., which renamed the road the "New England Central Railroad" and commenced operations February 4, 1995. Railtex, Inc. was sold and merged into RailAmerica, Inc. in 2000. The assets of RailAmerica, Inc. were in turn purchased by Genessee & Wyoming, Inc. in 2012. Throughout all these changes in ownership, the New England Central name has been retained, and operations continue today.

Over the years, the Boston & Maine (and successors Guilford and Pan Am Southern) had usually interchanged traffic with the Rutland Railway (and its successor Green Mountain Railroad) on what is called "the Patch Track" north of the Rutland's Canal Bridge in Bellows Falls. The Central Vermont never interchanged

traffic with the Rutland in Bellows Falls. However, after its purchase of the line between Brattleboro and Windsor from Amtrak in 1988, the CV began interchanging traffic with the Green Mountain in the Conn River Yard in N. Walpole in 1990, and Green Mountain trains began making regular interchange moves between Bellows Falls and the Conn River Yard. CV successor New England Central has continued to interchange traffic with the Green Mountain/Vermont Railway, alternatively using either "the Patch Track" or the Conn River Yard.

Green Mountain GP9 1850 passes the iconic Saint Peter's Catholic Church at Chapins in N. Walpole, May 1990. The church, built in 1877, has graced many railroad photos taken at this location over the years. Frederick G. Bailey photo.

CV 5809 meets Green Mountain RS1 405 switching interchange in the Conn River Yard, N. Walpole, July 1990. Frederick G. Bailey photo.

Guilford EDWJ meets Green Mountain GP9 1850 interchanging CV traffic in the Conn River Yard, N. Walpole, ca. 1990. Frederick G. Bailey photo.

Green Mountain GP9 803 switching Conn River Yard, N. Walpole, March 1999. Frederick G. Bailey photo.

Green Mountain GP40-2 305 is on the Connecticut River main line, backing a train over the Bellows Falls diamond and across the river to the Conn River Yard for interchange with the New England Central, March 2001. B. G. Blodget photo.

Guilford made little use of its trackage rights over the road to White River Junction from 1990 to 2010. In 2006, Guilford Rail Systems renamed itself Pan Am Railways. In 2008, Pan Am Southern, LLC, a 50-50 joint venture of Norfolk Southern Railway and Pan Am Railways was created to own and operate the 155-mile former B&M Fitchburg Route Main Line between Ayer, Massachusetts, and Mechanicville, New York, along with certain other lines and trackage rights, including the Connecticut River main line from Springfield to White River Junction.

Now making a light move back to Bellows Falls, the 305 approaches the Connecticut River Bridge in N. Walpole, March 2001. B. G. Blodget photo.

CHAPTER NINE

THE ASHUELOT RAILROAD: THE VALLEY ROUTE TO KEENE

East Northfield, Massachusetts (MP S49.67) to Keene, New Hampshire (MP S73.70)

A four-car, Keene-bound passenger train works its way up the beautiful Ashuelot Valley in the glory days of steam. The river lies shrouded in forest between the railroad track and the highway. The train has passed the paper mills and will soon make its station stop at Ashuelot, a village of Winchester, NH, ca. 1912. Postcard; B. G. Blodget coll.

The Independent Years, 1849–1890

Chartered under several acts of the New Hampshire Legislature (Dec. 27, 1844; July 10, 1846; and June 21 and 23, 1848) to build between Keene, New Hampshire, and South Vernon, Vermont, the Ashuelot Railroad Company, with the backing of the Connecticut River Railroad (CRRR), built its line up the Ashuelot River Valley in 1849–1850.

The Ashuelot Railroad (Ashuelot) crossed the Connecticut River from Hinsdale, New Hampshire, to South Vernon where the company hoped to secure trackage rights southward over the Vermont and Massachu-

setts Railroad (V&M) to West Northfield, Massachusetts where it would connect with the CRRR line from Springfield, Massachusetts. When Fitchburg Railroad interests objected to this plan, the Ashuelot built a half-mile parallel line to West Northfield, where it crossed the V&M and connected with the CRRR. The Ashuelot was thus technically—albeit barely—a three-state road.

On the New Hampshire side of the Connecticut River, the Ashuelot—surrounded much of its length by very hilly terrain—closely followed its namesake river up the valley to Keene. It was by far the easiest rail route

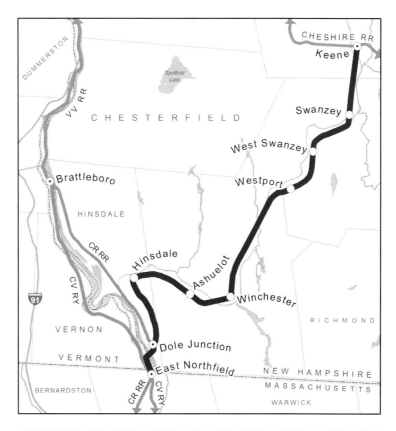

Springfield, Mass.	---	00.00
East Northfield, Mass. (*CV, CRRR*)	00.00	49.67
South Vernon, Vt.	---	49.97
East Northfield Bridge*	---	50.52
Doolittle, N.H.	---	50.87
Dole Jct.	2.28	51.90
Hinsdale	4.91	54.40
Cornville (Ashuelot Paper)*	7.28	---
Ashuelot	8.41	58.00
Winchester	10.60	60.20
Forest Lake	12.69	---
Westport	15.99	65.60
West Swanzey	18.53	68.20
Swanzey	20.73	70.40
Keene (*Jct. Cheshire, M&K*)	24.03	73.70
Joslin[1]	26.09	---

Mileage table for the Ashuelot Railroad, East Northfield, Mass. to Keene, N.H., showing stations and locations, junctions with other railroads, original distances from East Northfield and distances from Springfield, Mass. (Fitchburg Div., Ashuelot Branch, *B&M ETT No. 1*, April 29, 1928). On the Ashuelot, trains moving away from Springfield/Dole Jct. are northward/outward trains; Trains moving toward Dole Jct./Springfield are southward/inward trains. Stations are a compilation from various sources and not all were active in any given year.
[1]Became an Ashuelot Branch station after the Cheshire Branch east of Joslin was abandoned in 1972.
*Not a passenger station stop.

The Ashuelot's original Connecticut River bridge—perhaps best described as an upside-down covered bridge—was built in 1850. Trains ran along an open deck atop the structure, while the trusswork beneath was enclosed to protect it from the weather. Doors at each end and a walkway through the inside allowed access for inspection and maintenance. Using the same piers, the bridge was ironized in 1889 and it was replaced by a completely new bridge in 1929–1930. Richard Sanders Allen Coll., National Society for the Preservation of Covered Bridges Archives.

in or out of Keene. The Ashuelot River Valley below Keene lent itself to being harnessed for waterpower, and mills of every name and nature flourished up and down the valley in the nineteenth and early twentieth centuries. Paper, textiles, and woodenware were the major industries. The Ashuelot, for most of its existence, was a prosperous industrial switching road. It was the second road to reach Keene and would be the last to be abandoned.

As originally built, the Ashuelot was a twenty-four-mile, single iron road with 1.57 miles of passing sidings. Track structure consisted of fifty-eight-pound iron rail laid on gravel ballast. The maximum grade, between Hinsdale and Ashuelot, was 34.5 feet per mile (0.65 percent) and 3,712.5 feet or 0.70 miles in length. The average grade was eighteen feet per mile (0.34 percent), the total rise and fall in the road 429 feet. Curves totaled approximately eight miles, straight line sixteen miles. There were nineteen grade crossings. Wooden truss bridges totaled 1,223 feet, other wooden bridges 321 feet. Among the bridges were four over the Ashuelot River and one over the Connecticut River. The Ashuelot was never signalized and was train order territory its entire life. The total cost of construction was $506,000.

The Ashuelot's largest bridge, one of impressive magnitude in its day, was a single-track bridge that crossed the Connecticut River between South Vernon, Vermont, and Hinsdale, New Hampshire (S50.52). You hear this bridge referred to as either the Ashuelot, South Vernon, or East Northfield Bridge. For consistency, we will use the latter name. A timber truss bridge, it was constructed upon masonry piers resting on timber cribs with a deck height above the river bed of forty-six feet. There were four spans of approximately 150 feet each and two approach spans of about forty feet each, for a total length of 680 feet (*EM* Aug29, 3–4). This bridge was an important gateway into the Monadnock Region from the south and west.

The first trains were run December 9, 1850, and the road opened for business in January 1851 under lease to the CRRR for ten years. Rent was fixed at $30,000 per year. Since the Vermont Valley Railroad (VV) did not open between Brattleboro and Bellows Falls until the end of 1851, the CRRR briefly used the Ashuelot as part of a roundabout route from Springfield, Massachusetts to Bellows Falls, Vermont. After the opening of the VV, the CRRR's interest in the Ashuelot diminished and it allowed its lease to run out in 1860. The lease was then picked up by the Cheshire Railroad. In the 1870s, Ashuelot shareholders sued the Cheshire for unsatisfactory performance and embarked on a long struggle to regain control of their road.

In the meantime, by 1876 it had become apparent that the Manchester and Keene Railroad (M&K)—potentially a strategically important route to invade the Queen City and the industrial Merrimack Valley—was, after many difficulties, actually going to be completed. A. B. Harris, a twenty-four-year-old insightful investor, the son of CRRR president Daniel L. Harris, now entered the picture. During the latter part of 1876 and early in 1877, Harris—bankrolled by his father and Chester W. Chapin, president of the Boston & Albany Railroad—quietly bought up a majority of the Ashuelot's stock. General Superintendent H. E. Folsom described what happened next:

> On April 1st, 1877, John Mulligan, then Superintendent of the CRRR, without notice to and without the knowledge of the lessee, took possession of the Ashuelot Railroad with a Connecticut River engine and car, following the Cheshire Road's forenoon train from South Vernon to Keene, leaving South Vernon as soon as the regular train was out of sight. Mulligan stopped at all stations and where trackmen or other workmen were found, explaining that the Connecticut River had bought the Ashuelot Road and was taking possession—but that all of them would be retained in their places. He instructed stunned agents to make remittances

to Seth Hunt, treasurer at Springfield, and send all accounts and statements to Springfield, disregarding all instructions from the Cheshire. Upon arrival at Keene, Mulligan telegraphed the President of the Cheshire Railroad of the change in ownership of the stock and of the taking possession of the Ashuelot Railroad and its entire property (*EM* Oct24, 6).

While the Cheshire's operations on the Ashuelot came to an abrupt end, at least no shots were fired! The Cheshire made little effort to retain its lease and on April 20, 1877, the court, bringing an end to years of litigation, ruled that the Ashuelot shareholders could regain possession of their road. Shortly thereafter, the Ashuelot leased the road to the CRRR with terms specifying the lessees would operate the road under the management of the lessors (Indenture dated July 17, 1877). The Ashuelot now became the CRRR's Ashuelot Division.

In 1874 the Ashuelot Railroad Co., seeking additional room for expansion in Keene, purchased the Dr. George B. Twitchell house on Main Street and moved it to the rear of 96 Main Street on what is now called Cypress Court. On June 7, 1877, the *Sentinel* reported that the Dr. Twitchell House would be razed to make way for a brick passenger station to be shared by the M&K and Ashuelot roads. This station was never built as the railroads later arranged with the Cheshire for the use of their station. The Twitchell House was spared the wrecking ball and leased to other businesses (B&M Valuation Survey 1914, sec. 39.1).

The CRRR was clearly anxious to link up with the M&K. It had provided the M&K with a locomotive during its construction and subsequently agreed to lease the road from February 1879 through the fall of 1881. However, in 1880 the M&K entered receivership and a consortium consisting of the Boston & Lowell and Concord Railroads purchased the road at a bankruptcy sale held in the Cheshire House, Keene, on October 26, 1881, forever quashing the possibility it could be appropriated by a foreign road to invade the Merrimack Valley.

In the 1880s the Ashuelot and its lessee CRRR undertook a number of improvements. From the road's beginning, its terminal facilities at Keene consisted of only a three-stall engine house between the east and west legs of the wye (Sanborn map 1884). For turning its engines, we believe the road must have had an arrangement with the Cheshire for the use of their wye or turntable. However, in 1884 the Ashuelot installed its own turntable, followed by a three-stall roundhouse and freight house in 1885 on the four-acre site once occupied by the Twitchell House on Main Street. By 1887 the CRRR had converted most of its stove-heated coaches to be heated by steam from the locomotive. A major safety advance, it was

The newly-built Ashuelot and CRRR freight house, Keene, ca. 1885. Hist. Soc. Cheshire Cty.

the first road running into Keene to use this type of heating (*Sentinel* Oct. 17, 1888). In 1889 the road replaced the timber trusses on the East Northfield Bridge with deck iron trusses that raised the deck height from forty-six to seventy-one feet above the river bed (*EM* Aug29, 3–4). By the end of 1889, all the Ashuelot's original wooden bridges had been ironized (*Sentinel* Oct. 2, 1889).

As an independent company, the Ashuelot was always a leased road—at different times to either the CRRR (1851–1860; 1877–1890) or the Cheshire (1860–1877). The lessees always furnished the road with their own engines and equipment, which never wore the Ashuelot name. If you bought a ticket, however, you would see it was issued by the Ashuelot Railroad. On February 6, 1890, the CRRR absorbed the Ashuelot by merger, ending its forty-one-year run as an independent road.

Brand-new CRRR 9, a Schenectady-built 4-4-0, poses in the Ashuelot/CRRR Yard in Keene, 1890. Hist. Soc. Cheshire Cty.

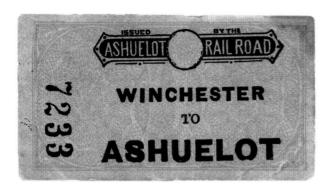

An Ashuelot ticket issued March 31, 1888. Brent S. Michiels coll.

After its absorption of the Ashuelot, the CRRR now owned a seventy-four-mile through line from Springfield to Keene. This attracted the eye of J. Pierpont Morgan's New York, New Haven and Hartford Railroad (New Haven), whose tracks extended up the Connecticut Valley as far as Springfield, Massachusetts. Seeing an opportunity to extend its reach up the valley into New England's northwest and a connection with the Vermont roads, as well as to tap into southern New Hampshire, the New Haven executed a lease with the directors of the CRRR in 1892 that was to take effect January 1, 1893. But, surprise! In a stunning *coup de majeur*, the road was leased instead to the Boston and Maine Railroad (B&M), at the time presided over by A. Archibald McLeod. While the

New Haven management, confident of routine approval by shareholders, had rested unsuspicious, McLeod had quietly secured a controlling stock interest in the CRRR and the road was leased to the B&M (Baker 1937, 173; Kirkland, 1948, 2, 28–30).

Even though McLeod's presidency was extremely short—lasting less than a year—it was historically very important. In addition to securing control of the CRRR for the B&M, it was also during his tenure—on March 6, 1893—that the New Haven and B&M reached a milestone agreement in which the two systems would divide New England on a line roughly following the Boston & Albany main line. In the future neither road would enter upon or oppose acquisitions in the other's territory (Kirkland 1948, 2, 31). When expedient, this arrangement worked pretty well, but, as we shall see in Chapter 14, it did not always work perfectly.

The Boston & Maine Years, 1893–1984

After the B&M seized the CRRR in 1893, the Ashuelot Branch together with the M&K, formed a through route between East Northfield and Nashua. This route for a time achieved some importance as a secondary east-west line, but in the end would not prove competitive with the road's Fitchburg Route Main Line to the south. In the B&M years, the Ashuelot was successively included in the

B&M trackage east of Main St., Keene, showing the approach to the Ashuelot turntable and roundhouse. In the days when the building was used by the railroad, it was accessed from the east side (rear), no doubt to avoid blocking Main St. Notations on this B&M track diagram indicate the turntable is gone and the 231-foot turntable lead was removed on May 25, 1918. Note there were four tracks across Main St. at this time. The Ashuelot Branch crossed Main St. on the southern-most track, the Cheshire Branch on the northern three tracks. June 1918.

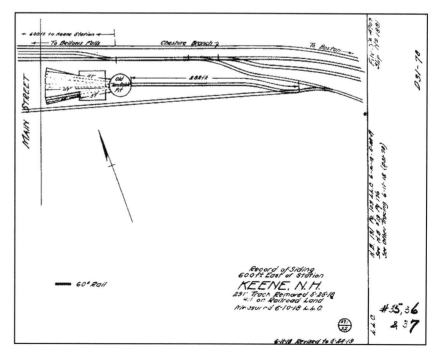

The New Cheshire Garage was an early tenant in the old Ashue-lot roundhouse at 82 Main St. Photogr. unknown; Sect. 39.1, B&M Valuation Survey, 1914; Benjamin Campbell coll.

Connecticut and Passumpsic Division (1893–1917), the Connecticut River Division (1917–1930), the Fitchburg Division (1930–1971), the Boston Division (1971–1974), and the New England Division (1974–1983).

As we discussed in Chapter 2, the Fitchburg had undertaken its expansion and modernization of the Keene Shops in 1895, making them the road's largest locomotive repair shops. After the B&M acquired the Fitchburg in 1900, the Keene Shops and roundhouse facilities came with the deal. The small "Main Street Roundhouse" that the Ashuelot had built in 1884–1885 immediately became redundant and was soon phased out and closed. In 1915–1934, the B&M rented the building as an automobile dealership and garage—initially to A. Gibson Smith, later to Perley Safford. A B&M crew came out from Fitchburg and razed the structure in 1943 (*EM* Win43, 35).

The East Northfield Bridge became a maintenance headache for the B&M. It was discovered that the concrete piers near the Vermont side of the river were subject to deep scouring action that exposed an underlying stratum of blue clay and silt. Over the years, settlement and slippage took place and repairs and extra protective measures were taken to strengthen the bridge.

In 1912–1913 the B&M built a new section of its Connecticut River Route Main Line on the New Hampshire side of the river between East Northfield and Brattleboro (see Chapter 14). The first two miles of the Ashuelot Branch—including the East Northfield Bridge—were appropriated, upgraded, and block-signalized as a part of the new main line. The Ashuelot Branch, now shortened about two miles, left the new main line at a location named Dole Junction, New Hampshire. Track structure on the branch between Dole Junction and Keene was upgraded by 1930 to mostly 100-pound with some 115-pound steel rail. However, the branch was never equipped with block signals.

Passenger Service. Early images of passenger trains on the Ashuelot show that trains usually consisted of the standard power of the day—an American-type engine—with a combine and one to three coaches. Power was turned on a turntable at East Northfield and was either wyed or turned on the turntable at the Keene roundhouse.

On June 20, 1910, during a period of notably strong New Haven influence, the *Keene Express*, a joint B&M/ New Haven through train service between Keene and New York began running (*Sentinel* April 19, 1910). Operating daily except Sundays, Train 38 departed Keene at 2:20 p.m. and arrived New York at 9:00 p.m., while Train 29 left New York at 11:00 a.m. and arrived Keene at 5:00 p.m. In some years Train 14, a morning train departing Keene at 7:25 a.m., ran as the *Keene Express*. Despite the train's name, it made all station and flag stops along the Ashuelot Branch. In addition to its through coaches, the trains also carried a through Pullman buffet parlor car. The *Keene Express* trains were discontinued when wartime nationalization began in 1918.

We know the Ashuelot was not among the early routes considered for a gas-electric rail motorcar or "doodlebug" (*EM* Jun26, 9 and Sep26, 3), but traditional steam power had in fact been replaced by a doodlebug by the early 1930s. The doodlebugs were bidirectional (with operating controls at both ends) and were really predecessors of the rail diesel car. The cars were operated by a three-man crew: engineer, conductor, and brakeman/flagman. People who remember them say you could always hear the doodlebugs coming as they made a distinctive sound that was audible in the distance. In the late 1930s, upon abandonment of a number of its low-density branch lines, the B&M began disposing of its rail motorcars. After World War II only eleven cars remained.

St. Louis Car/EMC gas-electric 150 on the east leg of the wye leaving Keene for E. Northfield, ca. 1930–1933. This is the earliest image we could find of a doodlebug running on the Ashuelot. Purchased in 1926, the 150 and sisters 151–152, were the first true gas-electrics on the B&M. Cutler Studios photo; B&MRRHS Archives.

Same car, now numbered 1150, pulled up to the station at E. Northfield, Nov. 11, 1937. All the B&M's fleet of twenty-four doodlebugs were renumbered in 1934 by adding 1,000 to their numbers. George Melvin photo; R. R. Richards Jr. coll.

Osgood Bradley/EMC-GE rail motorcar 1181 in the station at Keene, undated. S. J. Whitney coll.

Train 7301, gas-electric rail motorcar 1196, has come up from E. Northfield and sits in the station at Keene. The 1196 (and sister 1197) were the largest (seventy-six feet) of ten Osgood Bradley/EMC-GE rail motorcars purchased by the B&M in 1926. Dwight Smith, who rode the car this day and took the picture, recalled "it was a noisy smelly ride," Oct. 21, 1950.

Miles	Rail-road	Sun P M	exSun P M	exSun A M	Sun A M	READ DOWN		READ UP	Sun A M	exSun P M	exSun P M	Sun P M
0.0	N. H.	1230	1230	445	1210	Lv New York G.C.T.....N. Y.	Ar	....	410	1005	1005
55.6	"	141	141	625	144	...Bridgeport ... ...Conn.	...	...	250	846	846
72.3	"	205	205	f655	220	....New Haven............	"	....	225	820	820
108.9	"	308	308	800	345	....Hartford	Ar	....	127	717	717
134.3	"	343	343	f842	423	Ar Springfield............Mass.	Lv	....	1255	645	645
		7055	717	73	7051				712	74	74
0.0	B&M	400	400	930	455	Lv Springfield.............Mass.	Ar	...	1230	623	623
49.7	"	534	539	1137	607	Ar East Northfield	Lv	...	1050	457	457
		7353	7305	7301	7351				7350	7300	7302	7302
49.7	"	537	552	1149	945	Lv E. NORTHFIELD ..		934	1034	444	444
51.9	"	f542	f558	f1154	f950	...Dole Jct. .. ..N. H.	...	929	1029	439	439
54.5	"	f548	604	1200	f956	.....Hinsdale............	"	f920	1020	430	f430
58.0	"	f556	612	1208	f1004	....Ashuelot	"	...f912	1012	422	f422
60.2	"	f602	618	1214	f1010	....Winchester	"	907	1007	416	f416
65.6	"	f612	f628	f1225	f1020	...Westport	"	f857	f957	f405	f405
68.2	"	f618	634	1231	f1026	...West Swanzey	"	f852	952	359	f359
70.4	"			f1236	f1031	...Swanzey	"	...	...	f353	f353
73.7	"	630	646	1245	1040	Ar KEENE..................	Lv	840	940	345	345
		P M	P M	P M	A M			A M	A M	P M	P M

Ashuelot Branch   **81**

9-28-47   XL

Ashuelot Branch passenger train service shown in the B&M PTT, Sept. 1947. For symbols, see the Cheshire Branch schedule on page 75.

Passenger traffic consisted of commuters traveling to work in the various mills in the valley, students traveling to school, and summer vacationers. During periods of heavy summertime traffic, especially when there were summer campers traveling from New York to Winchester and Keene, the doodlebug would have an extra coach attached.

At mid-century, service consisted of two daily round trips from Keene to East Northfield and return. A hostler would bring the train up from the roundhouse in the morning. After the train returned to Keene in the evening and the car was unloaded, a hostler would take the car back to the roundhouse for the night, to be serviced and refueled. Even after the Keene Shops closed in 1940, three stalls at the east end of the roundhouse remained in use: one for the doodlebug, one for the Keene Switcher, and one for a spare.

Sunday service had been reduced to just one round trip by 1949 and was eliminated altogether in 1951. The last scheduled gas-electric run over the Ashuelot happened with scant notice Saturday evening January 5, 1952, as Train 7303, doodlebug 196, returned to Keene from East Northfield. On Monday, January 7, 1952, it was replaced by a weekday-only mixed train that ran from Dole Junction out to Keene and return. A timetable for this train appeared in the *B&M PTT* through October 1958. Thereafter, for an uncertain period of time extending at least into the mid-1960s, unpublished service was provided by B&M local freight EK-1/KE-2, which was obliged to provide transportation—usually in the caboose—on the rare occasions when someone (usually a rail buff) requested such.

Freight Service. While the Cheshire was most notable as a passenger route, the Ashuelot's forte was always freight. At its very beginning before the VV was completed in 1851, the Ashuelot formed part of the through route up the Connecticut Valley. Then after the M&K opened for business in 1878, the Ashuelot interchanged east-west traffic with that road's operators—initially the CRRR (1880–1881), later the Boston and Lowell Railroad (1881–1887), and finally the B&M. As an east-west through route, the M&K/Ashuelot route was not competitive and ultimately lost out to the Fitchburg's parallel main line route to the south.

However, the Ashuelot benefited from a robust industrial customer base. B&M local freight service along the Ashuelot was handled by locals EK-1/KE-2, East Deerfield–Keene and return. However, after a sharp dropoff in freight traffic in the 1950s, the B&M began to jigger freight jobs and frequencies to more efficiently serve remaining customers. There still was important railroad business in Keene, but Keene was becoming more of an outlier on the B&M's system.

The railroad struggled to find an efficient and responsive service plan for southwestern New Hampshire.

EK-1/KE-2 were annulled in 1960 and briefly replaced, first by locals EX-1/XE-2, East Deerfield to Bellows Falls and return via Keene (using the Ashuelot and Cheshire Branches), and then by locals E9/E10, East Deerfield to Keene and Troy and return. In October 1962, EJ-1/JE-2, East Deerfield to White River Junction and return, were established (EJ-1 ran via Keene and JE-2 ran via Brattleboro on the main line). EK-1/KE-2 were reinstated and ran off-and-on as traffic conditions warranted, at times alternating as EJ-1/JE-2 three days a week.

In October 1966 freights EJ-1/JE-2 were annulled. EK-1/KE-2 were revived as a six-day job and ran as such until the East Northfield Bridge failed in June 1970. EK-1/KE-2 were abolished and replaced by BK-1/KB-2, Brattleboro to Keene and return using the Fort Hill Branch to reach Dole Junction. With minor variations, this arrangement continued to the end of operations on the Ashuelot Branch.

East Northfield (South Vernon), Massachusetts—MP S49.67

The Ashuelot's original station here was known as South Vernon Junction (later shortened to South Vernon) and was in Vermont. In 1909, apparently for safety reasons, so that passengers did not have to cross the tracks to board Ashuelot Branch trains, the B&M relocated the South Vernon, Vermont, station from the west to the east side of its tracks and southward just across the state line into West Northfield, Massachusetts. The new station was so close to the state line you could almost throw a stone and it would land in Vermont! The station name "South Vernon" was retained, making for a peculiar situation where the passenger station was in Massachusetts and the freight house in Vermont (Dwight A. Smith, pers. comm., 2013).

The town of Northfield, Massachusetts is the only town in the Connecticut Valley that straddles the river. Most of the people who used the South Vernon station—both in its old location and after it was relocated to West Northfield—lived on the "wrong side" of the river—in the village of East Northfield. South Vernon was the closest station for students attending Northfield School for Young Women and for people attending the summer camp assemblies in East Northfield, but there was no easy way to reach the station.

To remedy this situation, the 515-foot Francis J. Schell

South Vernon Junction, VT, looking north. Central Vermont tracks are at left, B&M (Ashuelot Branch) tracks at right, ca. 1905. Postcard; Peter S. Miller coll.

(Highway) Bridge had been built across the river in 1903 to better connect the village of East Northfield with "its" station. Then in 1915, the Trustees of the Northfield Schools, claiming the name "South Vernon" was misleading and confusing to the public, successfully petitioned the Massachusetts Public Service Commission to change the station's name to East Northfield, which change was ordered on July 8, 1915 (Mass. Public Service Comm. 1916).

Looking south on the main line, this is the new South Vernon depot built in 1909 just south of the state line in W. Northfield, MA. The bridge is for E. Northfield Rd. and is still there today. Note the ball signal that governed movements of Central Vermont and B&M trains through the junction, Jan. 1910. Postcard; B. G. Blodget coll.

Here are the two South Vernon stations: the new station in Massachusetts and the original station in Vermont (beyond) that it replaced, Jan. 1910. Postcard; Peter S. Miller coll.

South Vernon depot in W. Northfield, MA, ca. 1913. Note that orderboards have been installed at the station as well as a siding for Ashuelot Branch passenger trains. The station's name would be changed to East Northfield in 1915. Photogr. unknown.

(below) Snowplow-equipped Osgood Bradley/EMC-GE rail motorcar 1195 at E. Northfield, April 17, 1948. S. J. Whitney coll.

Consolidation 2400, probably with EK-1, the East Deerfield–Keene local freight, is at E. Northfield about to pass beneath E. Northfield Rd., 1941. Dwight A. Smith photo.

Dole Junction—MP S51.90

Dole Junction was a flag stop and train register station that came into being when a new section of the Connecticut River main line was built through western Hinsdale in 1912. Located at a remote location on Northfield Road (Route 63), "Dole" became the new beginning point of the Ashuelot Branch after its first two miles had been appropriated for the new main line.

On this day, Consolidation 2424 has brought KE-2 down the grade from Hinsdale and the conductor is at the "cabin" to sign the train off the branch. It appears the engineer, fireman, and head-end "brakie" have stepped down off the engine to stretch their legs. Behind the crewmen is the main line bridge (S51.91) over Northfield Rd. (Rte. 63), Dole Jct., Nov. 11, 1937. Albert G. Hale photo; Brent S. Michiels coll.

Southward view at Dole Junction. That is the Ashuelot Branch leaving the main line at left, ca. 1954. LeRoy Frederick photo; Mike Bump coll.

Looking north, the railroad's bridge over Northfield Rd. (Rte. 63) has been dismantled, Dole Jct., NH, April 20, 1990. Photogr. unknown; Hinsdale Hist. Soc.

Hinsdale—MP S54.40

At Hinsdale, the railroad grade was well above the village and, except for coal dealers W. E. Fay and W. G. Smith, most consignees doing business at this station had to dray their freight to and from the station's team tracks. Consignees here included Hinsdale Woolen Mill, G. E. Robertson Paper Co. and several other tissue paper makers, Granite State Mowing Machine Co. (lawn mowers), M. S. Leach (wagon manufacturers), N. Barnes Co. and I. R. Holman (machinery), and F. W. Tilden (iron foundry). Hinsdale station—once a very busy place.

We believe this is a Connecticut River Railroad cabbage-stack, inside-connected American (4-4-0) engine posing at the original (ca. 1851) Hinsdale, NH, station with a northbound train, ca. 1877. J. A. French photo; Hist. Soc. Cheshire Cty.

Southbound train arriving at Hinsdale station, ca. 1905. Postcard; B. G. Blodget coll.

The original Hinsdale station was destroyed by fire and rebuilt ca. 1935. Here, Consolidation 2703 is at the second Hinsdale station with EK-1, Aug. 2, 1948. Donald S. Robinson photo; Brent S. Michiels coll.

Hinsdale station, Oct. 12, 1954. L. S. Twombly photo; Brent S. Michiels coll.

Hinsdale station, looking outward. From the town, located in the Ashuelot Valley below, it was a steep climb up Depot St. to reach the station. On the sweeping curve beyond the station, the section house is visible over the station roof, ca. 1930. William Monypeny photo; Brent S. Michiels coll.

Crew on EK-1, left to right: R. R. Richards Sr., brakeman; Bill Coffey, engineer; M. K. Robinson, flagman; Myron Mooney, conductor; and G. W. Berry, fireman; Hinsdale, 1954. R. R. Richards Jr. coll.

Ashuelot—MP S58.00

At Ashuelot, a village in the western part of Winchester, the larger consignees included the Ashuelot Manufacturing Co. (textiles), Sheridan Woolen Mills, New England (Winchester) Box Co., New Hampshire Box Co., F. L. Felch (coal), and three paper mills: Ashuelot Paper Co., Paper Service, Inc., and the Robinson Paper Co. Unlike the case at many stations, most of the consignees here had dedicated sidings into their plants.

Ashuelot, NH, station beside its namesake river. Note the covered auto bridge over the river to Rte. 119, ca. 1930. William Monypeny photo; Dale O. Russell coll.

Ashuelot station, looking north, Oct. 12, 1938. Albert G. Hale photo; R. R. Richards Jr. coll.

Winchester—MP S60.20

B&M customers in Winchester included New England (Winchester) Box Co., Wood Flour, Inc., Winchester Creamery, Winchester Tannery (A. C. Lawrence Co.), a paper mill, and commodity dealers A. D. Potter & Co. (hay & grain) and W. A. Sabin (coal). The A. C. Lawrence Co. was famous for the highly aromatic box-car loads of rawhides they received. When the wind was right, everyone in town would know when the cars had arrived.

Consolidation 2712 underway with KE-2 south of Winchester, NH, ca. 1940. George Melvin photo; R. R. Richards Jr. coll.

Because of the date, consist, and power on this train, it can only be EJ-1, which often ran with two to three units and sixty to eighty cars, many of them empty boxcars returning to the north country paper mills. On this day, RS3s 1544 and 1542 have the train at the Rte. 119 crossing south of Winchester Yard in Sept. 1963. Alfred S. Arnold photo.

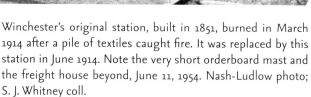

Winchester's original station, built in 1851, burned in March 1914 after a pile of textiles caught fire. It was replaced by this station in June 1914. Note the very short orderboard mast and the freight house beyond, June 11, 1954. Nash-Ludlow photo; S. J. Whitney coll.

EK-1, this day with Consolidation 2400 in charge, is at Winchester, undated. Donald S. Robinson photo; B&MRRHS Archives.

Alco S4 1270 with EK-1 is stopped for a break in Winchester. That crewman in the engine cab knows just how to cool off on a warm summer day—with a nice slice of watermelon. ca. 1960. Donald Virtue photo, courtesy of Sandy Sliviak.

One of the Ashuelot's four steel truss bridges over its namesake river, Winchester, undated. Photogr. unknown; R. R. Richards Jr. coll.

Westport—MP S65.60

At various times there were box, pail, chair shop, and other woodenware factories in Westport. Though once a "post-village," Westport today could almost qualify as a "ghost village." The B&M closed its freight agency here in 1927.

Westport, NH, station, ca. 1905. Hist. Soc. Cheshire Cty.

Looking north from the station, woodworkers pause from their labors for a group picture. Behind them a steam mill operated by J. C. Field and a B&M boxcar spotted at the freight house are visible. Left to right: the main line, passing track, and a spur to the mill. Westport, ca. 1895. Hist. Soc. Cheshire Cty.

West Swanzey—MP S68.20

This station was originally known as "Swanzey." In 1890, however, through the efforts of playwright Denman Thompson, its name was "properly" changed to West Swanzey (*Sentinel* July 16, 1890). Thompson, who lived almost across the road from the station, like many people in the region had a strong sense of place.

The first station here burned in 1908 and was replaced. The second station was closed December 18, 1953, and was taken down November 17, 1954.

At West Swanzey, the New England (Winchester) Box Co. and West Swanzey Box Co. (manufacturers of pails, buckets, and boxes) were each served by dedicated sidings. The station team tracks were used by Homestead Woolen Mills, Nash Bros. (wood turnings), Quinn & Grogan (coal/hides), F. R. Brown (hide shipper), E. J. Hanna and J. A. Howard (hay & grain dealers), and E. B. Holbrook (livestock shipper).

Most of the small towns along the railroad had poultry farms, and there were five in Swanzey alone. One of them, Perry's Poultry Farm, shipped eggs every week (1928–1945) to Brockleman Brothers Market in Fitchburg. If the weather was hot, they'd wait in the egg room until they heard the train's whistle in Westport and then rush the egg crates over to the station. The eggs traveled to Keene where they were transferred to a Cheshire Branch train for Fitchburg.

The first West Swanzey station, trackside, right to Keene, ca. 1900. Photogr. unknown.

The station agent (right) and the train conductor (left) and his crew pose with northbound B&M American 573 (ex-CRRR 10) at the first W. Swanzey station, ca. 1894–1900. Recall that the B&M had only just taken over the CRRR in 1893. Photogr. unknown.

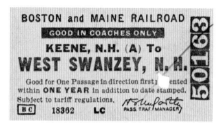

The first W. Swanzey, NH, station, street side, left to Keene. The horse in this image, his feet not touching the ground, appears to have been startled by the locomotive. In horse-and-buggy days, engineers were cautioned to approach horses with care to avoid startling them, ca. 1905. Photogr. unknown; Hist. Soc. Cheshire Cty.

The first W. Swanzey station, only recently updated with a bay window and orderboard mast, was gutted by fire in 1908 (NH Div. Hist. Resources. West Swanzey Village, p. 69). The railroad built a temporary siding and, as was the typical practice in such emergencies, rushed in some passenger coaches to serve as a temporary station/waiting room. Image from Swanzey Old Photos Website.

Looking inward from the Christian Hill Road Bridge (EN18.54), a Keene-bound train is arriving at W. Swanzey's second station. Box factory siding is at left. Franklin Mountain, the highest point in Swanzey, dominates the horizon to the south. Straddling the Winchester-Swanzey town line, 1,411-foot Franklin Mountain is one among a cluster of monadnocks in the area, ca. 1910. Postcard; B. G. Blodget coll.

A southbound plow train, pushing Vermont Valley (VV) wooden snowplow number 15, has just passed under the Christian Hill Road Bridge on a snowy winter's day, ca. 1895–1910. The VV plow on the Ashuelot is no mystery. The Ashuelot, VV, and the Sullivan County roads were all operating under the CRRR flag after 1880, and all four were under the B&M flag after 1893. The VV 15 was listed in a B&M MOW roster dated June 1917. It and others like it were built in the B&M's Concord Shops. Photogr. unknown; Swanzey Old Photos Website.

On March 22, 1911, while on a light move from Springfield to Keene, Sullivan County Mogul 603 derailed and toppled over on the fireman's side just north of the West Swanzey station at the Eaton Rd. crossing. In this image, a Keene to E. Northfield local is passing the scene of the accident. Photogr. unknown; Swanzey Hist. Museum.

Orderboards are in raised position at the second W. Swanzey station. It appears that the crew is waiting to meet another train and has moved the train (note shadow) to clear the crossing, W. Swanzey, ca. 1930. Keene is to the right. Photogr. unknown.

Consolidation 2400 is stopped just south of W. Swanzey station with an early postwar fan trip for the New England Model Railroaders in W. Swanzey, July 21, 1946. (The RRE New England Div. would not run its first postwar fan trip until April 27, 1947). Stanley H. Smith photo; Collection of Bob's Photo.

Swanzey—MP S70.40

After the original Swanzey station's name was changed to West Swanzey in 1890, the B&M opened a "new" Swanzey station—a flag station for the convenience of local residents—2.2 miles further north at Sawyer's Crossing Road in 1896.

In this later scene, the station is boarded up but now has a proper flag signal, Swanzey, undated. Photogr. unknown; Swanzey Old Photos Website.

Swanzey flag stop at Sawyer's Crossing Road, undated. Photogr. unknown.

Keene—MP S73.70

At the end of the line in Keene there was a very diverse customer base. In the first half of the twentieth century as many as thirty-six consignees were served on their own sidings at any given time. In the 1950s, there were about twenty-nine consignees in the city with their own sidings, receiving lumber, paper supplies, coal and oil, agricultural supplies, groceries, propane, minerals, metals, and other industrial raw materials. Outbound traffic included consumer products, specialty packaging, wood-enware and toys, machinery, textiles, and scrap metal. Shipments for even more consignees that lacked private sidings were handled at team tracks or at the freight house (Whitney 1997). A switcher was assigned to Keene to service the many customers' needs. The "Keene Switcher" would break down cuts of cars brought into Keene, spot inbound and lift outbound cars on/from sidings, and assemble outbound trains for the road jobs. (In Chapter 4, we discussed B&M consignees in Keene in more detail.)

Alco S1 1171, beginning her trip down the Ashuelot Branch, swings KE-2 around the east leg of the wye with a respectable hitch this day, Keene, ca. 1950. Stanwood K. Bolton photo.

EK-1/KE-2, this day with Alco S3b 1167 in charge, awaits the return of her crew from lunch break, Keene, ca. 1950. Victor M. Zolinsky photo.

Author R. R. Richards' father, Conductor Richard R. Richards Sr., on the rear platform of EK-1's caboose, Keene, Jan. 1970. Larry Kemp photo.

SW9 1231 has arrived in Keene with EK-1, Feb. 1970. Photogr. unknown; R. R. Richards Jr. coll.

The Fort Hill Branch Years, 1970–1983

One morning in June 1970, just as SJ-1, the Springfield-to-White River Junction freight, was starting out onto the East Northfield Bridge, Engineer Bernie Moon noticed a misalignment of track and notified the dispatcher's office in Greenfield. SJ-1 made it across the bridge, but it would be the last train to ever use the bridge. Inspection revealed that the bridge pier closest to the Vermont side of the river had shifted and was tilting about fifteen degrees. The B&M, which had just entered its second bankruptcy, was in no shape to repair the bridge and it was immediately taken out of service. It stood unused until 1985, when it was finally dismantled. The loss of the bridge severed the B&M's main line between East Northfield and Brattleboro, and henceforth all main line traffic shifted back to the Central Vermont on the Vermont side of the river.

Ashuelot Branch trains suddenly had no option to reach Dole Junction other than to cross the river at Brattleboro and run south on the now-former main line. Thus repurposed, the line between Brattleboro and Dole Junction was christened the "Fort Hill Branch." Since there was no runaround track at Dole Junction, the Fort Hill Branch functioned as a long switchback. Local freights serving the Ashuelot Branch now would make an eight-mile backup move from Brattleboro to a point south of Dole Junction known as Doolittle, then reverse direction and head out the branch to Keene. Returning from Keene, trains would pull down to Doolittle and then make a reverse move back to Brattleboro. Thus came about the peculiar situation whereby trains between Brattleboro and Dole Junction were always backing up!

Conductor Richard R. Richards Sr. (left) and his crew (left to right): Bernie ("B. C.") Moon, engineer; Francis Gamarlo, head brakeman; and George Fontaine, flagman, on BK-1/KB-2, the local freight Brattleboro to Keene and return, ca. 1971. R. R. Richards Jr. coll.

SW9 1231 and buggy C121 are tied down on the Barrow's Coal Spur, the equipment layover point in Brattleboro, VT. When BK-1's crew came on duty in the morning, they would tie onto any cars dropped for them by Connecticut River main line freights SJ-1 or SJ-3 and then head for Keene. Photogr. unknown; R. R. Richards Jr. coll.

Looking south (left) and north (right) at Dole Jct. on the former Connecticut River main line, now the Fort Hill Branch, shortly after the E. Northfield Bridge was lost. CTC has been discontinued and the searchlight signals turned aside. Note the dwarf signal on the Ashuelot Branch that protected the main line. Post-1970. Ron Rand coll.

BK-1 passing Hinsdale station, Spring 1972. Dane H. G. Malcolm photo.

1231 with BK-1 passing Hinsdale station, ca. 1976. Frederick G. Bailey photo.

BK-1, with SW9 1229 on the point this day, is in W. Swanzey, ca. 1978. S. J. Whitney photo.

BK-1 passing beneath the telltale just north of Christian Hill Rd. Bridge in W. Swanzey. The turnout once led to one of the two New England Box Co. plants in town, ca. 1976. Frederick G. Bailey photo.

The bustling life in downtown Keene appears to engulf the railroad on this day in 1976. BK-1's work completed, the 1231 idles patiently east of Main St., its crew on lunch break! After lunch, the train will depart southward as KB-2. Frederick G. Bailey photo.

1231 rounds the west leg of the wye, as it departs Keene with KB-2, ca. 1975. Richard Gibbons photo.

Standing about where the W. Swanzey depot once stood, two young railfans observe the passage of KB-2 south of Christian Hill Rd. Bridge, ca. 1978. Richard Gibbons photo.

KB-2 is about to step onto the first crossing south of Rte. 10, Winchester, ca. 1976. Frederick G. Bailey photo.

KB-2 has passed near Franklin Mountain on the Swanzey-Winchester line, ca. 1976. Frederick G. Bailey photo.

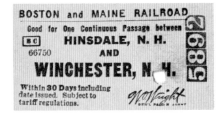

BOSTON and MAINE RAILROAD

Good for One Continuous Passage between

BC HINSDALE, N. H.

66750 AND

WINCHESTER, N. H.

5892

Within 30 Days including date issued. Subject to tariff regulations.

KB-2 at Winchester Box Co., Winchester, ca. 1976. Photogr. unknown.

KB-2 passing the Winchester freight house, ca. 1976. Frederick G. Bailey photo.

KB-2 passing Ashuelot station, ca. 1976. Frederick G. Bailey photo.

Approaching Hinsdale station. Here KB-2 will pick up outbound cars on the passing track and continue on back to Brattleboro, ca. Nov. 1973. George Melvin photo, R. R. Richards Jr. coll.

As the afternoon shadows lengthen, KB-2 rolls along Rte. 63 just north of Dole Junction, ca. 1976. Frederick G. Bailey photo.

Green Mountain Railroad Operations, 1978–1983

In the last years of Ashuelot Branch operations, the Green Mountain Railroad (Green Mountain) reached a lease agreement with the B&M in 1977 and took over all switching duties in the Keene Yard on January 21, 1978. Effective January 23, 1978, Keene was designated as an interchange point with the Green Mountain (B&M Bulletin Notice NE#7). The B&M continued to operate the Ashuelot Branch, dropping cars at Keene for the Green Mountain. As late as 1981, there were still a dozen regular consignees at Keene (Whitney 1997).

Effective January 1, 1982, the B&M transferred operation of the Fort Hill Branch between the Brattleboro Bridge and Doolittle, and the entire Ashuelot Branch, to the Green Mountain and established interchange with the Green Mountain at Brattleboro (B&M Bull. Order NE1-354). This arrangement would only last for one full year and it was a year from hell. The Ashuelot Branch's advanced state of disrepair, combined with unusually severe winter operating conditions and a rapidly eroding customer base, led to a suspension of all service north of Cornville (Ashuelot Paper) effective January 3, 1983. After a last revenue run out to Ashuelot Paper on November 1, 1983, all service on the branch ceased. Later the same month the B&M, which still owned the branch, abandoned the line and all remaining yard trackage in Keene.

After the line was given up, trucks had poor, and in some cases no access to the paper mills across the river from Route 119. The late Craig Weed, who purchased the Hinsdale station from the B&M in 1989, recalls speaking with truck drivers at that time that were backing up the railroad bed from the station to reach the paper mills. This practice continued until the paper companies built their own bridges across the river (C. Weed, pers. comm., April 27, 2013).

The Green Mountain has taken over switching duties at Keene. Here, leased B&M SW1 1115 is seen in the East Yard next to the freight house, which saw its last duty serving as the Green Mountain's operating headquarters, ca. 1978–1980. Photogr. unknown; R. R. Richards Jr. coll.

Here are some images captured, except where otherwise noted, by Green Mountain engineer, Scott J. Whitney, in the twilight years of Ashuelot Branch operations. The images sequentially follow BK-1 out to Keene with KB-2 back to Brattleboro.

Green Mountain 305 departs Brattleboro Yard with borrowed B&M snowplow 2740 for a trip out the Ashuelot Branch in the very snowy winter of 1982. The pigeons are feasting on grain spilled from a car. Frederick G. Bailey photo.

BK-1 starting out of Brattleboro with the backup move over the Fort Hill Branch to Dole Jct. The train is backing across the Brattleboro Bridge (S59.26), 1982.

Looking south on the Fort Hill Branch, this is the Rte. 63 Bridge (S51.91) just north of Dole Jct. All the bridgework on the Fort Hill Branch had been constructed to accept a second track if future traffic warranted it, 1982.

The cab view looking north at Dole Jct. The Fort Hill Branch is at left, the Ashuelot Branch at right. Note the heavier rail on the Fort Hill Branch (former main line), 1982.

Ashuelot Paper Co. shortly before rail service ended, looking north, Ashuelot, 1982.

Paper Service Co., looking north, Ashuelot, 1982.

Robinson Paper Co., looking north, Ashuelot, 1982.

Green Mountain Alco 305 is northbound with BK-1 approaching Ashuelot station, just out of the frame at right, 1982.

Green Mountain Alco 305, with BK-1, is at Ashuelot station. The station's roof is just visible over the diesel's hood. Directly ahead is the collapsing freight house, 1982.

Boxcar of hides being spotted by BK-1 at A. C. Lawrence Co. (leather tanning), Winchester, 1982. Railroaders couldn't drop these cars and get away from them fast enough because they smelled so bad.

Looking outward, the passing siding disappears into the grass at W. Swanzey. The station, razed about 1954, once stood down the tracks at left. Christian Hill Rd. Bridge is visible beyond, 1982.

The wye tracks at Keene mark the end of the Ashuelot Branch. The east leg of the wye swings right to Keene Station. Straight ahead are the old Keene Shops (behind the white building), 1982.

BK-1 has just crossed Main St. and the engineer is presented with this view of the weed-grown East Yard. Beech Hill is beyond. Keene, 1980.

Green Mountain Alco 305 has just come over the Main St. crossing and into the East Yard with BK-1, Keene, 1982. Richard Gibbons photo.

Green Mountain switching the Wetterau Foods warehouse, Keene, NH, 1980 (right and below).

East Yard in the last years of operation, now looking west toward downtown. A boxcar is spotted at the loading dock of the old Ashuelot freight house, Keene, 1980.

Here's the plow extra we saw earlier in Brattleboro. It has turned on the wye and is now ready to depart Keene for the return trip, Jan. 1982. Frederick G. Bailey photo.

The former Ashuelot Freight House, built ca. 1885, became B&M property in 1893. After 1900 the railroad had less use for the building and it was leased to others, including Keene Oil Co. in 1926–1955. In 1958, the B&M freight agent's office was relocated here when the station was demolished (EM AugSep58, 26–27). The B&M still had an agent on duty here at least as late as the fall of 1975. The freight house was last used as the Green Mountain's base of operations in Keene 1977–1982. Cypress St. is in the foreground. Keene, ca. 1980. Richard Gibbons photo.

Now en route back to Brattleboro, KB-2, approaches the Wood Flour, Inc. plant in Winchester. The Winchester Box Co. siding is at left, 1982.

Green Mountain Alco 305 at the Wood Flour, Inc. plant, Winchester, NH, 1982.

As seen from within the Ashuelot covered bridge, Green Mountain Alco 305 is returning from Keene light this day in the last full year of service out to the Elm City. The imposing building is the former Ashuelot School (1924–1971). Ashuelot, Jan. 1982. Frederick G. Bailey photo.

KB-2 approaches the Depot Rd. crossing at the now boarded-up Hinsdale station. The last B&M freight agent on the Ashuelot Branch had maintained an office here, 1982.

The old Ashuelot Freight House, the last building in Keene to wear a B&M sign, stands abandoned in what was once the East Yards. It's been seven years since the rails were lifted. Keene, 1991. W. Roger Meservey photo; B. G. Blodget coll.

SOURCES AND BIBLIOGRAPHY

In the preparation of our text, we made frequent use of the following important sources for which the citing of every reference individually is impractical: Annual Reports of the New Hampshire and Massachusetts Railroad Commissioners, ICC documents, Annual Reports of the Boston & Maine Railroad (B&M) and predecessor roads, the B&M's 1914 ICC Valuation Survey, and other original B&M paper materials, including Approvals for Expenditures, Roadway Completion Reports, equipment rosters, track charts, employee and public timetables, bulletin orders, and various notices, studies, and official correspondence.

We drew considerable material from the *Boston & Maine Railroad Employees Magazine*, the Boston & Maine Railroad Historical Society's *B&M Bulletin* and *Newsletter* and from various newspapers, including among others the *Keene Sentinel, Peterborough Transcript,* and *Bellows Falls Times,* for all of which we make abbreviated in–text citations.

The following list contains additional materials we consulted, some of which may not be specifically referenced in the text.

Anon. "The Ashburnham Branch." *B&M Bulletin* vi, no. 1 (1976):28–29.

____. "Big Boy on the Boston & Maine" *B&M Bulletin* 20, no. 2 (1995):17.

____. "Boston & Maine extension from Hinsdale, N.H. to Brattleboro, Vt." *Railway Age Gazette* 55, no. 15 (1913):661–662.

____. "Bus company reaches 20th milestone." *Boston & Maine Railroad Employees Magazine* (June 1945):vi–8.

____. "Engine crashes into caboose in No. Walpole railroad yards." *Sentinel,* (September 19, 1951).

____. "Last milk train from Bellows Falls leaves." *Bellows Falls Times* (July 23, 1964).

____. *The Monadnock Railroad—Its lease by the Cheshire Railroad Company—Sketches of Winchendon, Jaffrey, Rindge and Peterboro. Sentinel,* Jan. 8, 1880.

____. "New England Division Notes: The Ware River Trip." *The Enthusiast* (January 1939):20–21.

____. *Notes for Cheshire Branch ICC hearing dated April 1, 1959.* Boston & Maine Railroad Historical Society Archives (1959).

____. "Operating divisions on the B&M." *B&M Bulletin* vi, no. 4 (1977):15–16.

____. *Wachusett Lake and Park and Other Points of Interest Reached by the Gardner, Westminster & Fitchburg Street Railway.* Fitchburg, MA: William A. Emerson, ca. 1900.

____. [George B. Leighton/Monadnock Farms], "A pioneer in a great movement." *The Granite Monthly* 39, no. 1(1907):2–10.

Armstrong, John B. *Factory Under the Elms: A History of Harrisville, New Hampshire, 1774–1969.* Cambridge, MA: The MIT Press, 1985.

Atkins, J. R., ed. *Official Guide of the Boston and Maine Railroad.* Chicago: B&M Traffic Dept./Atterley Publishing Co., 1915.

Bachelder, J. Leonard. *'Half–Century Limited' Special Train Operated from Boston to North Adams and Pittsfield, Mass.* Trip brochure and route description. Ward Hill, MA: Massachusetts Bay Railroad Enthusiasts, Inc., 1984.

Baker, George Pierce. *The Formation of the New England Railroad Systems: A Study of Railroad Combination in the Nineteenth Century*. Cambridge, MA: Harvard University Press, 1937.

Ball, Donald L. *George Mansfield and the Billerica and Bedford Railroad*. Blue Springs, MO: Aubrey Publications, 2011.

Bauhan, William. "The Dublin Stage Company." *Dublin Historical Society Newsletter* no. 23 (1992):1.

Beers, F. W., & Co. *Atlas of Worcester County, Massachusetts*. (1870).

Blodget, Bradford G., ed. *Index to the Boston & Maine Railroad Employees' Magazine*. Unpublished (2013).

____. "The last ride of the Peterboro local." *Landmark* (April 3, 2003):41, 70.

____. *Marium Foster's Boston & Maine Railroad 1917–1958: The Story of Keene's Railroad Lady*. Keene, NH: Hist. Soc. of Cheshire County, 2011.

Boston & Albany Railroad. *Proposed Construction Plan for Templeton Street Railway and Boston & Albany Railroad for interchange track at Templeton, Mass. station* (September 18, 1912).

Boston & Maine Railroad. "Series of Numbers for Boston & Maine Freight Equipment." *Car Service Department Circular* no. 323 (July 20, 1909).

____. *System of Renumbering Locomotives*. Haverhill, MA: C. Archie Horne, (1911).

____. *Station and Siding Symbols*. Booklet (1918).

____. *Branch Lines—Passenger Service*. Information spreadsheet in Boston & Maine Railroad Historical Society Archives (May 6, 1942).

____. "A Boston & Maine Railroad Chronology: 1900–September 1945 inclusive." *B&M Bulletin* 25, no. 1–4 (1945). Compiled by the Passenger Traffic Department (see *Hurst*, below, for a continuation of this chronology).

Bradlee, Francis B. C. *The Boston and Lowell Railroad, the Nashua and Lowell Railroad, and the Salem and Lowell Railroad*. Salem, MA: Essex Institute, 1918.

____. *The Boston & Maine Railroad. A History of the Main Road, with its Tributary Lines*. Salem, MA: Essex Institute, 1921.

Byron, Carl R. "Boston & Maine's EMD FT diesel locomotives: A Golden Anniversary Gala." *B&M Bulletin* 20, no. 1 (1994):4–39.

____. *A Pinprick of Light: The Troy and Greenfield Railroad and Its Hoosac Tunnel*. Shelburne, VT: The New England Press, 1995.

Campbell, Victor. "Slow train to Keene." *The Railroad Enthusiast* 3, no. 2 (1966):2–8.

CHA, Inc. 2009. *Evaluation and Historic Recordation of the Cheshire Railroad Stone Arch Bridge over the Branch River*. City of Keene, NH: CHA Project No. 19959 (2009).

Cobb, Chandler, ed. "Turntables (from a listing from the B&M Chief Engineer's office, Jan., 1918)." *B&M Bulletin* 11, no. 2 (1981):28–31.

Conard, Richard. "Seventy–Five Years (1934–2010) of Rare Mileage. Parts I–VI." *Callboy* (December 2009–May 2010).

Cook, John E. "The Village Connection." *New England States Limited* 1, no. 1 (1977):4–6.

Cousins, Pearl M. *Westminster (Mass.) Depot*. Unpublished memoirs, Westminster Historical Society (1958).

Cowan, Robert F. "The Milk Trains—Transportation of Milk in New England." *B&M Bulletin* 7, no. 3 (1978):6–21.

Crouch, H. Bentley. 1979. "Collision at Nahor: An Historical Review." *B&M Bulletin* 9, no. 1(1979):27–30.

Cummings, O. R. "The Keene Electric Railway." *Transportation Bulletin* 46 (February 1958):1–16.

Earle, Alice Morse. *Stage–coach and Tavern Days*. New York: MacMillan Co., 1900.

Edson, William D. "Locomotives of the Fitchburg." *Railroad History* 146 (1982):64–102.

Fitzwilliam Bicentennial Committee. *Fitzwilliam Bicentennial, 1762–1962*. Booklet (1962).

Fitzwilliam Town History Committee. *Fitzwilliam: The Profile of a New Hampshire Town, 1884–1984*. Canaan, NH: Phoenix Publishing, 1985.

Fletcher, William J. Unpublished letters, 1953–1981. B. G. Blodget collection.

Foster, Marium E. "Transportation." *Upper Ashuelot: A History of Keene, New Hampshire*. Keene, NH: Keene Historical Committee, (1968).

Frizzell, Martha M. *A History of Walpole, New Hampshire, Vol. 1*. Walpole, NH: Town of Walpole, 1963.

Frye, Harry A. *Minuteman Steam: Boston & Maine Steam Locomotives, 1911–1958*. Boston & Maine Railroad Historical Society (1982).

____. "The Fitchburg Railroad: A Corporate Genealogy." *Railroad History*. 146 (1982):60–63.

____. "Boston & Maine predecessor railroads, Parts 1–7." *B&M Bulletin* 20, no. 2–22, no. 1 (1997–2000).

Garvin, James L. "The Cheshire Railroad Stone Arch Bridge." *SIA New England Chapters Newsletter* 27, no. 1 (2006):9–16.

Gauthier, Joseph H. "*Blueberry Special* Finale." *Worcester Gazette* (March 7, 1953).

Girr, Christopher F. *Mastery in Masonry: Norcross Brothers, Contractors and Builders 1864–1924*. Master's thesis, Columbia University, 1996.

Goodwin, Dana D. "Ashburnham Hill." *B&M Bulletin* 6, no. 1(1976):7–27.

Greene, J. R. *Quabbin's Railroad: The Rabbit*. Athol, MA: Highland Press, 2007.

Greenwood, Lois S. *Winchendon Years 1764–1964*. Winchendon, MA: Town of Winchendon, 1970.

Griffin, S. G. *A History of the Town of Keene (1732–1874)*. Keene, NH: Sentinel Publishing Co., 1904.

Herrick, Wm. D. *History of the Town of Gardner* (1878).

Hopkins, Doris E. *Greenfield, New Hampshire: The Story of a Town*. Milford, NH: Wallace Press, 1977.

Hostutler, Elizabeth J. *Cheshire Railroad Area Form*. NH Department of Transportation, 1994.

Harlow, Alvin H. *Steelways of New England*. New York: Creative Age Press, 1946.

Hinsdale, N.H. (Town of). 1976. Hinsdale, N.H., 103pp.

Holden, R. P. and B. B. Holden. *Ashburnham, Massachusetts 1885–1965*. Ashburnham, MA: Board of Trustees of the Stevens Public Library, 1970.

Hurd, D. H. *Town and City Atlas of the State of New Hampshire* (1892).

Hurst, Richard K. 2007–13. "A Boston & Maine Chronology: September 1945 through 1986." *B&M Bulletin* 26, no. 1–28, no. 3 (2007–2013). (A continuation of *Boston & Maine Railroad*, 1945; see above.)

____. "Cheshire Branch Passenger Service Discontinuance." *B&M Bulletin* 26, no. 4 (2009):37–39.

Hutchinson, Leroy C. 1977. "Boston & Maine Dining Cars, Part I: The Wooden Era." *B&M Bulletin.* 6, no. 4 (1977):17–25.

Hyman, Tom. *Village on a Hill: A History of Dublin, New Hampshire, 1752–2000.* Portsmouth, NH: Peter E. Randall Publishing, 2002.

Jones, Robert C. *The Central Vermont Railway: A Yankee tradition, Vol. VII, 1981–1995.* Shelburne, VT: The New England Press, 1995.

Jones, Robert Willoughby. *Boston and Maine—Three Colorful Decades of New England Railroading.* Glendale, CA: Trans–Anglo Books, 1991.

____. *Boston & Albany—The New York Central in New England.* Los Angeles: Pine Tree Press, 1997.

____. *Boston and Maine—Forest, River, and Mountain.* Los Angeles: Pine Tree Press, 1999.

____. *Boston and Maine—City and Shore.* Los Angeles: Pine Tree Press, 2000.

Karr, Ronald Dale. *The Rail Lines of Southern New England: A Handbook of Railroad History.* 2nd ed. Pepperell, MA: Branch Line Press, 2017.

____. *Lost Railroads of New England.* 3rd ed. Pepperell, MA: Branch Line Press, 2010.

Kirkland, Edward Chase. *Men, Cities and Transportation: A Study in New England History, 1820–1900.* Cambridge, MA: Harvard University Press, 1948.

Knoblock, Glenn A. *Images of America: New Hampshire Covered Bridges.* Charleston, SC: Arcadia Publishing, 2002.

Kyper, Frank. "Fatal Disaster at Long Bridge." *B&M Bulletin* 15, no. 2 (1987):33.

Ladoo, Raymond B. 1922. "Feldspar Mining and Milling in New Hampshire." *Rock Products* 25, no. 23 (1922):25–27.

Lindsell, Robert M. *The Rail Lines of Northern New England: A Handbook of Railroad History.* Pepperell, MA: Branch Line Press, 2000.

Lord, William G. *History of Athol, Massachusetts.* Somerville, MA: Somerville Publishing Co., 1953.

Lowe, Rosetta. *History of Hinsdale, New Hampshire–Transportation.* Unpublished, undated manuscript, Hinsdale Historical Society.

Lowenthal, Larry. Titanic Railroad: *The Southern New England—The Story of New England's Last Great Railroad War.* Brimfield, MA: Marker Press, 1998.

Massachusetts Public Service Commission. *Third Annual Report of the Public Service Commission,* 1 (1916):358.

Massachusetts Street Railway Investigation Committee. *Report of the Street Railway Investigation Commission of the Problems Relating to the Street Railways of the Commonwealth* (1918).

Melvin, George F. *Trackside Around New Hampshire 1950–1970 with Ben English Jr.* Scotch Plains, NJ: Morning Sun Books, 2009.

Moore, Esther Gilman. *History of Gardner, 1785–1967.* Gardner, MA: Hatton Printing Co., 1967.

Morison, George A. *History of Peterborough New Hampshire.* Rindge, NH: Richard R. Smith, 1954.

Morgan, Philip M. *The Boston, Barre, & Gardner Railroad.* Worcester, MA: Worcester Historical Society, 1964.

New Hampshire Department of Transportation. *Preserving the Railroad System: An Overview of New Hampshire's Activity, 1975–2000* (1999).

Nimke, R.W. *Green Mountain Railroad*. Rutland, VT: Sharp Offset Printing Inc., 1985.

____. *Connecticut River Railroads and Connections, Vol. I: Greenfield—East Deerfield through Westminster*. Rutland, VT: Sharp Offset Printing Inc., 1991.

____. *Connecticut River Railroads and Connections, Vol II: Bellows Falls, Vermont East and West*. Rutland, VT: Sharp Offset Printing Inc., 1991.

O'Gorman, James F. "O. W. Norcross, Richardson's 'Master Builder': A Preliminary Report." *Journal of the Society of Architectural Historians* 32, no. 2 (1973):104–113.

Opielowski, Philip. "The Ware River Railroad." In *One Town & Seven Railroads*, 40–47. Palmer, MA: Palmer Public Library Railroad Advisory Board/Palmer Public Library, 2008.

Patalano, Giro R. Behind the Iron Horse: *The People Who Made the Trains Run in the Bellows Falls, Vermont Area (1941–1980)*. Barre, VT: Vermont Historical Society, 1997.

Patch, Ronald. "Log Driving on the Connecticut River." *The Vermont Journal/The Shopper* (July 30, 2014).

Patton, Kenneth E. "B&M's Self–Propelled Passenger Equipment. *B&M Bulletin* 3, no. 3 (1974):5–14.

Peterborough Historical Society. *Our Changing Town: Peterborough 1939–1989*. Vol. I. Portsmouth, NH: Peter E. Randall Publisher, 1996.

Pfeifer, P. E. 1931. "New CTC (Centralized Traffic Control) Installations Are Largest in the World." *Boston & Maine Railroad Employees' Magazine* (April–May 1931):8,14.

Poor, Henry V. *Railroads and Canals of the United States of America*. Vol. I. New York: John H. Schultz & Co., 1860.

Proper, David R. "For Decades, Bridges Stood over Troubled Waters." *Sentinel*, March 28, 2006.

____. "Tourists Were Implored to Ride that Train." *Sentinel*, August 26, 2008.

Raymond, Charles. 1899. "Troy White Granite and Its Production." *Stone* 20, no. 1 (1899):13–18.

Richards, L. J. & Co. "Village of Winchendon, Plate 53," *New Topographical Atlas of the County of Worcester, Massachusetts*. Philadelphia, PA, 1898.

Rindge Historical Committee. *Town on the Border: Rindge, New Hampshire, 1874–1988*. Rindge, NH: Town of Rindge, 1989.

Roberts, Oliver A. *California Pilgrimage of Boston Commandery, Knights Templars August 4–September 4, 1883*. Boston: Alfred Mudge & Sons, 1884.

Roy Jr., John H. *A Field Guide to Southern New England Railroad Depots and Freight Houses*. Pepperell, MA: Branch Line Press, 2007.

Sanborn Map Co. Insurance maps of Bellows Falls. 1885–1886, 1906.

Sanborn Map Co. Insurance maps of Keene. Variety of dates 1884–1908.

Schexnayder, Clifford J. *Builders of the Hoosac Tunnel*. Portsmouth, NH: Peter E. Randall Publisher, 2015.

Shaw, Joseph N. "The B&M Transportation Story." *B&M Bulletin* 22, no. 4 (2001):10–23.

Smith, Dwight A. 1987. "Where Did the Freight Go?" *B&M Bulletin* 15, no. 2 (1987):26–32.

Spofford, Foster R. *Ware River Branch, N.Y.C.* Boston & Maine traffic analysis. January 31, 1962.

____. *Study–Cheshire Branch–Winchendon to Bellows Falls*. Branch Line Study Group, September 19, 1962.

____. *Study–Cheshire Branch–Keene to Bellows Falls*. Branch Line Study Group, February 19, 1962.

Stearns, Ezra S. *History of Ashburnham, Massachusetts, 1734–1886*. Ashburnham, MA: Town of Ashburnham, 1887.

Symmes, Richard W. and E. Robert Hornsby. "Elmwood Junction, New Hampshire." *B&M Bulletin* 4, no. 1 (1974):1, 10–19.

Tobey, Raymond E. "The Green Mountain Flyer." *B&M Bulletin* 11, no. 4 (1982):24–35.

Tuttle, Lewis C. "Travel Within and Beyond Hancock: Railroads." In *The Second Hundred Years of Hancock, New Hampshire*, 259–272. Canaan, NH: Hancock Town History Committee/Phoenix Publishing, 1979.

Twombly, L. Stewart. *Cheshire Railroad: Yearly Record (of Locomotive Changes, Mostly from Annual Reports 1846–1889)*. Typed manuscript, unpublished, undated.

Valentine Jr., Donald B. 1977. "A Brief History of the Cheshire Railroad." *New England States Limited* 1, no. 1 (1977):20–29. Includes a roster of Cheshire Railroad locomotives.

____. "The Forest Line—Central Vermont's Desperate Plan of 1880." *B&M Bulletin* 17, no. 1 (1990):6–11.

____. "The Marlboro Quarries." *B&M Bulletin* 19, no. 4 (1994):26–35.

Wadsworth, Samuel. *Historical Notes with Keyed Maps of Keene and Roxbury, Cheshire County, N. H.* Keene, NH: Sentinel Printing, 1932.

Walker, Ellis E., ed. "Boston & Maine Railroad Pits and Turntables (as of October 27, 1898)." *B&M Bulletin* 15, no. 3 (1987):9–12.

Walker, O. W. & Co. *Atlas of Winchendon Town, Massachusetts*, Washington, DC, 1886.

Wolmar, Christian. *The Great Railroad Revolution: The History of Trains in America*. Philadelphia: Public Affairs/ Perseus Books Group, 2012.

Walpole (NH) Historical Society. *Images of America: Walpole*. Charlestown, SC: Arcadia Publishing, 2009.

Ward, Margaret S. *My Skatutakee Story*. Unpublished memoir, Historic Harrisville, Inc., 1989.

Warsher, James L. " 'The 402 Is in WARE?' A Railroad Enthusiasts, Inc., Excursion on the Boston & Albany." *Central Headlight* 15, no. 1 (1985):16–23.

West, Nancy Weston. *I Remember Distinctly* [the railroad in Hancock, NH]. Unpubl. memoirs prepared for the Hancock Town History Committee. Hancock Historical Society, ca. 1975.

Westmoreland History Commission. "Transportation: The Railroad Era." *The History of Westmoreland, 1741–1970*. Westmoreland, NH: Town of Westmoreland, 1976.

White, John H. *The American Railroad Passenger Car. Part 2*. Baltimore: John Hopkins University Press, 1985.

Whitney, Scott. "From Ashuelot to Ashes, Part I." *B&M Bulletin* 14, no. 1 (1985):28–31

____. "From Ashuelot to Ashes, Part II." *B&M Bulletin*, 14, no. 2 (1985):32–35.

____. "Connecticut River Bridges." *B&M Bulletin* 17, no. 1 (1990):20–35.

____. "The Ashuelot: A Branchline Adventure." *Railroad Model Craftsman* (May 1997):84–91.

____. "Modeling the Boston & Maine's Ashuelot Branch." *Railroad Model Craftsman* (June 1997):86–93.

____. "The Conn River: Colorful Railroading (Parts 1 and 2)." *B&M Bulletin* 30, no. 1 (2017):16–39 and 30, no. 2 (2017):16–38.

Wilber, Clifford C. "Ashuelot Railroad Statistics." *Sentinel,* August 8, 1935.

____. "First Wreck on the Cheshire Railroad Involving Passengers." *Sentinel,* August 7, 1935.

____. "The Stone Arch Railroad Bridge." *Sentinel,* November 23, 1936.

____. "Iron railing on Stone Arch Bridge." *Sentinel,* December 10, 1936.

____. "Cheshire Railroad Repair Shops, Parts 1–3." *Sentinel,* April 5–7, 1937.

____. *Centenary of the Opening of the Cheshire Railroad to Keene, NH, May 16, 1848.* Keene, NH: Keene National Bank, 1948.

Live steam engine 206, the *Brass Betsy*, rounds a bend on the F. L. Railroad, an obscure, long–forgotten, miniature pike that once operated at Joyland, located in a pineland on Flat Roof Mill Rd. in E. Swanzey, NH The tiny road was 15–inch gauge and about a mile–long. The road's initials are for builder/operator Francis LeClair, late 1930s. Postcard; Brent S. Michiels coll.

On a warm summer's day, passengers enjoy a ride along the F. L. Railroad behind the 206/*Brass Betsy* at Joyland, E. Swanzey, NH, late 1930s. Postcard; Brent S. Michiels coll.

INDEX

Note: **bold entries** *denote major chapters*